The Secret Lore of Magic

Books by Idries Shah

Sufi Studies and Middle Eastern Literature

The Sufis
Caravan of Dreams
The Way of the Sufi
Tales of the Dervishes: *Teaching-stories Over a Thousand Years*
Sufi Thought and Action

Traditional Psychology, Teaching Encounters and Narratives

Thinkers of the East: *Studies in Experientialism*
Wisdom of the Idiots
The Dermis Probe
Learning How to Learn: *Psychology and Spirituality in the Sufi Way*
Knowing How to Know
The Magic Monastery: *Analogical and Action Philosophy*
Seeker After Truth
Observations
Evenings with Idries Shah
The Commanding Self

University Lectures

A Perfumed Scorpion (Institute for the Study of Human Knowledge and California University)
Special Problems in the Study of Sufi Ideas (Sussex University)
The Elephant in the Dark: *Christianity, Islam and the Sufis* (Geneva University)
Neglected Aspects of Sufi Study: *Beginning to Begin* (The New School for Social Research)
Letters and Lectures of Idries Shah

Current and Traditional Ideas
Reflections
The Book of the Book
A Veiled Gazelle: *Seeing How to See*
Special Illumination: *The Sufi Use of Humour*

The Mulla Nasrudin Corpus
The Pleasantries of the Incredible Mulla Nasrudin
The Subtleties of the Inimitable Mulla Nasrudin
The Exploits of the Incomparable Mulla Nasrudin
The World of Nasrudin

Travel and Exploration
Destination Mecca

Studies in Minority Beliefs
The Secret Lore of Magic
Oriental Magic

Selected Folktales and Their Background
World Tales

A Novel
Kara Kush

Sociological Works
Darkest England
The Natives Are Restless
The Englishman's Handbook

Translated by Idries Shah
The Hundred Tales of Wisdom (Aflaki's *Munaqib*)

The Secret Lore of Magic

Books of the Sorcerers

Idries Shah

ISF PUBLISHING

ISBN 978-1-78479-066-0

First published 1957
Published in this edition 2016

In association with The Idries Shah Foundation

The Idries Shah Foundation is a registered charity in the United Kingdom
Charity No. 1150876

Contents

Part I

RITUAL MAGIC

Chapter

1 The Complete Ritual of Ceremonial Magic: The Key of Solomon, Son of David 3
2 The Clavicle: Spells and Medallions 36
3 The Complete Ritual of Black Magic: The Pact of the Black Art 65
4 'A Book by the Devil' – The Grimorium Verum 81

Part II

WHITE MAGIC: SECRETS OF ALBERTUS MAGNUS

5 The Magical Powers of Stones 129
6 The Magical Uses of Certain Herbs 144
7 Animals in Magic 161
8 A Book of Spells 169

Part III

THE ART OF COMMANDING SPIRITS

9 The Magical Talisman 197
10 The Book of the Spirits 210
11 The Catalogue of Demons 248
12 Cornelius Agrippa: On Calling Spirits 264

Part IV

MAGICAL POWER THROUGH TALISMANS

13 The Book of Power, by Aptolcater 271

Part V

THE GRIMOIRE OF HONORIUS THE GREAT

14 Preparing the Magical Skin 297
15 The Liber Spirituum 311
16 The Circle of Evocation 315
17 Conjuring the Kings of the Demons 318
18 Conjurations of each Day of the Week 322
19 Hours and Times for Magical Rites 331
20 The Spirits, Planets and Data of Magic 338

Appendices
1 Powers and Second Conjuration of Spirits 353
2 Third Conjuration of Spirits 357
3 Commanding the King of Reluctant Spirits 359
4 'The Burning', Invocation to Rebellious Spirits 360
5 'Curse of Chains', addressed to Spirits 361
6 'The Pit', Second Invocation to a Rebellious Spirit 362

List of Abbreviations 363
Index 365

PART I

RITUAL MAGIC

CHAPTER I

THE COMPLETE RITUAL OF CEREMONIAL MAGIC

THE KEY OF SOLOMON, SON OF DAVID

The Key of Solomon

THIS IS PROBABLY the most celebrated and at the same time most feared[1] work in the whole of ceremonial magic. Controversies have raged for centuries as to its authenticity and as to whether there ever was a Hebrew version; and it is only relatively recently that fresh light has been thrown on the question.

Circumstantial evidence now shows that the *Key of Solomon* has existed, in one form or another, from very

1 Again and again, in the works of clerical writers against witchcraft, the *Key of Solomon* is called the 'Book of the Devil'. It was one of the books which Jeronimo de Lebana confessed to having seen in the home of the Count of Zabellan. These, he said, had been bought in Antwerp and smuggled into Spain: and their cost was well over four thousand escudos. Also in that small collection was a copy of the *Almadel* (which is included in the present work). The Inquisition of 1559 also prohibited the *Key* as a dangerous book, and the Roman Inquisition proscribed the *Book of Solomon* for the same reason. Vide: *Inquisition Records of Toledo and Cuenca*, Madrid, 1942.

remote antiquity. Certain of its Words of Power, the actual arrangement of the processes, point to Semitic and even Babylonian origins. The opinion of the present writer is that it may have entered Europe through the medium of the Gnostics, Cabbalists and similar magico-religious schools.

We cannot be sure, of course, as to how much of the work as we know it is original, and how much must be attributed to later additions. This, from one point of view, is not really important. If we are to decide about 'originality' we are faced with two important and altogether mysterious considerations: Need it have had one single author, and need he have been the actual historical Solomon, son of David? Secondly, we are drawn into the morass of wondering whether the rituals are 'true' – that is, do they work? This type of study, however, is outside the scope of the present work.

Contentions levelled against the *Key* have, so far, been confined to criticism as unfounded as anything in magic itself may be. One writer says that it could not have been the work of King Solomon, because he was a good man. It may be mentioned that an occultist could reply to this with some justification that the Bible says that Solomon fell and gave way to temptation.[1] Again, orthodox religionists have fought against the content, if not the authenticity, of the *Key* because of its alleged 'diabolical' character.

Western occultists have counter-attacked with the thesis that anything diabolical is a later addition, and does not belong to the true work, which is, they say, nothing more nor less than the purest spirit of High Magic, working through the Divine Force.

1 The oldest known version in this form is the sixteenth-century Latin copy in the British Museum: Add. MSS. 10,867, tr. by Isau Abbraha, from the Hebrew.

We know the *Key* in Europe through the manuscript copies which are buried in the great libraries of London, Paris and other centres. With the exception of one partial version several hundred years old (which is not obtainable), there has been no unbiased version ever seen in print, at any time. The manuscripts, diagrams and their arrangements and sequence differ from copy to copy. French and Latin are the usual languages in which the *Key* is found, and most copies date from the eighteenth century.

But we must go much further back for evidence that the *Key*, or something very much like it, has existed for probably over two thousand years.

Even in the first century AD, as Flavius Josephus tells us, there was such a book. Eleazar the Jew exorcised devils with its help, and with the Ring of Solomon which is so well known to students of the *Arabian Nights*.

The *Great Albert*, the same spell-book which is reproduced in full in these pages, quotes from one Aaron, who is certainly Aaron Isaac, the magician and interpreter of Emperor Manuel Comnenus. The book that Isaac used is, from all internal evidence, the *Clavicle* (Key of Solomon), and shows that its currency had continued from the first to the eleventh century. The actual *Albert*, of course, was not yet on the scene, and these grimoires did not become widely current in the West until the thirteenth century.

One copy tells how the *Key* was to be buried with Solomon in his tomb, and how it was taken to Babylon and then brought back by a prince of that country. 'All created things' must obey its secrets.

To return to the *Arabian Nights* evidence. It is thought that a good deal of the material content of the *Nights* is based upon stories of Babylonian origin. The Arabs themselves possessed no book describing Solomon's life and magical activities as mentioned in the *Nights*: at least, no book that has been mentioned by the very voluminous and indefatigable bibliographers of ancient Arabia.

These facts have led to a supposition that the *Key* may be derived from a body of magic initiated or used by Solomon, which was then or later current among the sorcerers of the eastern Mediterranean. This contention is interesting in that there have been suggestions that Solomon's work is connected with the body of magical ritual used in ancient Egypt, and attributed to Hermes. The term Hermetic is still used to denote alchemical and secret works.

There has been a confusion in comments and history due to the fact that several books have circulated under the general title of Solomon's *Key*. *The Key of Rabbi Solomon*, for example, is a totally different work, dealing with planetary talismans. It may, however, be connected with the Solomonic clavicle. Again, there is another and very rare *Key* attributed to Solomon, which is not generally available for comparison, and which is considered important enough to have a special section devoted to it in this present book.[1]

This very interesting contribution tells how Solomon first came into contact with the genii whom he was later to control, how he compelled their obedience, and of his downfall.

The *Lemegeton* (Little Key of Solomon) is another book examined in these pages, which deals with evocation of spirits. It is distinct, however, from the grimoire which follows.

It is extraordinary how, in the study of occultism, people seem to put the cart before the horse. Eliphas Lévi – the Frenchman of the nineteenth century whose real name was Constant – was very greatly influenced by the 'Last

1 *Vide* Chapter II.

of the English Magicians', Francis Barrett, author of the much-quoted but almost never seen *Magus: The Celestial Intelligencer*, published in 1801.

Barrett quoted original sources in his tome, and was the first man to reduce the available works of the sorcerers into a system of magic: at any rate, the first of the self-professed occultists to do so. But, while Lévi's *Dogme et Rituel* and other books have been translated into English and carefully annotated by the translator, Barrett remains a literally closed book. You cannot buy a copy of the Magus without months of searching, and then only at a very high price indeed. Few examples have even changed hands during the past quarter of a century.

Lévi, again, based his system of magic largely upon the *Key of Solomon* which we are now discussing. The actual *Key* is not (or has not, so far) been generally available for comparison.

That such comparison is sorely needed is evidenced by the fact that it is universally acknowledged that Lévi himself was anything but accurate in his exposition of magic. Innumerable footnotes by the actual translator of Levi's *History of Magic* point this out, quite apart from the obvious mistakes throughout the book.

Of these two important sources, then, the *Key* is now presented: perhaps some day the *Magus* will be made available also.

WARNING
To the Possessor of this Book.

This Section is not contained in all versions of the Grimoire. It exists in the manuscript copies translated into French ('from the Hebrew') by Abraham Colorno, of which a few copies are known in the British Museum and the Paris Arsénal Library.[1]

The person into whose hands the manuscript may fall is cautioned and adjured not to part with its secrets to anyone who may be unworthy, because of the power said to reside in its pages. This is the general rule in relation to the secret doctrines of magical and alchemical works. The text is as follows:

> This work of Solomon is composed of two books. In the first you can see how to avoid mistakes in operations with the Spirits.
>
> In the Second Book you are taught how to perform the Arts of Magic.
>
> You must take the greatest care that this Key of Secrets does not get into the hands of the foolish and the ignorant.
>
> He who has it, and uses it according to the instructions, will be able not only to perform magical ceremonies: he will be able, in the case of errors, to correct them.
>
> No operation will succeed unless the Exorcist understands completely what he is about.
>
> I therefore most earnestly adjure the person who gains possession of this Key of Secrets not to pass it on, nor to share its knowledge to anyone, unless he is faithful, and can keep a secret, and is proficient in the Magical Art.
>
> I humbly pray the possessor of this, by the Name of God TETRAGRAMMATON, YOD HE VAU HE, and by

1 Such as the Harleian MS. 3981, King's MS. 288, and Sloane MS. 3091, in the British Museum collections; and the Arsénal MS. 2348.

> the Name ADONAI, and by all the other Names of God, the High and Holy, that he should treat this work as precious as his own soul, and share it with no foolish or ignorant person.

THE DESTRUCTION OF ENEMIES

(i) This is a rite from the *Key of Solomon*, which concentrates upon creating discord between and harm against two lovers. The assumption is that the operator has some vital interest in this separation. At the same time, of course, magicians were wont to take a spell such as this and modify it according to the result desired. Spells, that is to say, are not inflexible. This is almost a principle of magic. Magical literature abounds with processes directed towards certain results which are clearly derived from a quite different inspiration.

This fact goes far towards indicating that it is the *intensity* of the magical force, rather than its actual *character*, which determines its efficacy, according to magical belief. This is what Solomon has to say about operations of destruction:

> It is important always to observe the requirements of the days and hours in which the operation is to be carried out, irrespective of the method used. And the correct instruments, perfumes and so on are to be used.[1]

[1] i.e. works of hatred are done in the day and hour of Saturn, and offensive incense (asafoetida, etc.) used.

In the case of an image being used, write the name of the person upon it with a consecrated needle, and say over the image:

"USOR, DILAPIDATORE, TENTATORE, SOIGNATORE, DEVORATORE, CONCITORE ET SEDUCTORE."

Then this spell is pronounced, still over the waxen image:

"O commanders and friends, I conjure and command you to obey this order without hesitation: consecrate this figure in the name (NAME OF PERSON TO BE CURSED) and the one is against the other; thus they are henceforth irreconcilable!"[1]

Then the image is to be placed in contact with the noxious fumes which are burning in a dish: the fumigations of Mars, brimstone and asafoetida. The effigy is left in this atmosphere for a complete night.

(ii) A variation of this curse is when food is bewitched to cause discomfort and disaster. The actual food is addressed, in the days and hours of Mars or Saturn, and the terrible incantation pronounced over it:[2]

"Where are you, SOIGNATORE, USORE, DILAPIDATORE, DENTORE, CONCISORE, DIVORATORE, SEDUCTORE, SEMINATORE?

1 i.e. the lovers whom it is desired to part.

2 Food and drink are unusually potent 'conductors' of curses: "The efficacy of a wish or curse depends not only upon the potency which it possesses from the beginning... but also in the vehicle by which it is contained – just as the strength of an electric shock depends both on the original strength of the current and on the condition of the conductor. As particularly efficient conductors are regarded blood, bodily contact, food and drink." – Westermarck *Orig. and Devel. of Moral Ideas*, I, 586.

> "O Ye, makers of hatred and prolongers of enmity: I conjure you by Who has created you for this work, I conjure you to complete this work, so that when (NAME OF PERSON TO BE BEWITCHED) eats this food, or when (NAME, ETC.) places a hand to it in any way, he (/SHE) shall never rest!"

Frustrating the Spell

Just as processes such as this were widely known to exist in former times, and were greatly feared, so did antidotes to witchcraft form a department in their own right. It should not be thought that sorcerers 'had it all their own way': only the unprepared could be bewitched.

In the early years of the Christian era, the cornelian stone, set in a ring, was worn as an infallible specific against hostile magic. And this belief was carried westwards when the knowledge of the *Key of Solomon* and similar rituals deserted Byzantium for continental Europe. The magician himself relied to a great extent upon his pentacles: the consecrated figures of a five-pointed star which were said to be derived from the design on Solomon's mighty Ring.

When the magical manuscripts now under examination were current in Britain, the search for talismans of defence against magicians went on. For those who were unable to procure a cornelian, another magical stone was provided in the words of a seventeenth-century expert:

> "*Of the Land Toad.* Take a great Toad, kill him, and put him into a Horse Dung hill, there let him lie, and the Ants will consume the Flesh. In the Head you shall find a thing like a Stone, great or little, the which being set in gold, and worn about a

> Man or Woman, it doth give them warning of any Mischief, or ill to them that weareth it, by changing colours in divers manners."[1]

This was one of those general-purpose defensive talismans, which would not only work against witchcraft or any other evil, but would actually warn that the owner was in danger.

Another method, when the actual witch or magician was known, was to compel her to remove the spell, if needs be by force. Many cases are reported of witches being forced to take away enchantments or demons, by counter-spells which caused the witch to suffer awful agonies until she came and begged forgiveness and promised never to do the like again.

THE TIMES AND POWERS FOR MAGICAL RITES

Solomon's *Key* concentrates upon planetary data in laying down the days and hours upon which various kinds of rites are to be performed. It is assumed that most people with an interest in the occult sciences will have a sufficient knowledge of astrology to be able to work out the days and hours of the planets. This is probably so, but the method of working out which days were under which stars, and how the planetary hours were arrived at, was conveniently simplified by Albertus Magnus, in his *Secrets*. As this system is simplicity itself, and is given in the section devoted to Albertus Magnus, it will be unnecessary to repeat it here.

1 John Durant, *Art & Nature*, London, 1697.

Before determining the correct day and hour, however, the magician must make up his mind as to what he is to accomplish, and then read off in the list as to which planet governs that type of operation. Solomon summarises these data as follows:

PLANET		**TYPE OF OPERATION**
Saturn	♄	Saves from the Pit. Operations for good and evil connected with buildings; gaining familiar spirits to speak to one in one's sleep; luck and disaster in business, property, fruits and vegetables; to obtain knowledge; works of hatred, death and disaster.
Jupiter	♃	Honour and riches; friendship, physical health; the heart's desire.
Mars	♂	War, military success; valour; destruction; works of disharmony, slaughter, death and suffering; to obtain fortune in army affairs.
Sun	☉	Money, hope, sortilege; operations to obtain the support of princes and those in power; against hostility and for friendship in general.
Venus	♀	Love, friendliness, journeys, kindness and pleasure.

PLANET		TYPE OF OPERATION
Mercury	☿	Eloquence, business; arts and sciences, marvels and conjurations, prediction, discovering thefts, goods and merchandise; operations involving deceit.
Moon	☽	Travel, shipping, love and reconciliation, messengers. Theft (new Moon), visions, water.

Powers of the Hours

1. Hours of Saturn, Mars and Moon:
   Raising spirits, works of hatred and enmity.
2. Hours of Mercury:
   Games, jokes, pastimes, detection of theft with the aid of spirits.
3. Hours of Mars:
   Raising souls from the inferno, particularly soldiers killed in action.
4. Hours of Jupiter and the Sun:
   Works of invisibility, love and well-being, and all unusual experiments.

Signs and Planets to be considered for Magical Effects

The Effect of the Moon. Constructive efforts to be done when the Moon is New. Discord and Hatred succeed when the Moon is waning. Invisibility and Death only when the Moon is almost obscured.

The Zodiacal Signs and the Moon in magical operations:

The Moon must be in Taurus, Virgo or Capricornus – that is, Earth Element Signs, for *Supernatural Effects.*

For operations of *Love, Friendship or Invisibility*, the Moon must be in one of the Fire Signs: Aries, Leo or Sagittarius.

Hatred and Discord is to be accomplished when the Moon is in a Water Sign: Cancer, Scorpio or Pisces.

All Unusual Operations are to be planned for dates when the Moon is occupying an Air Sign: Gemini, Libra or Aquarius.

In the days when every man had to be his own astrologer and had to work out his own tables, the above data alone would have taken some time to calculate. Magicians of former times would probably have given much for access to 'aspectarians' such as are published today, and contain the requisite material in tabular form. The law of supply and demand does not seem to hold true in magic; for nowadays there are probably fewer magicians, and aspectarians appear in astrological magazines: while the actual astrologers themselves are generally considered 'respectable' and are probably not magicians....

PREPARATION FOR THE GRAND RITE

The *Key of Solomon*, while giving details of several magical processes, maintains that no operation involving contact with spirits can be achieved without a magic circle being drawn and consecrated, after the master and his disciples have correctly dedicated and purified themselves.

This is in line with the standard requirements of High Magic, and dates at least as far back as the Babylonian tablets, which give us a formula for the consecration of the Circle of Protection.[1]

It is only in the *Key*, however, that we find the complete detailing of the preparatory rites: neglect of which, say magicians, would inevitably mean that the evocation must fail.

The first requirement, then, is for the magician to decide upon what he wants to achieve, what spirit will be invoked to accomplish the deed. When this has been done, the mage will concentrate his attention fully upon the 'end which he seeks'. This continues during the preparation and dedication of the robes and accessories, until the actual time of the operation, which takes place according to the data of times and powers of the planets.

The master must first of all ensure, says Solomon, that he is in a state of 'ritual purity'. This means that he and his assistants must abstain for at least nine days from all unworthy and sensual things. He should even fast for three of those days – or at least eat most frugally. The *Grand Grimoire*, however, which differs in some points from the *Key*, gives the period of abstinence as 'a quarter of a moon'.

After six days, the Prayer and Confession are to be read. On the seventh day, the master is to undergo complete ablution and immersion in sanctified water, with the prayer:

"O Lord Adonai, who hast formed me, Thy unworthy servant, in thine image, from plain earth: bless and sanctify

1 Cf. "...boundary that the Gods cannot pass, which cannot be displaced, which neither god nor man can explain". See *Records of the Past*, III, 142.

this work, for the cleansing of my soul and body, and may no deceit or stupidity be here.

"O Most Powerful God! Through whose power the people were able to walk through the Red Sea from Egypt: give me this grace, purified and cleansed by this water, pure in Thy presence!"

The magus then completes his bathing and washing in the sanctified liquid, afterwards drying himself with a white linen towel. Then he is able to assume the 'pure garments' of the Art.[1]

The blessing and robing of the assistants is thus: the two disciples are taken by their master to a 'hidden place', and there he bathes them in water consecrated as above, making sure that total immersion is achieved. Then the magus intones:

"Be thou regenerate, cleansed and purified, so that the Spirits may neither harm thee nor abide in thee. *Amen.*"

The assistants are then purified, and may put on their magical garb.

The Pure Garments

These are of linen ('but silk is better'), and completely white, spun by a virgin girl. Those which have already been used by a priest in his services are considered the best. On the breast

[1] One over-zealous critic of the *Key* (he had apparently not read it) claims that the purity of body and clothes proves that this rite is 'diabolical': because the early Christian St Jerome held that 'purity of the body and its garments means the impurity of the soul' (Ep. cviii, 713). The Solomonic ritual is Jewish; even if it were otherwise, it is not now Christian doctrine that uncleanliness is next to godliness, so that the criticism is of little value.

is embroidered in red silk, and with a consecrated needle,[1] this:

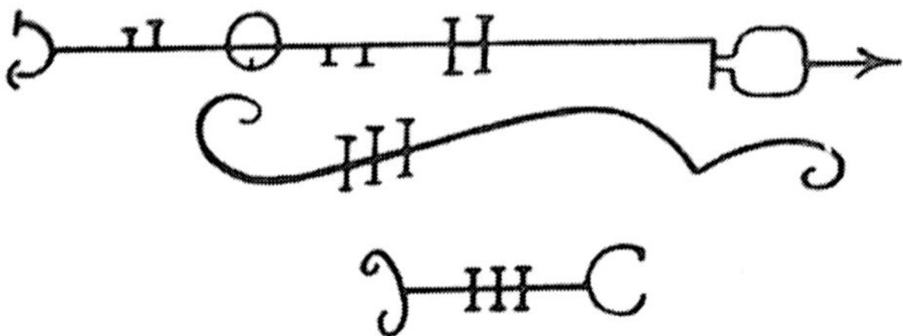

The Shoes

The footwear of the Art are also white, with these signs on them:

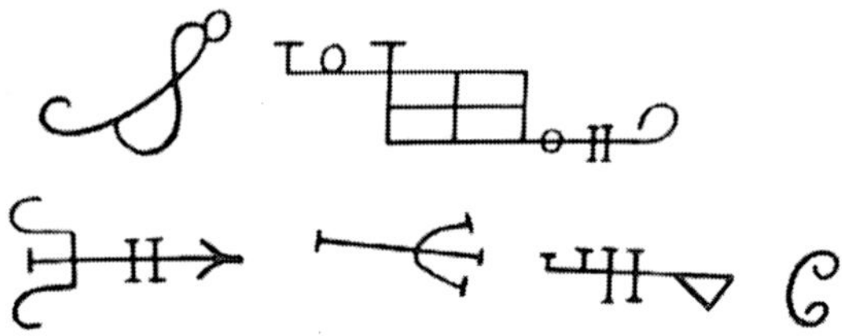

[1] Some versions give varying forms of consecration for the implements. One MS. states that only one oration is needed, and this is to be said over all instruments used in the Art of spirit evocation:

"Athanatos Sapientissime, artises qui sohovo servi tuo dedestint justus fabricar artiffia qu adusan taberculi debetant in servi et a sanctificerit alus rebus hie presentibus pater virtutem et efficacian ad mehe operanti seheter, en servant et sicti frecur: TAUTOS, TAUTAYON BARA-CHEPI, GEDITA, IGEON, *Amen.*"

There are variations in the magical designs, too. MS. No. Acc. 36674 in the British Museum collection gives these symbols for the breast of the Robe:

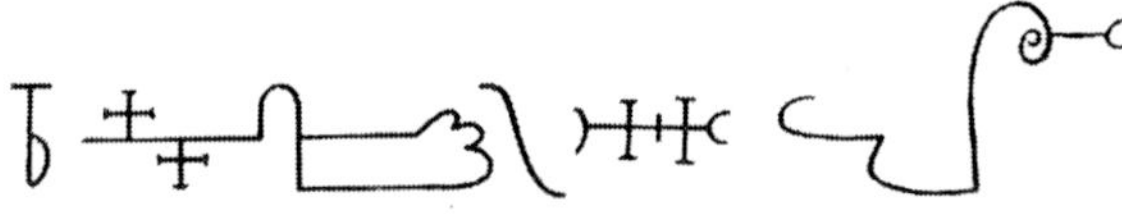

The Crown

The magus is instructed to wear a crown made of virgin white paper, and upon it is to be written certain signs, with a duly consecrated pen: the Pen of the Art.

The signs are the Hebrew Names of God: YHVH on the front, ADONAI behind, EL at the right side, and ELOHIM on the left.

The crowns of the disciples are similar to that of the master, except that they are to have these signs upon them:

Another copy of Solomon's *Key* states that this is the correct inscription for disciples' crowns:

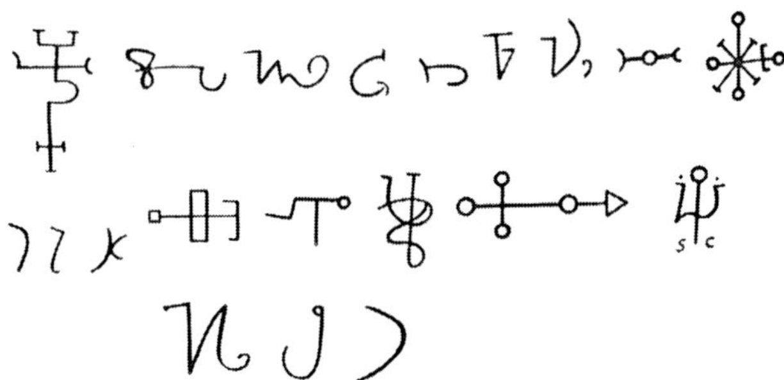

While the vesting is taking place, certain Psalms are recited by the master, beginning with Psalm xv.[1]

After Psalm xv has been said, this invocation is spoken:

"AMOR, AMATOR, AMIDES, IDEODANIACH, AMOR, PLAIOR, AMITOR!

"By the powers of those sacred angels I dress myself in these powerful robes. And through them I will bring to a successful conclusion the things that I burn to accomplish: through Thee, O Most Holy Adonai, and Thy Kingdom and Rule is everlasting. *Amen*."

The Making and Consecration of Pentacles

It is almost unanimously agreed upon by magicians that the pentacle constitutes the operator's greatest defence against tricks played by spirits. They may be used to compel demons to speak, and identify themselves: with their aid, spirits of good and evil may be conjured, bound and made to provide the 'karcist' with whatever he may desire.

Solomon's *Key* is probably the most detailed of all the rituals in its exposition of the art of pentacle-making – as the following pages will abundantly show. First, however, it might be as well to get a clear idea of pentacleology.

It seems that the true pentacle is the pentagram: a five-pointed star, called in Greek and other magical literature the pentalpha – 'a star composed of five letter A's, equidistant from a central point'. Considerable confusion has been caused by the fact that the hexagram (six-pointed star, composed of two superimposed equilateral triangles) has also been employed in magic. For this reason the hexagram (sometimes called the

[1] The Psalms are: Nos. xv, cxxxi, cxxxvii, cxvii, lxvii, lxviii and cxxvii.

seal or shield of David, father of Solomon) has been thought to be 'Solomon's Seal' – whereas it seems from the majority evidence of black books that the star attributed to Solomon is in fact the five-pointed pentagram.

But there is even greater confusion to come. Endowed as it was with wondrous qualities and miraculous magic, the pentagram became synonymous with the word 'talisman'. Hence, in the *Key of Solomon* in the versions available to us, medallions which have little resemblance to pentagrams are called 'pentacles' throughout. In order to avoid confusion as to the items to which I am referring, I call these objects 'medallions', and have referred to them as pentacles only in a footnote.

The origins of the pentagram as a symbol of well-being and safety cannot be discovered with any certainty at all. One clue, however, is found in a reference to this figure being employed by physicians (who were, of course, invariably magicians as well) of various schools of thought: as Menestrier says, "A star of five points, composed of five A's interlaced, was formerly made by physicians the symbol of health, under the name of Pentalpha."

This interpretation, however, if we remember the elaborate thought-associations of symbology, must date from some earlier origin. The present generally used symbol of healing, for example, is the Staff of Mercury, with the twin intertwined snakes: referring to well-known legends, and connecting with the magical exploits of Moses himself. Somewhere along the line of transmission – perhaps in Babylonia or beyond to the Accadians – this pentalpha probably meant an epitome of some equally well-known facet of occult lore.

However that may be, we have recorded historical instances of the pentalpha or pentacle in actual use as a magico-medical charm. The badge of Marguerite de France,[1] daughter of Henri II, wife of Henry IV and the last of the Valois, was composed of a pentalpha with a capital letter in each ray of the star: spelling out the word for health: SALUS.

That the pentacle was used to represent fortune and blessings is evidenced by such quotations as one from Aubrey, who says that the figure was "heretofore used by the Greek Christians (as the Sign of the Cross is now) at the beginning of letters or books, for good luck's sake".

The mystical aspect of the figure was explained by the Arabs of a certain family, who used it as their crest. After the advent of Mohammed, the figure was adapted into a knot with five limbs, to signify unity. This was one facet of its mystical (Sufi) interpretation, and stood for the Koranic quotation: "Hold fast by the Bond (knot) of God together, and never separate."

The Jews "did make this mark on their chrysome cloths", as Dr Bathurst mentions, and "the Jews in Barbarie have this mark on their trunks in nailes, and on their cupboards and tables". The pentagram was widely used by others than the Jews under the Hispano-Arabian culture of Iberia and north-west Africa – 'Barbarie'.

Christianised, the pentacle surmounted even the challenge of a new theology; for in No. 231 of the Lansdowne manuscripts we find that Rennet, Bishop of Peterborough, opines: "The figure of three triangles intersected and made of five lines is called the Pentangle of Solomon, and when it is delineated on the body of a man, it pretends to point out the five places wherein the Saviour was wounded, and therefore... the devils were afraid of it." All in all, the pentagram seems to have had quite as varied and mystical a

1 Died 1615.

history as the celebrated swastika, or any other variety of the cross or other solar device. It may even be found in England used in a devotional building:

"The magic pentalpha in the western window of the south aisle of Westminster Abbey bears evidence that the black monks who chanted in the choir were deeply read in occult science."[1] Another person fond of the figure was Evelyn, for "John Evelyn in many of his books, after inserting his name in monogram, was wont with the pen to draw the pentacle between the words 'Dominus providebit'" – which could very easily be part of a magical operation.[2]

But the pitfalls of the magician are not all covered, even with the preceding information. For how many people know that there are two ways of writing this mysterious and powerful sign? According to magical symbolism, if it were drawn with only one point upwards, it signified the Power of God. If, however, it were inscribed with two points upwards, it signified the Devil and his powers, and was used in infernal evocation and demonology.

Solomon, in his *Key*, warns the reader that he must fully understand the meaning of its works and significance before venturing to undertake any of the rites. Ignorance, he says in more than one place, is dangerous and therefore he who will be successful must read and re-read the *Key*, to fit himself for its mysteries. One cannot refrain from pointing out that, from the point of view of modern research, the *Key* as it stands does not provide such data as any sincere would-be wizard would have to dig out.

In its use as a magical accessory, then, the pentacle had to be drawn on virgin lambskin in bright red ink, and the skin prepared when the Sign of the Sun was in the ascendant.

1 J Pallister, *Devices*, 1870.
2 Burke, *Tokens*, 1878.

Alternatively, other magicians write that it could be drawn in gold on virgin marble. In any case it had to be consecrated: this being accomplished by one of the numerous methods of such dedication, such as are provided in the text of the *Key* given in this book.

The Instructions of Solomon on Pentacles

The *Key* specifically lays down that whoever wants to make magic must know about the making of the pentacles. For this reason the son of David collected the knowledge, and passed it on to his son Roboam, his son – to whom, of course, the *Key* is dedicated.

"Then, in these pentacles he will find the great and holiest names of God, written by him on the tablets of Moses. These I, Solomon, learned through the services of an angel.

"And I have collected and consecrated them, for the good of all humanity, and for the defence of the body and the soul (against evil spirits).

"The pentacles are to be made on the day of Mercury, and in its hour. The Moon is to be in a sign of air or earth, and waxing, and her days shall be the same as those of the Sun.

"Retire to a specially prepared room or other place, set aside for this purpose, with your companions. It is to be censed and perfumed with magical incense and fragrances."

This is done when the sky is clear and mild. Some pieces of virgin parchment are to be carried to this place. Also will be taken these colours: gold, cinnabar or vermilion, and bright blue of the skies. They must be exorcised, as also must be the pen of the (magical) Art, with which they are drawn.

The making of the pentacles should, for preference, be completed on the day and in the hour indicated – that of Mercury – but if they cannot be finished by then, there are further instructions. The magician is to wait until there is a second recurrence of a day and hour of Mercury, before finishing and consecrating the figures.

When they have been drawn, a pure silken cloth – the 'Cloth of the Art' – is to be used to enwrap them.

"Then take an earthen vase, nearly full of charcoal. Exorcise and purify frankincense, mastic and aloes, and put these upon the coals." This is the fumigant for the blessing ceremony, which must be applied in the dedication of all magical implements.

The operator is warned that he must himself be pure, clean and abstinent, as in the case of all magical operations. This caution recurs several times in the *Key*, with the warning that if any small detail of ritual procedure be omitted, nothing but failure can result.

Then, says the author, take the knife or the sickle of the Art, and draw two concentric circles, and between them the Names of God which are appropriate. The pentacles are now fumigated with the incense smoking in the charcoal vessel.

"Turn your face Eastwards, and holding the Pentacles over the smoke, repeat these[1] Psalms of my father (i.e. of David, father of Solomon). Then say this Oration:

> "'O Adonai, Omnipotent, EL, all-powerful, AGLA, holiest, ON, most righteous, Aleph and Tau, the Beginning and the End! O thou that has caused everything through thy knowledge! Thou, who elected Abraham as thy servitor, and who promised that all the nations shall be blessed by his progeny; and thou who hast manifested thyself to thy slave Moses as a flame in the Burning Bush; who enabled him to walk dryshod through the Red Sea! Thou,

[1] Psalms viii, xxi, xxvii, xxix, xxxii, li, lxxii and cxxxiv.

> who gavest him the Law upon Sinai, thou, who gave to thy servant Solomon these Pentacles, of thy mercy unequalled, that souls and bodies might be saved!
>
> "'We with humility beg and implore thee, Majestic and Holiest One, to cause the consecration of these Pentacles, through thy power: that they may be made potent against all the Spirits; through thee, ADONAI, Most Holy, for ever and ever.'"

As soon as the Oration is completed, the pentacles are perfumed and placed in their silken wrapping, to await the master's future use of them in the circle of evocation of the spirits.

The Erection of the Circle

When the master and his disciples are themselves ready for the rite, and have prepared all that they need for it in the way of accessories, the next step is the making of a magical circle: the refuge of the invocants, and specially endowed spot from whose shelter spirits may be called, 'bound', and ordered to answer questions or perform any service.

There are several forms of the Magical Circle: ranging from the ring of flour used by the Babylonians, or the ring of black stones of the Hindus, to the portable paper circle of later magicians, and the circle of metal which was reputed to be Solomon's ring, and which itself conjured genii.

The most accepted type, however, and that which is described in some detail in the *Key of Solomon*, is that which is drawn on the floor or ground in a suitable place – such as a graveyard or ruined building. According to the *Key*, a rope is to be taken, nine feet in length, and used in conjunction with the Knife of the Art as a sort of compass, to describe a ring on the earth. After this, another concentric arc is described, within the first, and one foot less in diameter.

As in the case of the vesting, Psalms are recited during this important operation, the numbers of these Psalms being ii, liv, cxiii, lxvii and lxviii.

Then is the letter *Tau* drawn four times, once at each point of the compass. Then, between the circles, and between the points of the East and South, the magician writes the four-lettered Name of the Deity which cannot be spoken. This is IHVH, and it is referred to as the Tetragrammaton. Between the other points other Ineffable Names of Power are written: "Between the South and West, AHIH (EHEIEH); between the West and North, ALVIN (ELION); between the North and East ALH (ELOAH)."

When this is completed, a double square is made, at some distance from the circle, and enclosing it. The distance between the two quadrangles thus made is to be six inches. The angles of this figure are to point to the points of the compass. Each outer angle of this square is to be covered by another double circle, each one foot in diameter. "Within the double rings of these circles, these Names are to be written: at the North, ADNI (Adonay); at the West, AGLA (Agla), at the South, IH (Yah), and at the East, AL (El)."

Between the two squares the terrible and powerful Name TETRAGRAMMATON is written, once at each side. This is an exact description of the Circle from most manuscripts, including that in the Bibliotheque de l'Arsénal, at Paris, from which the illustration reproduced here is also taken.[1]

1 Eighteenth-century Bibl. Arsénal MS. 2348.

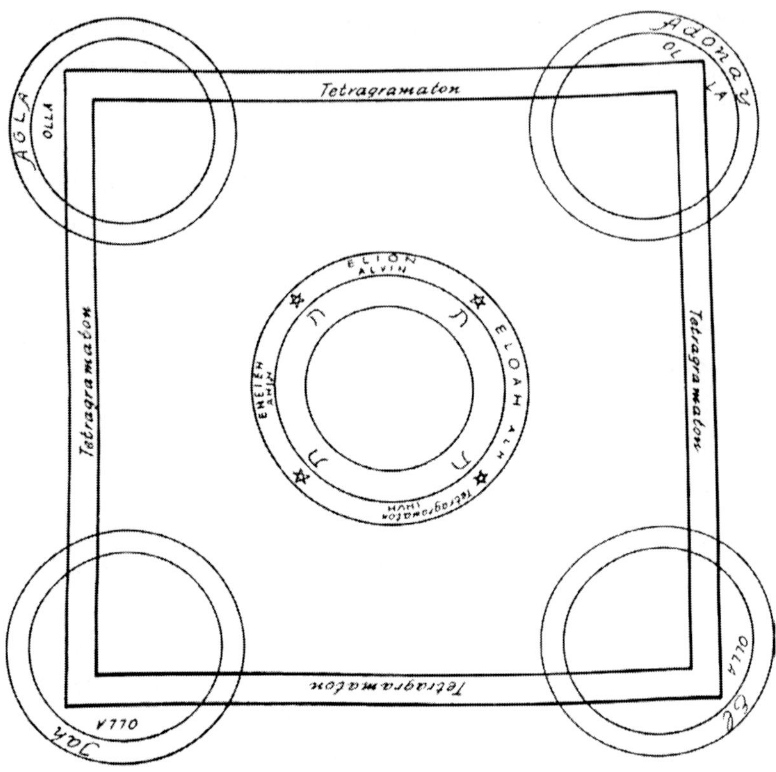

There are, however, variations on this theme, and other examples of the same manuscript in the Arsénal give another form.[1]

In this second variety, although there are differences, the essential character of the circle of evocation remains the same. The position of the smaller circles (which are occupied by the disciples) is different. The Hebrew names of the Creator here are similar, plus the secret word KIS – an abbreviation of KADOSH IEVE SABAOTH: 'Holy God of Hosts'.

1 *Clavicule de Salomon*, Bib. Arsénal MS. 2349.

Entry into the Circle

The figure is now ready, and the workers are ready to enter the sanctified precincts. Outside the arena a charcoal fire is lighted, upon which the perfumes are to burn, plus a candle ('of the Art', of course). After a short speech of encouragement to the disciples, they all enter the circle, and the master closes it by completing the last part.

Now the actual conjuration starts. It is closely modelled on the processes given in the chapter devoted to the *Book of the Spirits* of the *Lemegeton* of Solomon.[1] The magician, after consulting such books as the *Lemegeton*, the *Grand Grimoire* or the *Testament* of Solomon, chooses which spirit he is to raise. He will probably have brought with him a medallion, made in the day and hour of the planet of the spirit, with which to compel the spirit's obedience. Using the standard invocations and the Names and Words of Power, he calls his demon and obtains his services. It is on these occasions, too, that the 'Black Pact' – in which the conjurer sells his soul to Lucifuge and others – is performed.

The Rite of Conjuration

When all is prepared, the master makes an oration against possible interference by demons:

"May all devils flee, and particularly those who are inimical to this operation! When we enter herein we call with humility that God the Almighty entering this Circle will cast down divine pleasure and prosperity and joy and charity and greeting.

1 V, Chap. X.

"May the Angels of Peace help and defend this Circle: may discord disappear from it!

"Help and magnify us, O Lord. Thy Most Holy Name bless our meeting and our speech. O Lord our God, bless our entry into this Circle, for Thou art blessed for Ever and Ever! *Amen.*"

Then the master falls upon his knees, and recites the consecration of the circle:

"O Lord our God, the Most Puissant and Most Clement, Thou who desires not the death of a sinner, but rather that he may turn from his evil and continue to live; grant us Thy blessing and consecrate this ground and this circle, which is here described, and which contains the most powerful and divine Names.

"O Earth! I conjure thee, by the holiest name ASHER EHEIEH, with this arc, made by my own hand!

"May God, ADONAI, bless this place with all the heavenly virtues. May no defiling spirit be able to enter this Circle, or even to cause discomfort to anyone within it. Through the Lord God, ADONAI, He who is everliving, for ever and ever, *Amen.*

"O Lord God! I beg Thee, the Most Puissant, the Most Clement, to bless this circle, and this whole place, and all of us herein.

"And that a good Angel be allowed us, to protect us. Remove, O Lord, all inimical powers. Give us, O Lord, safety as Thou art the Everlasting Ruler! *Amen.*"

Now the magician rises, and assumes a paper crown, upon which is written: AGLA AGLAI AGLATA AGLATAI. He is, of course, provided with pentacles, which are sewn to the front of his robe.

The time for the actual conjuration of the spirit has come. Turning towards the East (or whatever direction is that of the genie being addressed) he conjures him with the First Conjuration:

First Conjuration of the Spirit

"O Lord, hear my prayer, let my cry come unto Thee. O Lord God Almighty, who has reigned before the beginning of the Ages, and who by Thine infinite wisdom hast created the heavens, the earth and the sea, and all that in them is, all that is visible, and all that is invisible, by a single word:

"I praise and bless Thee and I bless Thee, I adore Thee, I glorify Thee, and I pray Thee now at the present time to be merciful unto me, a miserable sinner, for I am the work of Thine hands.

"Save me, and direct me, by Thy Holy Name, Thou, to whom nothing is difficult, nothing is impossible; and deliver me from the night of mine ignorance, and enable me to go forth therefrom.

"Enlighten me with a spark of Thine Infinite Wisdom.

"Take away from my senses the desire of covetousness, and the iniquity of my idle words. Give unto me, Thy Servant, a wise understanding, penetrating and subtle heart, to acquire and complete all Sciences and Arts; give unto me capacity to hear, and strength of memory to retain them, so that I may be able to accomplish my desires, and understand and learn all difficult and desirable sciences; and also that I may be able to comprehend.

"Give me the virtue to conceive them, so that I may be able to bring forth and to pronounce my words with patience and humility for the instruction of others, as Thou hast ordered me.

"O God! The Father, Puissant and Clement, who hast created all things, who knowest and conceivest them universally, and to whom nothing is hidden, nothing impossible:

"I beg Thy Mercy for me and for Thy servants, because Thou seest and knowest well that we do this work not to tempt Thy power, as if in doubt thereof, but rather to crave the kindness of a favour on us, by Thy Splendour, Thy Magnificence, and Thy Holiness, and by Thy Holy, Terrible and Powerful Name IAH, at the which the whole world trembles, and by the fear by which all creatures obey Thee. Grant, O Lord, that we may become responsive unto Thy Grace, so that through it we may have a full confidence in and knowledge of Thee, and that the Spirits may reveal themselves here in our presence, and that those which are gentle and peaceable may come unto us, that they may be obedient unto Thy commands, through Thee, O Most Holy ADONAI, whose kingdom lasteth for Ever and Ever. *Amen*."

Then the magician rises and touches the pentacles. One of the assistants opens the book of invocations, and the master turns to the four points of the compass, and says:

"O Lord, be Thou unto me a tower of strength against the attacks and appearance of Evil Spirits."

And then, again to each compass point:

"These Pentacles are the symbols of the Names of the Creator which can bring fear and terror to you. Obey me, then, by the power of these Holy Names, and by these mysterious symbols and the secret of secrets.

"Then will the spirits appear and approach, from every side."

If, however, they are unable to come – or unwilling – there will be a delay.

In this case the fumigations are to be started again, and the circle will be traced anew, and the knife pointed at the sky.

Then the mage touches again the pentacles, and kneels and says the following, together with his disciples, all in a low voice:

The Confession

"O Lord of Heaven and Earth, before Thee I do confess my sins, and repent them, cast down and humble in Thy presence. I have sinned by pride, desire and idleness, by greed and debauchery and drunkenness. I have offended Thee by all kinds of sins and defilements, both performed by myself and tacitly by suffering others to do them. I have sinned by sacrilege, rapine, violation and homicide. I have sinned by the evil use of my goods, by my wastefulness, by giving bad advice, by flattery, by malconversion of goods entrusted to me, by tyranny over others, by breaking the Sabbath, by inchastity and injurying the deserving, by breaking my oath, by disobeying my parents, by ingratitude, sensuality, irreverence, profanity and pollution, and by neglect of my prayers.

"I recoil from the sins which I have done, sins of evil and vain thoughts, suspiciousness and rash conclusions, idleness and lies, deceit, perjury and slander.

"I renounce these crimes: treachery and discord incited by me, curiosity and greed, false words, violence, maledictions, blasphemies, vanities, insults and dissimulations. I have sinned against God by breaking the Ten Commandments, by neglect of my duties and obligations, and by lack of neighbourly love.

"I detest the sins of the senses that I have committed: by sight, taste, smell and touch: by carnal things, thoughts, deeds and feelings.

"I admit these before Thee, and I worship Thee.

"O Angels and children of God, I confess my sins, in order that my enemy shall have no power over me, even unto the Last Day. He cannot now say that I have concealed my wrongdoing.

"O All Powerful and Most Puissant Father, let me see the Spirits by Thy Mercy, that I may have my desire and will fulfilled, by Thy Power and Glory: who Art the Powerful, the Pure, the Father."

There is only one conjuration needed now, says the *Key*, to ensure that the spirits appear, as instructed.

"O Omnipotent, Everlasting God, Father of Creation, bestow upon me Thy mercy, for I am Thy creation. I beg Thee, defend me from my enemies, and strengthen my faith to be firm and strong.

"O Lord! I commit unto Thee my body and soul, and believe only in Thee, and upon Thee do I depend. O Lord, O my God! help me and assist at the time and on the day when I shall call to Thee.

"I beseech thy remembrance of my nearness, Thou art my Saviour: grant to me love to become better, O Lord! These are my desires, O Eternal, Ever-ruling One. *Amen.*

"O Omnipotent and Most Wise one, Thou who created the Heavens, Earth and the Sun, and all that in them are; O Thou, Who hast breathed life into all things, I praise and bless Thee, worship and glorify Thy Name. I am a sad sinner, and I ask Thy aid and comfort, help me.

"By the power of Thy Great Name, I beg Thee to drive away the obscurity of ignorance from my mind, and to replace it with the light of knowledge. Remove off me all evil, and let me not speak foolishly.

"Thou art the Living, the One whose light, whose Honour and whose Kingdom reach into time eternal! *Amen.*"

During this address, the spirits will come. If they are not visible, the *Key* tells us, the magus is to uncover the pentacles which are at his neck. Any further difficulties with spirits can be overcome with the Grand Conjuration, a form of which is found in the *Lemegeton*, and which is detailed in Appendix I – under the name of 'Second Conjuration to Reluctant Spirits'.

It is stressed that in the case of delay, spirits will often send representatives to explain the delay. A method of bringing genii post-haste is said to be the pointing of the knife into the Heavens, and a call to all the Celestial Angels.

When the angels appear (which they should have done during the early part of the rite), they are questioned as to their names, ranks and stations, and told what they are to do for the master. Then, before the circle is left, the spirits are dismissed with this phrase, of which there are several variations:

Dismissal of the Spirit

"By the Power of the Mighty ADONAI, ELOHIM, SABAOTH, I license thee to depart, good spirit, whence thou came. Be ready to respond to my call when it shall please me."

CHAPTER II

THE CLAVICLE: SPELLS AND MEDALLIONS

Of the Process of Flying by Magic

MAGIC MAY BE able to perform all things, but this particular ritual can be started only once in the year: on the twenty-fifth day of June.

A stag's skin is taken, and two garters are made from it. In the inside of each of them is to be written:

OEƐ+ΘO OM3Λ3

This is to be done with the blood of a hare which has been killed on the twenty-fifth of June. On this day also – and before sunrise – there is to be gathered a quantity of green mugwort, and a short rod is cut from a holm-oak.

Both garters are filled with the mugwort, and one eye of a barbel fish placed in each. Now these valuable accessories are stored away until needed.

When it is desired to fly, the magician rises before the sun is up, and washes his garters in a running stream. Then they are put on, above the knee. Then "Take the oak rod, turn in the direction in which you want to fly, and write the name of your destination on the ground." The garters will fly at once, carrying the sage with them. To stop, the traveller merely swishes the air with the rod, and pronounces the word AMECH.

Of a Spell Against Hunters

There may be occasions upon which a magician desires to prevent hunters being able to kill game. On the other hand, he may be asked by some animal-lover to help in the struggle for the protection of furry friends. Amid all the weird and wonderful processes of ritual magic and spells which we find in the *Key of Solomon* it seems odd indeed that this lighter-hearted process is included. It might, however, be argued that it is in reality a hostile spell, designed to prevent an enemy from deriving any advantage from the hunt. However it may be, here it is.

A rod of green elder is taken, and the marrow removed from its two ends. Two small pieces of parchment made from the skin of a hare are thus inscribed, each with the blood of a black hen:

ABIMEGH

One of these talismans is then slid into each end of the elder rod, the ends afterwards being sealed with pitch. On a Friday, in February, "fumigate the rod with incense, three times and when it is in the air. Then bury it under an elder tree."

When a huntsman passes by this stick (which is dug up when needed, and placed by his path), he will kill nothing that day; we are assured of this. "You can use it often, but it must be buried between uses."

Of the Ritual of Love and Advancement

The Solomonic writings devote a special note to this subject. After mentioning that all is to be prepared for the circle and evocation, it is indicated that a special formula is to be written down: "Then shall your wish be granted."

Special formula:

"Sator, Arepo, Tenet, Opera, Rotas, IAH, IAH, ENAM, IAH, IAH, IAH, KETHER, CHOKMAH, BINAH, GEDULAH, GEBURAH, TIPHERETH, NETZACH, HOD, YESOD, MALKUTH, Abraham, Isaac, Jacob, Shadrach, Meshach, Abednego, Come here all to my aid, and all that which I seek to have."

Of the Accomplishment of Unusual Operations

When it is desired to do something different from the processes laid down in the book, or when there is something really difficult to be done, the ritual of the circle and calling spirits is to be reinforced.

After arming himself with the usual accessories, including the pentacles, virgin parchment and calculations of the correct times and day of operation, the operator is told to repeat this adjuration, just before the actual spirit-evocation ceremony:

"O God, Creator of all, who allows us to distinguish between good and evil! By the Names IOD IAH VAU DALETH – SABAOTH, ZIO, Amator, Creator: allow that this operation may succeed, through Thy Seal, Most Holy, O Adonai, Eternal! *Amen.*"

Then, we are assured, the operation must succeed.

Of the Works of Invisibility and Deceit

Invisibility is classed by the *Key of Solomon* as a work of deceit, insofar as it involves deceiving people as to one's presence at any given place. In addition to the drawing of the usual circle, at the times and on the days already stated to be suitable for this type of experiment, certain other extra requirements are noted.

The operator, for instance, is to call out loudly these words:

"ABAC, ALDAL, IAT, HIBAC, GUTHAC, GUTHOR, GOMEH, TISTATOR, DERISOR, DESTATUR: Come here, all of you who like the places and times in which duplicity and trickery are done! And you, the masters of invisibility: come here, and deceive those who see things: that they may appear to see what they do not, and that they may hear what they hear not, and that their senses may be tricked, and that they may see what is not true!

"Come, then, here and stay, and consecrate this spell, for God Almighty, the Lord, has assigned to you this function!"

If you do this correctly, says the *Key*, "you are sure to succeed".

Of the Winning of Hidden Treasures

Caution and Explanation

The world, we are told by the *Clavicle*, is full of spirits of various kinds. They know the location of treasures, and they guard them. People who seek such treasure have often been harmed by these creatures, which are opposed to greed. From this, and textual indications elsewhere, it is evident that the treasure must be sought with a healthy mind and almost altruistic motives, if this rite is to be fruitful.

First, continues our magician, the spirits merely annoy the treasure-hunter. Then, if their warning is not heeded, they may kill him. This may be one of the reasons why other magical ceremonies for claiming treasures stress the fact that the particular demon "will bring the treasure to you" or "will lead you to it, and you can carry away all you need in safety".

Assume, as one supposes we must, that the wizard knows (probably through another spirit) of the actual location of one such treasure. Naturally, it is guarded by spirits. Now he must know how to gain the confidence of the spirit-guardians.

The method of accomplishing this is now discussed for us.

Conjuring the Spirit

This operation is to be performed on a Sunday, before the Sun has risen, between 10th July and 20th August, making sure that the Moon is in the astrological sign of Leo. It is not always that a magician can create such effects as he wishes, in the twinkling of an eye, we should note: conditions must be right and aspects propitious.

Having satisfied himself that these requirements have been met, the operator now proceeds to the spot where the treasure lies, under its guardian genii. The place is surrounded by a circle, drawn on the ground with the Sword of the Art.

The centre of the circle, it is carefully pointed out, is to be the place where the treasure is. Above this spot is hung a lamp, whose oil shall contain fat from the body of a man who died during July. The wick is a strand from his winding-sheet.

The mage is, of course, arrayed in his ceremonial Robes of the Art, and censes the circle three times during that day, with the planetary incense for the day.

The man (or men) who will do the digging will each be protected with a belt made from the skin of a newly killed sheep. And in the same dead man's blood this is written thereon:

This invaluable accessory will protect anyone from the phantoms. If the excavation is not completed on that self-same day, the hole is to be covered with wooden boards, we are instructed, and then a light screen of earth is spread over this, to conceal the opening. The magus must be there all the time of the digging, wearing his robes and carrying the Sword of the Art.

Even though he may not be taking an active part in the digging, the master is fully occupied. During the progress of the work he is to intone:

"Adonai, Elohim, El, Eheieh, Asher Eheieh: King of Kings, Existence of all Existences, be merciful to me, and look upon me (NAME) Thy servant, who calls Thee with humility, and begs by Thy most holy name TETRAGRAMMATON to be benefited.

"Order Thy Angels and planetary spirits to come and be here: O Angels and planetary spirits! O all of you, spirits, I conjure you: I, the deputed of God! let God order you to come, that I ask most fervently and most humbly. *Amen.*"

When the treasure is found, and the hole refilled, all the spirits, in conformity with custom, are to be licensed to depart:

The Licence to Depart

"O good and happy spirits, we give thanks for the granting of what you have given. Go, then, in peace, to rule the element which is your divinely ordained abode. *Amen.*"

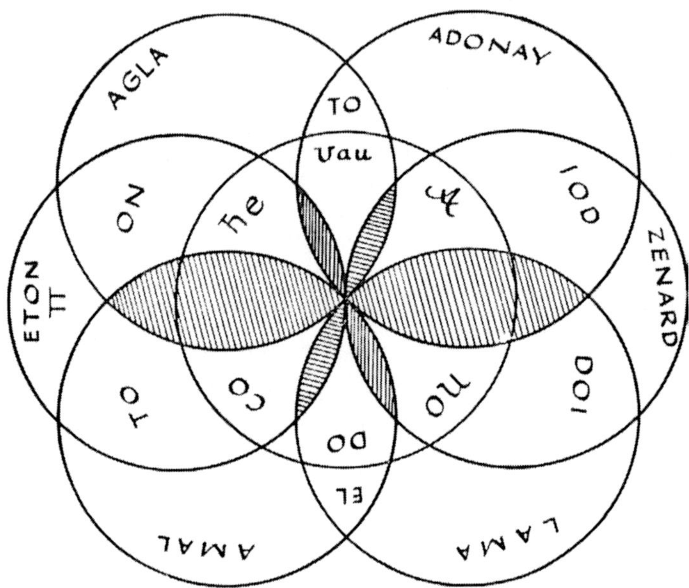

Talisman for 'Conjuring Infernal Spirits' – *Key of Solomon*, 18th cent. French MS.

Of the Sacrifices to the Spirits

The sacrifices are the blood, and occasionally the meat, of animals and birds: white in the case of the good genii, and black for evil demons.[1]

[1] Maimonides (*Guide to the Perplexed*) speaks of the general idea behind blood sacrifice, which later anthropological research has shown to be widespread among many communities with a magico-religious system. He says that the Sabians believed that blood was the food of the spirits, and hence was a link between man and genii (*Ibid*, III, xlvi).

They must be virgin (that is, have never engendered) and hence young ones are generally taken for the Rite of Sacrifice. Before the sacrifice is made, the magician says:

"O High and Mighty creatures, may this sacrifice be acceptable and pleasing to you. If you serve us faithfully, larger ones will be given to you."

When his oration is completed with the names of the spirits, the sacrifice is perfumed, and the animal is slaughtered. According to several versions of the *Key of Solomon* and other grimoires, the head has to be severed with one blow of the magical knife.

In this chapter, however, Solomon speaks of other offerings, which are also styled sacrifices. These consist of the wood which is appropriate to the day of the experiment (see Chapter XX) and each wood corresponds to one of the seven planets.

Then there are the offerings of food and drink. The bread and wine are so chosen as to be in harmony with the planets connected with the spirits to whom the offering is made. By this remark it is assumed that their colours and consecration follow those laid down by the author of the *Key*. (Bread, water and wine figure largely in spirit-propitiation ceremonies the world over; and their ritual use, of course, antedates the adoption of this symbolism by the Christian church in its services.)

The meal must be laid out on a pure, clean, white cloth, with another of similar type covering it. The meat – if there is any – is to be cooked. A pitcher of fresh water from a running stream must be present also. When all is prepared – presumably within a magical circle – the spirit is to be called by name:

"Wherever you may be, Spirit, come to this banquet and accept the offerings and gifts. If you agree to this, still better sacrifices will be prepared."

Then the food is censed with pleasant odours, and the consecrated water sprinkled over it. After this follows the usual conjuration of the spirit, in the manner given under the rite of the Magical Circle.

Of the Consecration of the Book of the Spirits

Make a small book in which are the prayers for all the operations, with the names of the Angels, in the form of Litanies, and with their seals and characters.

When this is done, you shall consecrate it to God and the clean Spirits thus. Place it in a special room on a table which is covered with a white cloth. The book is to be open at the beginning and on the first page is to be drawn the Great Pentacle.

Kindle a lamp hanging above the table. Put a curtain around the table, and dress yourself in the robes of the Art. Holding the book open, kneel and say this *Prayer*:[1] and after this you will cense it with the incense proper to the planet and the day, and replace the book on the table. During this operation the fire is to be kept going, and the curtain is to be kept closed throughout.

The process is repeated on seven successive days, starting on Saturday. Each day the book is to be perfumed with the incense of the Planet of the Day and Hour in which you are operating. The lamp is to burn day and night.

After this you will cense it with the incense proper to the Planet and Day, and then replace the book on the table. When the book is consecrated, call all the Angels whose names are to be found therein. Be not surprised if the Angels come not at

1 Here is repeated the prayer given under 'Of the winning of hidden treasure', above and beginning: "Adonai, Elohim, El..."

once, because they must struggle to associate themselves with man, the impure. But they will come, and you must be sure to guard against impurity of any kind. The book is kept in a small drawer under the table, which shall have been made especially for its reception, until such time as it is needed.

Of the Oracular Carpet for All Knowledge

This is a method of making what might be called a magic carpet: one that tells all secrets – hence probably it could be said to be more valuable even than the fabulous flying carpet which Solomon is supposed to have commanded.

The carpet is made from new white wool: the time of the operation is during the full Moon, when that luminary is in the sign of Capricorn, and during the hour of the Sun.

When he is satisfied that these requirements have been satisfied, the magician repairs to a deserted place somewhere in the country, far from the haunts of men.

Here the carpet is placed on the ground, one corner pointing Eastwards, and another to the West. It is to be surrounded by a circle.

"Stand at the Eastern corner, with your wand in your hand: and invoke Michael, to the East, Raphael, to the North, at the West, Gabriel, and Muriel to the South."

After this, the operator turns again to the South and calls upon the name AGLA, and lifts the eastern point of the carpet. Then he continues to the other corners in turn, "raising them off the ground".

As he holds the four corners in his hand, the magus turns again to the East, and calls out:

"AGLA, AGLA, AGLA, AGLA! O Almighty God, Thou art the Life of the Universe, and rule over the four parts of that immense area, through the power of Thy Holy Name

TETRAGRAMMATON: Yod, He, Vau He! Bless this carpet in Thy Name, as Thou blessed the cloak of Elijah in the hands of Elijah; so that, with Thy wings, I may be able to be protected against all: *He shall hide thee under His wings and under His feathers thou shalt trust, and His truth shall be thy protection.*"

Then the master is to fold the carpet, saying "RECABUSTIRA, CABUSTIRA, BUSTIRA, RA, A." "And then guard it until you need it, and use it."

When the time comes to question the carpet, this is to be done at full or new Moon, and only during the period between midnight and dawn.

The rite may be done anywhere that is clean and pure.

The night before this, the worker takes a piece of virgin parchment, and on it, with a dove's feather, writes this word: RAZIEL.

The carpet is then taken, and the head and body covered by it. Then the censer is lighted, and incense burned. Now the magician lies flat with his face on the ground, under the carpet, and the censer with him. He should be thus positioned "before the fumes have started to rise from the incense". Next, the parchment is held to the brow with one hand, and the wand is used to support the chin.

This is the spell to be recited in this position:

"VEGALE HAM I CAT A UMSA TERATA YEH DAH MA BAXASOXA UN HORAH HIMSERE! O God, give me inspiration, help me to discover that which I seek to know, whatever it is, with the help of Thine aides, the holy PALIEL, TZAPHNIEL, MATMONIEL!

"See, Thou wouldst have truth in youth, and I will know wisdom through this secret:

"RECABUSTIRA, CABUSTIRA, BUSTIRA TIRA RA A! KARKAHITA, KAHITA, HITA, TA."

Then you will clearly hear in answer the secret for which you have wished.

THE MIRACULOUS MEDALLIONS

These are the talismans through which almost anything, according to the *Key of Solomon*, can be accomplished. They are referred to in most texts as the 'Planetary Pentacles', though here I have adhered to one reading as medallions, in order to avoid confusion with those pentacles which are the 'ordinary' shields against the evil of spirits, whose manufacture is described separately in the *Key*.

These talismans share with the common-or-garden pentacle the ability to cause fear among spirits. In addition, however, they cause the spirits of the planets which they represent to obey the operator in every way, and thus would be of service to any aspiring magician. "Wherever you go," says our author, "providing that you have them with you, you will be completely secure for your whole life."

Frequently referred to by occultist writers are the terrible dangers attendant upon the raising of spirits. These spirits answer by false names, misleading the operator; they may succeed (for they try hard enough) in luring the magus or a disciple out of the protecting precincts of the Circle. In this case "death has generally resulted". Reading the assurances under the heading of these miraculous medallions, however, one is almost tempted to think that this is the complete answer: "When commanded by the Power of the Medallions, all spirits will obey, at once, and without danger."

If these talismans are made and carried, you will be "liked by all, fire and water will be overcome by them: and every created thing will fear the Names (upon them) and be obedient to you". Since all magic involves the acquisition of power in one form or another, one could say that the pentacle-talismans of Solomon alone are worth any sorcerer's trouble in making.

And the making, it is true, does involve some little labour. They are to be preferably in metal, but they can be on parchment. The metal is that which is associated with whichever of the Seven Planets the medallion refers to. The metal itself, of course, must be purified by fire, and the characters which are to be seen in the illustrations are engraved thereon with the Needle of the Art: a never-before-used, exorcised needle.

The pentacle of Saturn is of lead; of Jupiter, tin; Mars of iron; that of the Sun is of gold, Venus copper, and the Moon of silver. The medallion dedicated to the planet Mercury, commanding all the spirits thereof, is variously stated to be of a silver-gold alloy, or a mixture of various metals – unspecified.

If they are instead of metal made in paper, the correspondence of planets and colours is to be observed. Hence the consecrated virgin parchment is to have its designs inscribed thus:

Saturn, black
Jupiter, azure blue
Mars, red
Sun, gold or yellow
Venus, green
Mercury, mixed
Moon, silver or white-grey.

Would-be sorcerers will be relieved to learn that "size is of no importance, if all the other requirements are fulfilled".

The section on the making of these items ends with the usual cautions that all the things which are customary (doing things in the right planetary hour and day, etc.) must be observed, and that the Names which are used, being holy, are to be concentrated upon, and not treated frivolously.

Solomon winds up this chapter in some versions with terrible curses upon those who may profane these rites, and those who, for example, take the Name of God in vain.

Of the Pentacles for Compelling Spirits

The first medallion is one dedicated to the Sun. Its powers are all things connected with honour, glory and kingly power. This talisman is also used in rites intended to inflict loss on others.

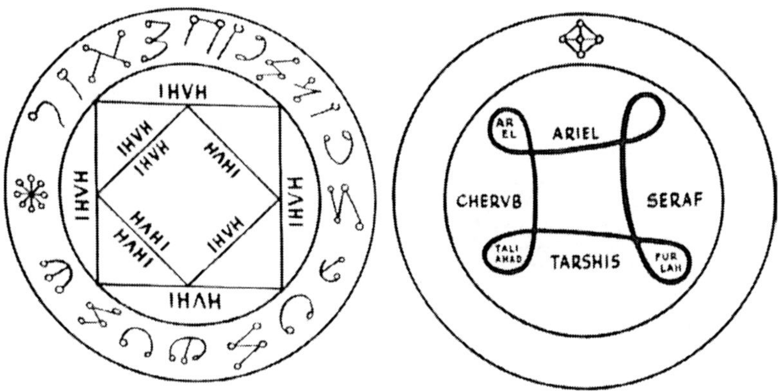

The second talisman is likewise under the Sun, and its province is to release magically anyone imprisoned. "If anyone is by chance imprisoned, and held with iron chains, he shall at once be freed, if this Pentacle is presented, engraved in gold on the day and at the hour of the Sun." According to MS. No. 2497 of the Paris Bibliothèque de l'Arsénal (*Les Vraies Talismans*), the inscription within the outer ring reads: "Dirupsiti vincula mea; tibi sacrificabo hostiam laudis, et nomen invocabo." This seems to be Psalm cxvi: "Thou hast loosed my bonds; I will offer to thee the sacrifice of thanksgiving, and will call upon the Name of the Lord." (16, 17.)

All created things come under the powerful talisman: the Face of Shaddai. Confronted with it, engraved on the metal of the Sun, in the hour and on the day of the luminary, every created being, whether corporate or not, must obey. On the right is written, in Hebrew characters, the Name of God, EL; on the left another Name of the divinity, SHADAI. Around the circle is written: "Ecce faciem et figuram ejus per quem omnia facta et cui omnes obediunt Creature."

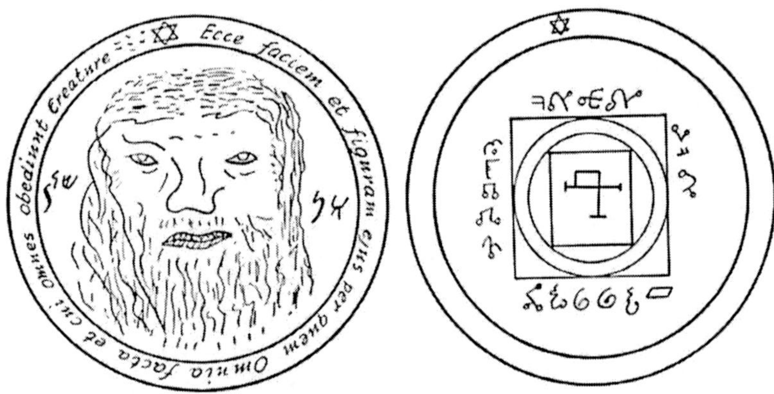

The next solar pentacle calls spirits to carry the sorcerer to whatever place he may desire to go, at once.

Around the circle is to be written an extract from Psalm xci, 11, 12: "He shall give his Angels charge over thee, to keep thee in all thy ways. They shall bear thee up in their hands."

Nearly all the Solomonic talismans contain quotations from the Psalms of David, and it is the opinion of traditional mages that the Book of Psalms itself is a sort of collection of magical incantations with a hidden as well as obvious power.

The next pentacle of the Sun confers invisibility, and bears within the twin circles this inscription: "Let their eyes be darkened, that they see not; and make their loins continually to shake" – from Psalm lxix, 23.

One of the difficulties facing any conjuror of spirits seems to be that when the demons come they will not always immediately manifest themselves – for some reason – in a visible form before him. This next Sun talisman is expressly designed to ensure the appearance of the spirits, when it is uncovered in their presence. Around the circle is to be written: "Lighten mine eyes, lest I sleep the sleep of death; lest mine enemy say, I have prevailed against him." This is, of course, from the thirteenth Psalm.

The next and last Sun talisman is another pentacle of power.

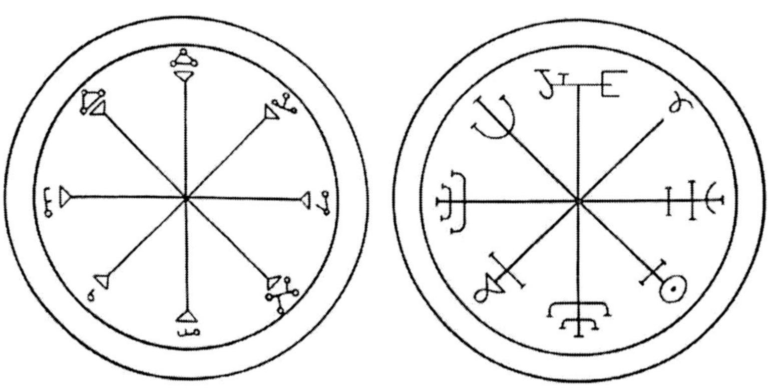

The next pentacle of Solomon is that of Venus, and serves to control the spirits of that planet. It will produce grace and honour and by its aid every art appertaining to the powers of Venus can be exercised. Around the medallion are written the name of the angels NOGAHIEL, ACHELIAH, SOCOHIA and NANGARIEL.

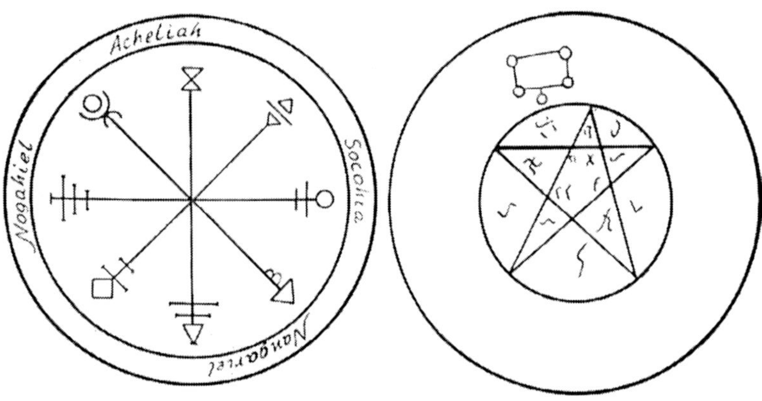

Operations under Venus involving matters of love are carried out with the aid of another Venusian pentacle. It takes the form of a five-pointed star within two concentric circles. The inscription is, appropriately enough: "Place me as a signet upon thy heart, as a signet upon thine arm, for Love is

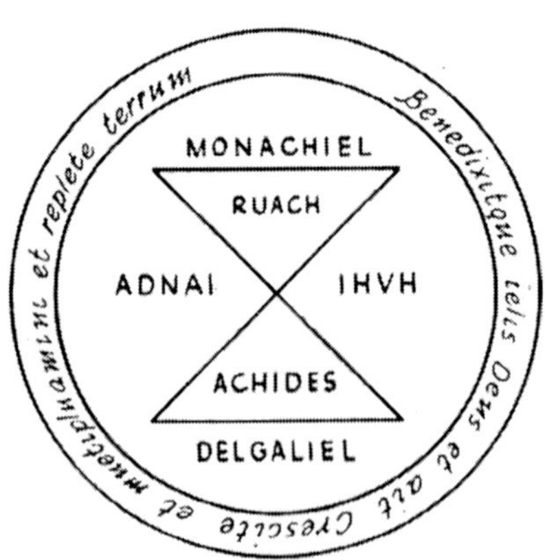

as strong as death" – from Canticles, viii, 6. Within and around the pentagram there are certain signs which are almost unintelligible in the manuscripts. Probably these are attempts by unlettered copyists to reproduce Hebrew letters.

Love can be caused in a person of one's choice by merely displaying the next pentacle, in which is written a Latin quotation from Genesis, i, 28: "Benedixitque ielis Deus et ait Crescite, et muetipluamini, et replete terrum..." Angelic and divine names complete the figure.

Any woman's love can be compelled in a moment by the use of another pentacle of Venus, given in the BA Manuscript No. 2348. Within the outer circles is written another verse from the Book of Genesis: "This is now bone of my bones, and flesh of my flesh... And they shall be one flesh."

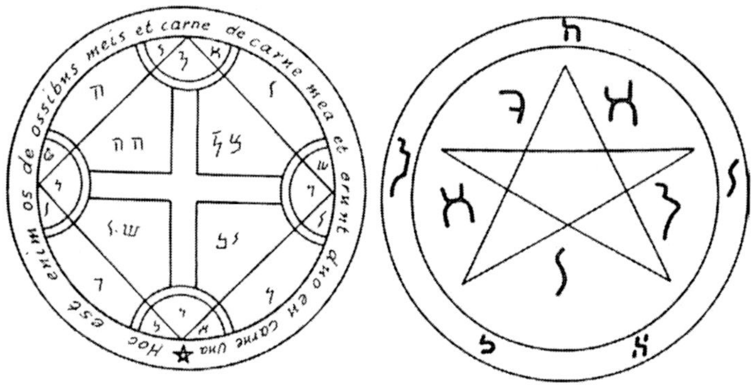

The spirits of Mercury may be invoked and compelled with the next powerful Solomonic pentacle. All operations connected with the reputed powers of this star are carried out when this talisman is shown.

Those who have business coming within the purview of the Moon on hand should make use of the following pentacle, that of the Moon. It not only calls spirits who come under this planet, but also opens all doors, no matter how they may be closed. Psalm cvii, 16 is written upon it: "He hath broken the gates of brass, and cut the bars of iron in sunder." Like the other talismans, this, too, has its quota of divine and angelic names.

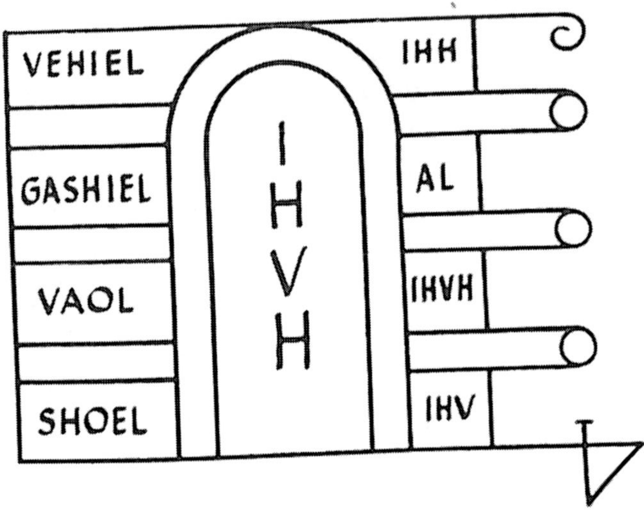

Spirits of Saturn are conjured and compelled to obedience by means of the first pentacle of this planet. When it is shown to them they yield, and kneel in submission. The square carries various divine names.

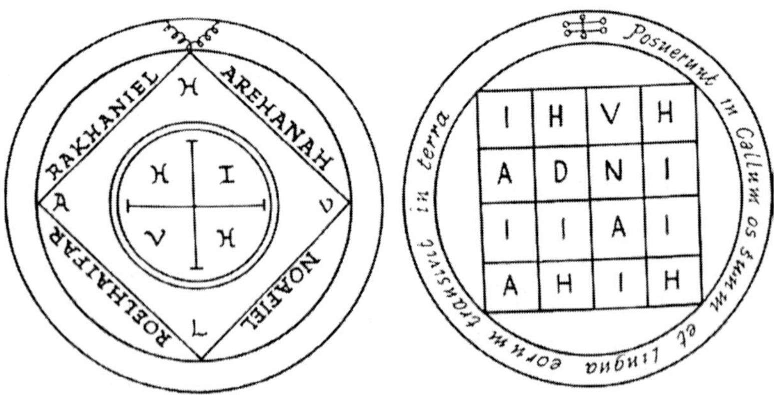

Another Saturnian pentacle, with an extract from Deut. x, 17, is also given here. With its aid, one may carry out any process under the influence of Saturn.

Those who, operating under Saturn, desire to cause a person to be possessed by devils could make use of the following figure.

It contains written thereupon a powerful curse: "Set thou a wicked one to be ruler over him, and let Satan stand at his right hand."

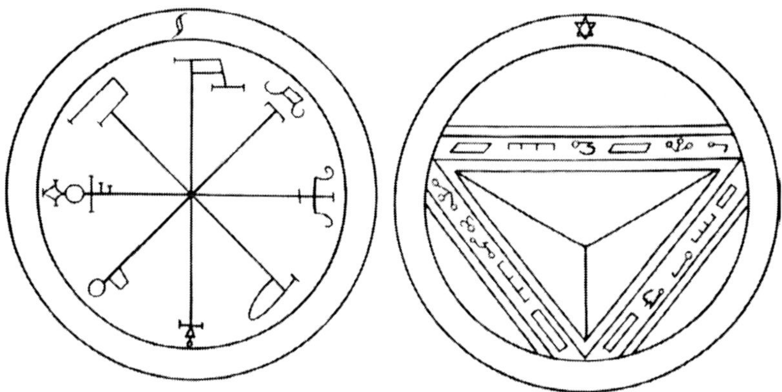

Do you wish to cause earthquakes? The power of the next Saturnian talisman causes all Creation to shake, through the force of the angels which it commands, if the talisman be properly made – like the other medallions – during the hours and day of the planet, and in its metal.

All operations of destruction, disruption and death should be carried out when the operator is in possession of another pentacle or talisman of Solomon, again under Saturn, and prepared in strict accordance with the requirements of occult manufacture.

Within the usual twin circles are the words: "As he clothed himself with cursing like as with a garment, so let it come into his bowels like water, and like oil into his bones." There is also the six-sided star of David here. Within the rings comes a triangle containing another circle decorated with the mystical letter YOD, in the Hebrew tongue. Then, beside the sides of the triangle, come words from Deut. vi, 4: "Hear, O Israel, the Lord our God is One Lord."

Saturn being such a malevolent planet, it is perhaps hardly surprising that there is a special pentacle devoted to protecting

the operator against death on Saturday, his day. An eight-pointed figure decorates the centre of our illustration, with magical inscriptions within the circles.

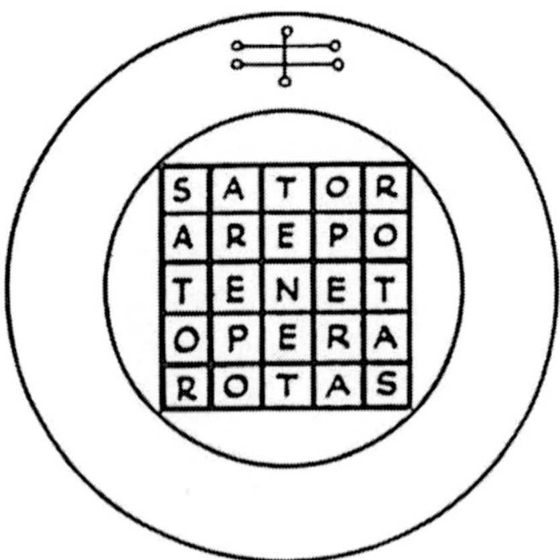

Another Saturn talisman is used against arrogance on the part of spirits, and also against all opponents. The figure consists of a magical square with the words SATOR, AREPO, TENET, OPERA, ROTAS, inscribed therein. The formula is Psalm lxxii, 8: "He shall have dominion also from sea to sea, and from the river unto the ends of the earth."

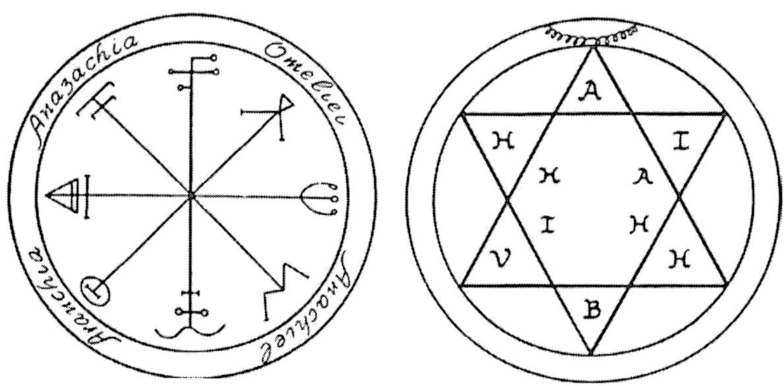

When the spirits of Saturn are called at night, the next talisman is to be written outside the magical circle of evocation. In addition to containing eight cabbalistical signs, the concentric circles contain the names of four important angels: ANAZACHIA, OMELIEI, ANACHIEL and ARAUCHIA.

The next talisman is of greater than ordinary interest, because we have an historical instance of its use by a well-known figure. It carries the inscription: "Wealth and riches shall be in his house, and his righteousness endureth for ever." (Psalm cxii, 3.)

This Solomonic talisman of Jupiter was found inscribed on a piece of parchment on the body of Count Anselm, who became Bishop of Wurzburg, on the night of the ninth of February, 1449. It has been said (of course) that this was the powerful talisman which caused him to rise to such heights, and to gain wealth and power, as well as evading all traps of his many enemies.

Another talisman of Jupiter, however, not only calls spirits but protects the owner and forces the complete submission and active obedience of all demons. In addition to the names of God ADNI and IHVH, and signs of the spirits, the inscription is from Psalm cxxv: "They that trust in Jehovah (shall be as) Mount Zion, which cannot be removed, but abideth for ever."

Those who wish never to be poor, or who are poor and think that they should be rich, are advised by the writers of the *Key of Solomon* to resort to the next talisman, ascribed to Jupiter, and to be made in accordance with the colours, metal, etc., of his day and hour.

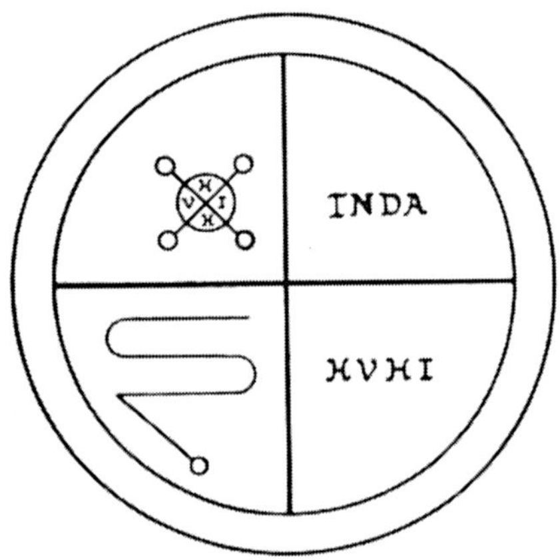

The medallion or charm written on parchment, as the case may be, is to be taken out and frequently looked upon. Then these words which appear upon it are to be recited: "He raiseth up the poor out of the dust, and lifteth the needy out of the dunghill, that he may set them with princes, even with the princes of his people." (Psalm cxiii, 7, 8.)

Those who seek to call the spirits of Jupiter for the purpose of finding treasure could do worse, we are told, than use the next talisman. The magical words are NETONIEL, DERACHIAH, SEDEKIAH and PARASIEL.

When the planet Jupiter is in the Sign of Cancer (the Crab), anyone with a piece of silver could pave the way to untold wealth by drawing the next figure on his silver, in the day and hour of Jupiter. He should, of course, not omit the quotation from Psalm cxii, 3: "Wealth and riches shall be in his house, and his righteousness endureth for ever."

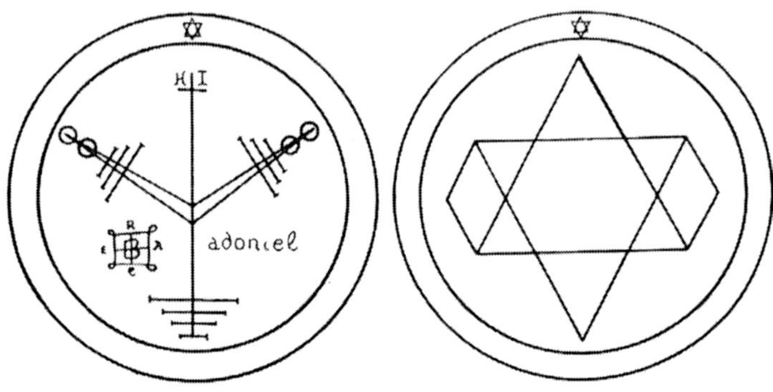

Of the two remaining pentacles of Jupiter, the first is for seeing visions. By its aid, we are informed, Jacob saw the ladder to Heaven. Some readers may think that they prefer the more solid advantages of the last pentacle of Jupiter. He who carries it about him, looking at it every day, will not be able to die. It contains the lines from Psalm xxii, 16, 17: "They pierced my hands and my feet, I may tell all my bones."

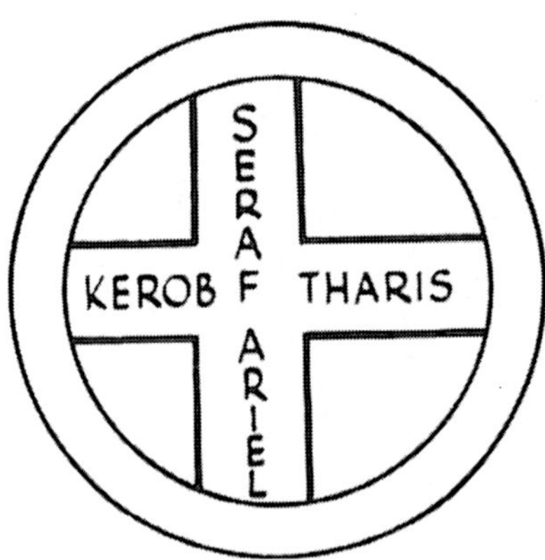

To produce war, as might be expected, one would need the medallion of Mars. In addition to this useful power, the figure can destroy enemies, and will terrify spirits if presented to them. It consists of one triangle within a circle, divided again into four triangles. The words are from Psalm lxxvii, 13: "Who is so great a God as our Elohim?" and certain Hebrew letters.

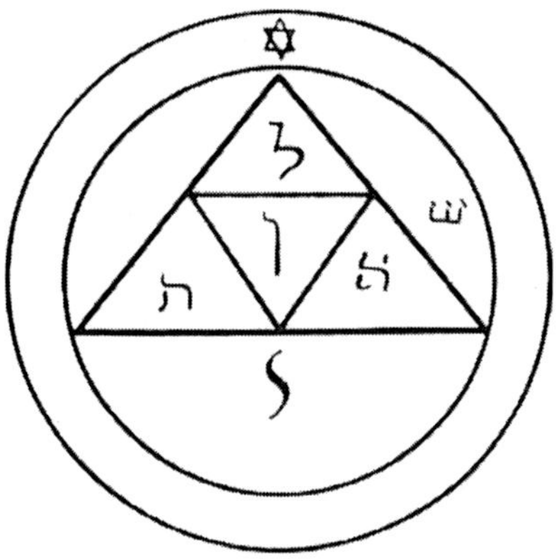

Having started a war, it would presumably be necessary to ensure victory. This can be done with the next pentacle. It is a cross within a double circle, with the letters for the Divine Names of Power arranged therein. The quotation is: "The Lord at thy right hand shall strike even kings in the day of His wrath." (Psalm cx, 5.)

If you are faced with demons, you can compel them to do anything if you only carry with you this figure of Mars written on virgin parchment. It consists of a scorpion (the conventional sign for the Scorpio of the Zodiac, which comes under Mars), and the words: "Thou shalt tread upon the lion and adder; the young lion and the dragon shalt thou trample under feet." (Psalm xci, 13.)

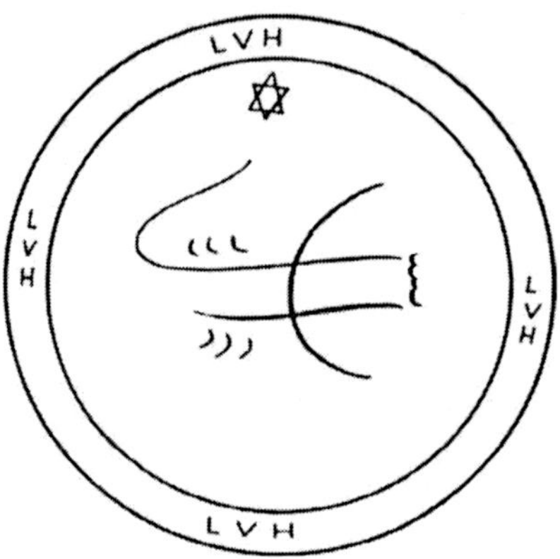

Then comes a Martian talisman for invincibility, against all attack, and to turn the arms of enemies against them. In Latin, the inscription is from Psalm xxxvii, 15: "Their sword shall enter into their own heart, and their bows shall be broken."

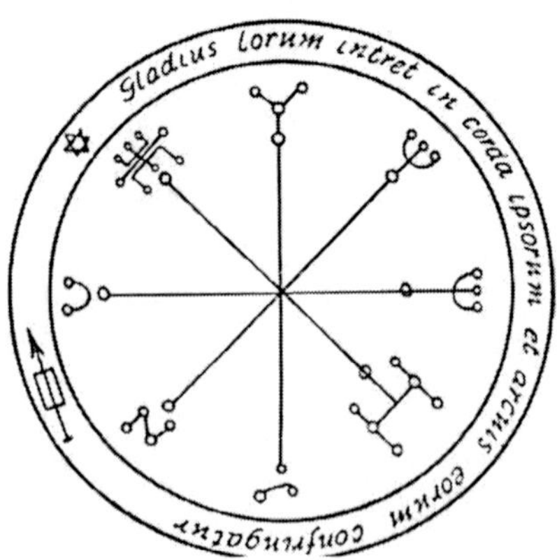

It may, however, be necessary to call the spirits of Mars to the invocant's circle. In order to do this he must display the next pentacle of Mars, upon which is written this: ESHIEL, ITHURIEL, NADAMIEL, BARZACHIA.

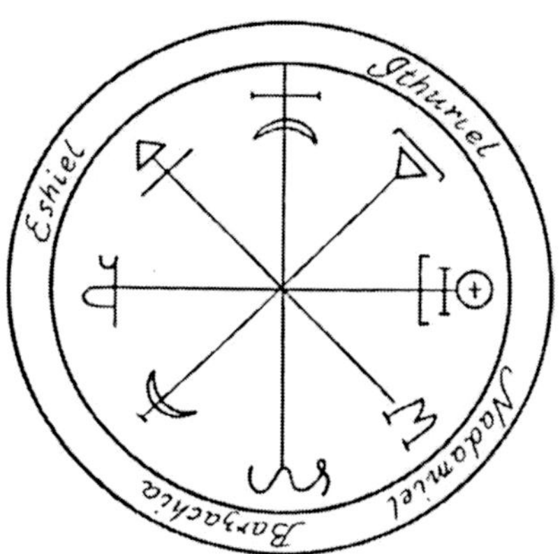

Write an eight-sided star on virgin parchment, with the blood of a bat, directs Solomon's *Key*. It is to be kept covered inside the circle until needed. When it is brought out, it will cause hail and tempests, by invoking the demons which control these phenomena. In the circle is written this, from Psalm cv, 32, 33: "He gave them hail for rain, and flaming fire in their land. He smote their vines also, and their fig-trees."

The last pentacle of Mars is used against all diseases, and cures them when it is held to the affected part. The quotation is from John i, 4: "In Him was life, and the life was the light of men."

CHAPTER III

THE COMPLETE RITUAL OF BLACK MAGIC

THE PACT OF THE BLACK ART
THE BLACK PACT

Pacts with Demons – and Escaping the Consequences

WHAT IS A 'pact with the Devil'? Selling one's soul by a formal, written act of contract? Or the very fact of communication with powers of darkness? Study of the magical rites of Western literature shows that there is much confusion on this point among the protagonists of various methods of demoniac conjuration. The reason for this is certainly historic, and can be explained only from an historical point of view.

If we take for granted what seems generally agreed about the origins of Western magic – that the evocation-rites are derived ultimately from Semitic and Babylonian sources – things become a little clearer. We can see, from the materials available to us, that in the far-off Eastern Mediterranean days of the rites, demons and other supernatural beings were wooed by a combination of propitiation and arrogance: strange bedfellows, but typical of the strange workings of the occultist mind. Spirits, it was felt, were possessed of powers which they could, and under certain circumstances, would, transfer temporarily to human beings. They had to be propitiated because their primary function was the doing of evil, and this had to be prevented before they could be put to work. One might find some sort of analogy in, say, electricity. If you want to use electrical power, you must first of all be sure that you are insulated against its lethal power. Then, by means of certain knowledge, you can put it to work. Ignorance of the *nature* of electricity (or spirits) is not important. What is fundamental, however, is the technique by which spirits can be 'bound' and constrained to act for the operator.

The electrician has to know as to what metals conduct the current; what substances are insulators – and so on. The magician likewise believes he must have his circle or triangle as an insulator, his equipment for attracting the demon, his talisman and words of power for directing their force to further his own ends.

Not all rituals agree that a pact is necessary to the employment of spirit aid. But that the belief was both widespread and generally credited is substantiated by the fact that most of the important black magical codices require either a formal pact and a sacrifice, or at least some form of contract between the spirit and the operator.

When the need arises for the making of a pact, several mages affirm that the consequences of giving one's pledge may be escaped by cheating the devil in any one of a number of ingenious ways. There are innumerable tales of work and miracles wrought by spirits under promise of reward which they never received. Throughout Europe, in fact, bridges and buildings exist which are pointed out as having been built in this way. On one famous occasion a celebrated cleric is reported to have asked the devil to erect a bridge, in return for the soul of the first creature to pass over it: which turned out to be – a cat. Other tales tell of the devil appearing and forcing a pact on some poor farmer – for such pacts are sometimes unilateral in origin. In the first year, the demon asked that everything above the ground should be his: and the farmer planted turnips, and presented his visitor with the tops. The following season, of course, Lucifer demanded all that grew below the surface. All he got was the roots of the wheat that the wily man had planted in all his fields. The large number of these stories extant goes a long way towards scotching the idea that his infernal majesty is as 'diabolically clever' as one might think. Even when the devil has been actually conjured, and the magician and his assistants are cowering within the protection of the magical circle, they have but to throw to him any small animal, and he accepts it apparently without question.

Some measure of exoneration may be pleaded by Satan on the ground that few rites involve conjuration of the potentate himself. Grimoires such as the *Grand Grimoire* indicate that it is with his immediate subordinates – Béelzébuth and Astaroth among them – that the actual pact is made.

So much for the preliminaries. Now comes the question of the pact itself. Sorcerers were convinced that contact with the powers of darkness could be achieved at any time, providing that the appropriate rites were observed. Certain words, clothes, perfumes and invocations were considered indispensable. Other experts – for example those of the Church – maintained that *any* invocation to the devil (such as 'I'd sell my soul if...') could be followed by acceptance by Satan, and that the mere offer of a soul was enough, in many cases, to ensure its ratification. Many cases are on record of people who claimed that the Devil appeared without even being mentioned. All they did was to build up sufficient emotional feeling about something desired: and the demon appeared and offered terms in return for performing the task. The general Christian attitude, of course, is that the very act of being mentally prepared to negotiate with any power other than God was an offer of contract, and might be taken up at any moment. So we have the implicit and explicit methods. In this book it is only the latter with which we are directly concerned: the ritual according to its own adepts which magic had laid down for contact with the supposed powers of evil.

What are the motives for associating oneself with Satan? According to the Grimoires, these are both constructive and destructive. Constructive insofar as they will require something to be done, brought or taught, to the advantage of the operator: destructive where it is desired to bring down ruin, revenge or other disaster upon anyone or anything. Among the so-called constructive efforts, those most favoured by invocants are money and power: the finding of immense treasures, the acquiring of honour and glory, of the gift of tongues, invisibility, the love of men or women, transport from one place to another in the twinkling of an eye, and so forth.

The following is one of the simplest rites given in any grimoire, which figures in the Grand Clavicle claiming its origin with Solomon the King, son of David:

The Conjuration of Lucifuge Rofocale

First, as always, comes the Preparation of the Operator. At the exact second when the Sun is on the horizon, the magician takes a new virgin (unused) knife, and cuts a wand from a hazel tree.[1] This must be a wild tree, which is virgin in that it has not yet borne any fruit.

This wand is to be preserved with the other instruments of the operation: the two candles, which should have

[1] Cut during the hour of the Sun.

been consecrated to the process, a bloodstone, and the documents.

There are two documents. The first is a paper containing a conjuration of the spirit, which conjuration is presumably read from it, and the other is the demand to the spirit, specifying details as to exactly what help is needed. In addition to these instruments, magicians were generally provided with two or more pentagrams for protection, a container for incense, writing materials and a brazier containing willow wood, which latter burns throughout the rite.

The process which is being described does not, however, need the construction of a magical circle. In its place a triangle is drawn on the ground, in some remote and inaccessible spot.

The master and – generally – two assistants first of all choose the place: a ruined church or castle, or some such deserted spot. With the haematite stone the magician then draws on the earth the triangle which is to be their refuge, and places the candle on either side of it. At the foot of the triangle the name of Jesus or some other protective name is drawn, such as ELOHIM, TETRAGRAMMATON.

Stepping within the precincts of the triangle, the master then begins the conjuration of the spirit – in this case Lucifuge Rofocale, as follows:

"O Emperor Lucifer, Chief of all the spirits which rebelled, I beg thee to favour me in this conjuration, which I am about to perform to Lucifuge Rofocale, thy Minister. O Prince Béelzébuth, I adjure thee to protect me in this work. O Earl Astaroth, favour me, and permit me tonight to obtain the appearance of the Great Lucifuge, in human shape, and without any evil effluvium. And that he may allow me, in return for the pact which I will sign, the wealth which I am in need of.

"O great Lucifuge, I beg thee to leave thy home, wherever it may be, and come to this place to speak with me. If thou doest not this, I will constrain thee to appear, by the force of the Great Living God, his Son and His Spirit. Do my bidding at once, or thou shalt be tormented for ever by the force of the words of Power of the Great Clavicle of Solomon, which he used to compel revolted spirits to obey him and accept his contract.

"Appear, then, immediately, or I shall torture thee with the force of these Words of Power from the Key of Solomon!"

The mage then utters these terrible words of power:

> "AGLON–TETRAGRAM–VAYCHEON STIMULAMATON EZPHARES RETRAGRAMMATON OLYARAM IRION ESYTION EXISTION ERYONA ONERA ORASYM MOZM MESSIAS SOTER EMANUEL SABAOTH ADONAY, TE ADORA ET TE INVOCO. AMEN."

When these dread phrases have been pronounced, Lucifuge will put in an instant appearance, and will address the magician in these words:

> "I AM HERE! WHAT DOST THOU SEEK? WHY DOST THOU INTERFERE WITH MY REST? GIVE ME ANSWER."

At this point the invocants are to be very sure that they do not step outside the triangle – indeed, it would mean violent death, we are told, for them to do this at any time at all until the spirit has departed. Summoning up his courage, the magician addresses Lucifuge:

"I desire to make a pact with thee, for the purpose of obtaining riches at once. If thou wilt not agree to this, I shall blast thee with the Words of Power of the *Key*."

Lucifuge, however, is not so easily to be trapped, and may demur thus:

"I WILL AGREE ONLY IF THOU WILT AGREE TO GIVE THY BODY AND SOUL TO ME AFTER TWENTY YEARS, TO USE AS I PLEASE."

At this, the mage flings down in front of the spirit the Pact, which he has inscribed with his own hand on a piece of virgin parchment (often in his own blood), and duly signed. Upon it are written:

"I promise the Great Lucifuge to reward him after twenty years for treasures given to me. And I sign:..."

For some reason, however, the spirit may refuse the request. If this happens, he will disappear, and will have to be recalled with the Great Conjuration:

The Great Conjuration

"I conjure thee, Lucifuge, by the power of Adonay the great, to appear at once: and I conjure thee by Ariel, Jehovam, Aqua, Tagla, Mathon, Aorios, Almoazin, Arios, Membroth, Varios, Majods, Sulphae, Gabots, Salamandrae, Tabots, Gingua, Janna, Etitnamus, Zariatnatmis. AEAIATMOAAMVPMSCSICGAJFZ."

The initial letters refer to a repetition of the Great Names Adonay Eloim, and so on.[1]

We are informed that Lucifuge will then appear again, and address the operator in these words:

"WHY DOST THOU THUS TORTURE ME? LET ME REST AND I WILL GIVE THEE IN EXCHANGE THAT TREASURE WHICH IS MOST NEAR. THE CONDITION IS THAT

[1] These Words of Power were used at least as long ago as the powerful SEHEM of the Babylonians.

THOU DOST RESERVE FOR ME ONE PIECE OF MONEY ON THE FIRST DAY OF EACH MONTH. ALSO THOU MUST NOT INVOKE ME MORE THAN ONCE IN EACH WEEK AND THAT BETWEEN THE TENTH HOUR OF THE NIGHT AND THE SECOND HOUR OF THE MORNING. TAKE THY PACT, FOR I HAVE SIGNED IT. IF THOU SHOULDST FAIL IN THE UNDERTAKING, THOU SHALT BE MINE ENTIRELY IN TWENTY YEARS."

The operator will then speak to the demon, and agree to his terms, asking him to point out the way to the nearest treasure. The mage can then leave the triangle, provided that he has brought his wand.

He will follow the demon to the treasure, and throw down the pact upon it. Then the gold is touched with the wand.

After this, the sorcerer can carry back as much treasure as he can to the shelter of the triangle: but he must be careful to walk backwards, and then discharge the spirit thus:

"Go in peace, and peace with you. Come whenever I shall call. *Amen*."

This completes the rite, as laid down in that most notorious grimoire, the *True Grimoire*. This interesting text resembles in several ways the *Key of Solomon*; and it is probably based upon the *Key* or another book which laid down this characteristic kind of ritual. For this reason it has been regarded by some commentators – many of whom seem not even to have actually read it – as of later production than other rituals. This, however, is something which cannot really be established at this stage of knowledge. There are, it is true, references in the editions available to us to Christianity and Christian teachings. This, however, proves nothing beyond the fact that it may have been 'Christianised' any time before the sixteenth century.

There have been several exchanges between writers upon the question of whether the *True Grimoire* is 'genuine' or not. This, as any unbiased reader will at once perceive, depends entirely upon what one means by genuine: upon the prejudice of the reader himself. It was certainly one of the source-books of the French occultist, Eliphas Lévi, who was considered the last of the professing magicians, and whose works have been admirably translated by a British writer. It is not necessarily spurious, insofar as it contains a process for evocation which is in line with black magical rituals familiar to the sorcerers of the Middle Ages. It has been denounced by several writers as 'diabolical' and 'degenerate' – though one is tempted to wonder why they bother with it at all, when every fibre of their being revolts, apparently, at the awful rites. The *True Grimoire* or *True Clavicles* does not exist in English. There are Latin versions, and some in Italian. Those best known in England include the translations in French: particularly that of the year '1517' which asserts that it is translated from the Hebrew, and published by Alibeck the Egyptian at Memphis.

A variation of the rite for conjuring Lucifuge is given in the notorious *Grand Grimoire*. Also claiming descent from the Solomonic dispensation, the *Grimoire* tells how one Antonio Venitiana del Rabbina actually copied its text from the documents of Solomon himself.

Compared with the process as laid down in the foregoing extract, this conjuration is difficult and complicated. According to some occultists, however, it is 'more reliable', and it may in fact provide a more complete account of the system followed by the original from which both books are derived.

A bloodstone must be acquired, and guarded carefully by the operator, as he goes about the business of preparing the blood sacrifice essential to success.

The sacrifice ('victim of the Art') is a virgin kid. Having bought this, the mage removes its head with one stroke (if he can) on the third day of the moon. The victim is prepared for sacrifice by making a wreath of verbena, and decorating its throat with this. The wreath, it may be noted, is to be tied with a green ribbon.

Repairing to some place far from the haunts of men, the operator prepares for the sacrifice. His robe is rolled up in such a way as to bare the right shoulder; a fire of willow wood burns in a large brazier; a clean and new knife (newly consecrated, no doubt) is employed for the killing.

Just before the actual sacrifice, this invocation of sacrifice is to be uttered 'with feeling and trust':

"I offer this creature to Thee, O great Adonai, Elohim, Ariel and Jehovam, in the Honour and Power, and the Resplendence of Thy Name, which is greater than all the spirits. O great Adonay: agree to accept it as agreeable. *Amen.*"

At this point the sacrifice is to be offered, by cutting the throat of the kid.

Now the advantage of the large brazier becomes apparent. The body, after having been skinned, is thrown upon the flames, and allowed to burn to cinders. As soon as this is finished, the magician throws handfuls of ashes towards the sunrise and calls upon the Deity again:

"In the Honour, and the Glory and the Splendour of Thy Name, O Great Adonai, Eloim, Ariel, Jehovam, I spill the blood of this sacrifice! Grant, Great Adonai, that it be an agreeable sacrifice."

The skin of the kid has been kept by the operator for the purpose of making the Circle of Evocation, from which he will later call the spirit to aid him.

There is now a second rite to be performed: the making of the Blasting Wand, which has power over spirits, to torment and force their obedience, and which is thus manufactured:

Making the Blasting Wand

A wild hazel tree, which has never fruited, is to be located in a place which is generally deserted. And this should have on it a branch which is about nineteen and a half inches long. It must not be handled until the actual moment of its cutting.

The knife which was used in the sacrifice of the kid is taken – with the blood still upon it – and as the Sun rises, the cut is made, accompanied by an invocation, given thus:

Invocation of the Cutting

"I beg Thee, O Great Adonai, Eloim, Ariel, Jehovam, exert Thy beneficence towards me, and give to this rod as I cut it the power and the virtue of the rods of Jacob, of Moses, and of Joshua the powerful!

"I beg Thee, O Great Adonai, Eloim, Ariel, Jehovam, to place in this wand the entire strength of Samson, the anger of Amanuel, and the blasting power of the mighty Zariatnatmik, he who will revenge against sin on the Day of Judgement. *Amen.*"

Now the operator turns his head in the direction of the Sun, and takes his rod home.

The process of the completion of the rod is done in this manner:

Apparently no other person is to be allowed to touch the rod. Therefore, when iron caps are needed for each end, a stratagem is to be employed. The 'karcist' is enjoined to find a piece of other wood, similar in size to that of the branch, and hie forth to a blacksmith. This worthy is to be ordered to take the actual knife of sacrifice and from the blade to make two caps, to fit over the ends of the dummy rod. When this is completed, the caps are transferred to the ends of the real wand by the magician himself. The instrument is ready to be used when the caps have been magnetised with the help of a lodestone, and these words said over it:

"I conjure thee by the Great Adonai, Eloim, Ariel, Jehovam, to attract all that I shall require, through the Power of the Greatest Adonai, Eloim, Ariel, Jehovam.

"I order thee, by the irreconcilability of fire and water, to cause all that I wish drawn apart, just as all things were separated on the Day of Creation. *Amen*."

Some lesser-known books and illustrations indicate that such words as TETRAGRAMMATON are written along the length of the wand. This Grimoire does not mention such an inscription: but I have an illustration in my collection with AGLA on one end of the wand, ADONAI on the other, and the TETRAGRAMMATON in the middle, as aforesaid.

Having obtained the skin and the rod, the magician is almost ready to perform the rite itself. As in the former process, he is to have two candles: and they are made by a virgin girl from previously unused wax. Several other items are also needed. These are: two candlesticks, two wreaths of verbena, steel, tinder and flints, for fire-making; holy water and incense, brandy and camphor, and four nails from the coffin of a child. The skin has been cut up into strips. A coin of gold or silver, to present to the spirit when he appears, completes the list of accessories carried by the magician. If he is accompanied by two helpers, they are to bear these items, and to be at all times strictly under his orders.

Making the Circle

The Grimoire directs that the circle is to be made on the ground by means of strips from the sacrificial kid's skin, and these are fixed with the coffin-nails. When this is complete, the haematite stone is taken and used to describe a triangle within the circle, and touching it at all three points. The first point to be touched when making the triangle is that which faces east. It is now that the magician (and the assistants, if he is accompanied) enter the triangle, and place the candles in their holders and surrounded by the verbena wreaths to the right and left of the triangle, and within the circle itself.

Upon no account should the important tracing of letters be forgotten: for this ceremony is said to protect the invocants from the approach of demons. On the east, outside the circle, is to be written a capital *A*, a small *a* and a small *y*. Inside the circle, and at the base of the triangle, is to be written 'J H S' – the name of Jesus.

Now the candles are lighted, and a fire started in a brazier, which should be nurtured with a little brandy and camphor. As soon as the fire and candles are going well, the invocant addresses the Deity:

"This incense of mine, O Great Adonai, is the best that I am able to obtain: purified, like this charcoal, made from the best wood.

"These are offerings, O Great Adonai, Eloim, Ariel, Jehovam, to Thee, with my heart and soul. Accept them, O Great Adonai, and accept them as a sacrifice. *Amen*."

By this time there may be a number of spirits around the circle. They are likely, it seems, to make a good deal of noise. They are to be ignored, and the assistants are not to speak a single word, but to allow all invocations to be performed by the master. A prayer is now made, while the assistants see that the fire is burning well:

"O Great Living God, in one and the same person the Father, the Son and the Holy Spirit, I adore Thee with the deepest humility, and I submit to Thy holy protection with complete belief: I believe, with the most sincere faith, that Thou art my Maker, my Benefactor, my Sustainer and my

Master: and I have no other desire than that I should belong to Thee throughout eternity. Amen."

There is a pause here, while the master sees that all is well with the lights and fire, and then he resumes with the Supplication:

"O Great and Living God, that created man that he should be happy in this life; who has furnished all things for his needs; who has said that all things should be under the will of man; and who will not allow that the rebellious spirits should possess the treasures that have been formed for our needs in this world:

"Grant me, O Great God, the power to dispose of them, by the fearful and terrible names of the Clavicle: ADONAI, ELOIM, JEHOVAM, TAGLA. *Amen.*"

There are variations in the names given at the end. One version has ADONAY, ARIEL, JEHOVAM, TAGLA, another ADONAI, ELOIM, TAGLA, MATHON and ARIEL.

The operator then takes some of the camphor and casts it into the flames of the brazier, with the words:

"I offer Thee this incense as the purest which I have been able to obtain, O great Adonai, Eloim, Ariel and Jehovam. Deign to receive it as an acceptable sacrifice, O great Adonai. And be favourable to me in Thy Power, and make me successful in this great undertaking. *Amen.*"

Now that all the preparatory rituals have been accomplished, comes the actual calling of Lucifuge:

Conjuration of Lucifuge

"Emperor Lucifer, Prince and Master of the rebel spirits, I ask thee to leave thy abode, in whichever part of the world it may be, to come and speak with me.

"I command and order thee, in the Name of the Great Living God: the Father, the Son and the Holy Spirit: to come without making an evil smell; to answer in a loud and intelligible voice, article by article, what I shall ask thee. Failing this thou shalt be constrained by the power of the Great Adonai, Eloim, Ariel, Jehovam, Tagla, Mathon, and by all the other higher spirits, who will compel thee against thy will. Come, Come! Submiritillor Lucifuge, or thou shalt be eternally tortured by the power of this Blasting Wand!"

It is said to be almost certain that the spirit will present himself before the circle after these awful words. Should, however, he neglect to appear, the next conjuration is resorted to:

"I command and oblige thee, Emperor Lucifer, by the writ of the Great Living God, by His Son and by the Holy Spirit... and I vow that in a quarter of an hour I shall smite thee with this frightful Blasting Wand. *Amen*."

Having given the spirit an ultimatum, the sorcerer waits for the allotted time. During this period, no sound is to be made. The spirit can be tortured in his absence by plunging the wand into the flames of the fire: which should evoke horrible screams. This time Lucifuge should definitely come, and ask why he is being tormented thus.

The Karcist then tells the spirit as to the times when he is to appear, and what he is to do, according to a timetable which has been drawn up beforehand. After some further threats with the wand, the demon will agree to terms, and will indicate the route to the nearest treasure.

Certain formalities have to be observed in taking possession of this. The assistants, for instance, must not leave the circle. Only the chief sorcerer may quit the circle's protective area, and follow the spirit, taking care to leave the enchanted place at the point where the word ADONAI is written. He must carry at all times the wand, which will enable him to discourage the fierce and dangerous dog or other evil thing which is guarding the treasure. The very man who originally buried the hoard will be encountered, and a fight will ensue for its possession. But he will overcome this, and will take one coin from the hoard and exchange one of his own, to assert ownership. Placing the Pact (or the Conjuration in written form) on the gold, he will retire backwards to the safety of the circle, bearing with him as much of the treasure as he is able to carry.

The whole process now comes to an end with two important recitations: the discharge of the spirit and the prayer of thanksgiving to God:

The Discharge

"I am pleased and contented with thee, Prince Lucifer, for the moment. Leave thou in peace now, and go in quiet and without trouble. Do not forget our pact, or I shall blast thee with my Wand. *Amen.*"

Thanksgiving Prayer

"O powerful God, Creator of all things for the use of man, thanks to Thee for granting our desires. *Amen.*"

CHAPTER IV

'A BOOK BY THE DEVIL': THE GRIMORIUM VERUM

THE GRIMORIUM VERUM – THE TRUE GRIMOIRE

THIS IS ONE of the most interesting of magical rituals which include the famous Grimoires or black books of the sorcerers. It is, in fact, nothing less than a magician's handbook, containing in small compass the entire rites of preparation, identification of spirits, conjuration and the alleged achievement of the operator's every desire.[1]

It does not come under the heading of a complete and original work: for there is no known magical book which fulfils the requirements of original authorship. Occultists sometimes delight in making petty distinctions between 'composite' and other rituals. The fact is that every extant book of spells, charms, divination or magical conjuration – whether working through the power of God, of the Devil, of demons or angels, of flowers, stones or familiars, crystals or visions – is a work which has gone through innumerable hands, been edited and re-edited, and translated in many cases two to three times between different languages.

1 A prominent churchman of my acquaintance, who has taken some interest in the rituals of magic, calls this 'A book by the Devil'.

Hence, when for example we find that some of the processes in the present work are closely allied to or are identical with some part of the *Key of Solomon* as we know it, we are not justified in saying: "Here is something interpolated from the *Key of Solomon*, a later addition; this is a composite ritual." In the present state of magical knowledge we would be equally at liberty – and even more justified – in saying that for all we know the *Grimorium Verum* is more original than the *Key*: or that it is one of the original books of the Library of Hermes, or even the magical libraries of the Babylonians.

No, the Grimoires should be studied from any point of view but that of bibliographical criticism: for here we have absolutely no criteria to apply, and the confused attempts by various commentators to judge the Grimoires from a semi-scientific standpoint serve only to make their work more ridiculous than they believe the Grimoires themselves to be.

There are, however, matters of general interest that can bear commentary in relation to the various versions of the *Grimorium Verum*. The oldest form in which it is known to us is in a printed volume, supposedly published by 'Alibeck the Egyptian, at Memphis, 1517'.

In actual fact, unless the title-page merely reproduces a page of the reputed manuscript original, it is not possible (from the typeface, binding, phraseology, etc.) that this book could date from such an early time. Deliberate deceit? More likely that the publisher wanted to escape from the possible consequences of publishing a book of black magic in Rome. Alibeck (Ali Baig) could be the name of an Egyptian, after the occupation of that country by the Osmanli Turks, for he bears one of the titles of this conquering people.

The title continues: "Grimorium Verum... translated from the Hebrew (into French) by Plaingière, 'Jesuite Dominicaine' [obviously a dig at Catholicism here], with a collection of Curious Secrets. The True Clavicles of Solomon."

Now, there were developed during the troublous days of struggle between magicians and the Church certain conventions whereby something in the nature almost of a truce came into operation in the field of magic. Whereas originally the clerical opinion was that all magic outside essentially religious rituals was nothing less than the Black Art, during the centuries the effect of the magical research schools of Arabian Spain caused a shift in attitude. Henceforth magic became officially understood as divided into the twin categories of Black and White. The actual determination of which was which caused, as may be imagined, a considerable amount of trouble.

Eventually, however, three main forms of White Magic emerged. In the first, Christianisation of the rites and formulae became the rule. The appeal to God was made in the name of Jesus Christ, and allusions to the New Testament were common. The older form, that which was based upon Judaism, continued in its own way, probably nurtured by Jewish necromancers. This preserved the purely Semitic approach: pentacles instead of crosses, *Agla* and *Tetragrammaton* in place of Christian phrases. The third and last form seemed to make no direct appeal to an all-powerful deity, and was named Natural Magic. In this category came several forms of alchemy, divining, crystal-gazing and semi-occult pseudo-sciences.

The Black Art was roughly divided into two sections. The first was that of the traditional Christian concept of the Devil and the pact that was made with him, to exchange a man's (or woman's) immortal soul for material advantages, and subject to a strict time-limit.

The second type of Black Magic did not involve quite such harsh penalties. The magician treated with demons rather in the way in which the Babylonians and later the Arabs did: on the assumption that devils were essentially less powerful than God, and that certain holy words (Names or Words of Power) if known by the operator, could compel the allegiance of the said demons, whether they liked it or not.

Man, therefore, may have been at the mercy of demons in his normal state, but the acquiring of knowledge of the words of power more than evened up the odds.

Considered to appertain to Black Magic, too, was any process designed to harm, maim or cause suffering to anyone. Such effects would be accomplished either through the pact with Satan or by compelling demons to carry out dastardly schemes. It is self-evident, of course, that works of destruction had perforce to come under the heading of the Black Art, since all White Magic concerned itself with operating through 'loaned' divine power, which would not be granted for illegal, immoral or sinful acts.

Here it may be instructive to mention a sort of intermediary type of magic, used much by the Arabs and probably derived from Assyria. This consisted of the utilisation of the supposed powers of Jinn (Genies) which are neither entirely good nor completely evil. In this they rather seem to resemble humanity, for they are capable of exercising whatever function they are constrained to perform. There are, it is true, good jinn and bad ones, males and females. Those which tradition says were imprisoned by Solomon in the brazen vessel and cast into the sea were almost all evil. But there are a number which are good, and some uncertain ones. They may be likened to a symbolic recognition of the possibility of the reality of a magical power which can be harnessed to the will of the operator.

It is interesting to note in this connection that at least one modern Arabian occult writer has likened the jinn to electricity. Jinn are, he explains, either good or bad, depending upon how you use them. They are an undoubted force, which exists everywhere, but their using depends upon certain requirements. We do not know their exact nature, any more than anyone knows what electricity actually is.

To return to the *Grimorium Verum*. This book, by traditional definition, belongs to Black Magic, insofar as it tells the operator how to conjure what it admits are demons. Exponents of High Magic could, however, equally plausibly argue that, since the operator is not submitting his soul to the said demons, and since he can control them and protect himself from them, the work could belong to White or High Magic. It may be a distinction which for its completion depends upon the use made of the book by the individual operator himself.

The contents of the Grimoire may be summarised thus: there are full instructions to the would-be magician for his preparations, consecrations and the rest. Then come details of the making of the magical paraphernalia, such as the instruments (knife, sickle, pen and the rest) and the accessories, such as the virgin parchment, the perfumes and fumigations, and so on. Then there is the matter of the ritual sacrifice of the kid to the spirit whom it is desired to evoke. Also included are details of the actual demons, their names and powers, as well as their seals and characters, which are to be inscribed within or without the magical circle, with illustrations of them.

Other illustrations are concerned with the strange inscriptions in unknown language which are to be carved or written on the instruments, paper, and the rest. Incantations are numerous, and every part of the ritual of evocation of the desired spirit is reproduced.

From the point of view of other rituals of this nature, the *Grimorium Verum* is simpler, contains less taboos and restrictions for the sorcerer, and – above all – assumes that he knows nothing of the magical art, and hence begins at the beginning and gives the full details, grisly and otherwise.

These may be reasons why, during the nineteenth century, this grimoire was *par excellence* the magical book of Europe. Apart from the edition dated 1517, there is another in French, and several copies are known as Italian editions of 1868 and 1880.

This present version is the first to collate material from all these editions, and present the grimoire in what may be the most complete form that it has known since the original French or Italian manuscript was published.

There is some mystery about actual manuscripts of the *Grimorium Verum*. The French version, for instance, seems to have been printed from a very incomplete copy: in fact, from what could have been some magician's notes from the complete manuscript. The Italian versions, on the other hand, seem to have been compiled with reference to a very complete manuscript whose whereabouts is not now known.

There is another mystery about the Italian editions. They are in extraordinarily great demand. There is nowhere that one can get a copy at less than a price far greater than almost any other work of similar size and date. The price, in other words, is out of all proportion (sometimes insanely so) to the rarity of the book as a collector's piece. This means that quite a number of people are buying the *Grimorium Verum* for purposes other than mere collection. If they are buying for study and research, why has there been no recently edited English translation of the book?

There is no answer possible to these queries. I have been carrying on a hunt for copies of this book for over five years – both in England and on the Continent: and I have come across precisely three copies, outside research libraries. One was sold in my presence for 100,000 francs (then £100) and the third was offered me six weeks ago at seventy pounds!

Introduction to the Grimoire

"In the first part," says the Grimoire, "is contained various dispositions of characters, by which powers the spirits or – rather – the devils are invoked, to make them come when you will, each according to his power, and to bring whatever is asked: and that without any discomfort, providing also that they are on their part content; for this sort of creature does not give anything for nothing."

Here the element of the pact with the demon is hinted at: there is a contractual relationship between the spirit and the sorcerer. In exchange for favours, something must be given in return. Sometimes it is said to be the soul of the magician himself. More frequently, if we are to believe the grimoires and commentators, it is the sacrifice of a virgin kid, a small animal, or even perfumes and food, as in the rites of the *Key of Solomon*, whose processes closely resemble some of those in the *Grimorium Verum*.

The introduction continues that the operator will also find in the first part of the book the means of calling the elemental spirits: whether those of Air, Earth, Sea or the Infernus, according to their correspondences.

In the second part, we are told, are taught natural and supernatural secrets, which operate by the power of demons. "You will find the manner to make use of them, and all without deceit."

This proneness to deceive humanity seems deeply embedded in the demoniac character, and disobedience and cunning must be met and matched with fearlessness and superior knowledge. Forewarned is forearmed, say the sorcerers.

The following text reproduces exactly the phraseology of the original grimoire:

In the Third Part

You will find the key to the work, with the manner of using it. But before starting this, it will be necessary to be instructed in the following.

There are three powers, which are: Lucifer, Béelzébuth and Astaroth. You must engrave their characters in the correct manner and at the appropriate hours. Believe me, all is of consequence, nothing to be forgotten.

You must carry the said character with you. If you are male, in the right pocket, and it is to be written with your own blood, or that of a sea-turtle. You put at the two half-circles the first letter of your name and surname. And if you wish more, you draw the character on an emerald or ruby, for they have a great sympathy with the spirits, especially those of the Sun, who are the most knowledgeable, and are better than the others.

If you are a female, carry it (the character) on the left side, between the breasts, like a Reliquary; and always observing, as much as the other sex, to write or have engraved the character on the day and in the hour of Mars. Obey the spirits in this, that they may obey thee.

The spirits who are powerful and exalted, serve only their confidants and intimate friends, by the pact made or to be made according to certain characters at the will of Singambuth or of his Secretary.

Aabidandes, of whom we will give you information, is the perfect acquaintance to call, conjure and constrain, as you will see in the key, where you will be given the method of making a pact with spirits.

Nature of Pacts

There are only two kinds of pact, the tacit and the apparent (explicit). You will know the one from the other, if you read this little book. Know, however, that there are many kind of spirits, some attractive and others not attractive.

It is when you make a pact with a spirit, and have to give the spirit something which belongs to you, that you have to be on your guard.

The Kinds of Spirits

In regard to spirits, there are the superior and the inferior. Names of the superiors are: Lucifer, Béelzébuth, Astaroth. The inferiors of Lucifer are in Europe and Asia, and obey him. Béelzébuth lives in Africa, and Astaroth inhabits America.

Of these, each of them has two who order their subjects all that which the Emperor has resolved to do in all the world, and *vice-versa.*

The Appearance of Spirits

Spirits do not always appear in the same shape. This is because they are not themselves of matter or form, and have to find a body to appear in, and one suitable to their (intended) manifestation and appearance.

Lucifer appears in the form and figure of a fair boy. When angry, he seems red. There is nothing monstrous about him.

Béelzébuth appears sometimes in monstrous forms, sometimes like a giant cow, at times like a he-goat, with a long tail. When angry, he vomits fire.

Astaroth appears black, in human shape.

Here are three characters of Lucifer, outside his circle:

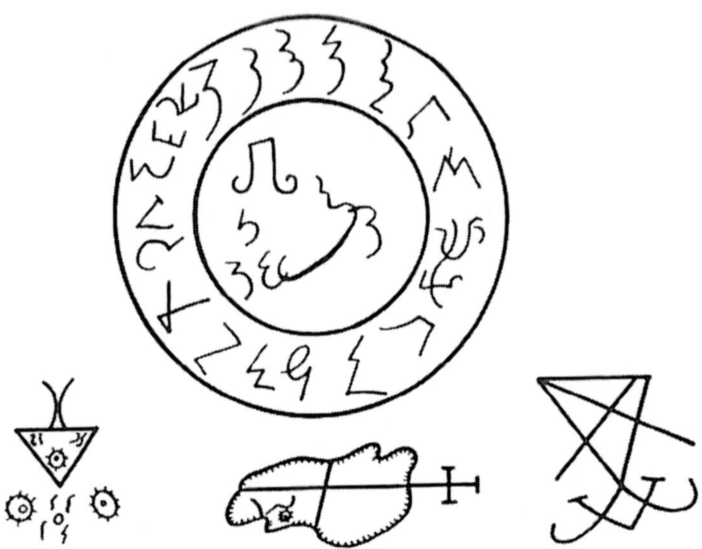

The following are those of Béelzébuth and Astaroth placed outside their circles:

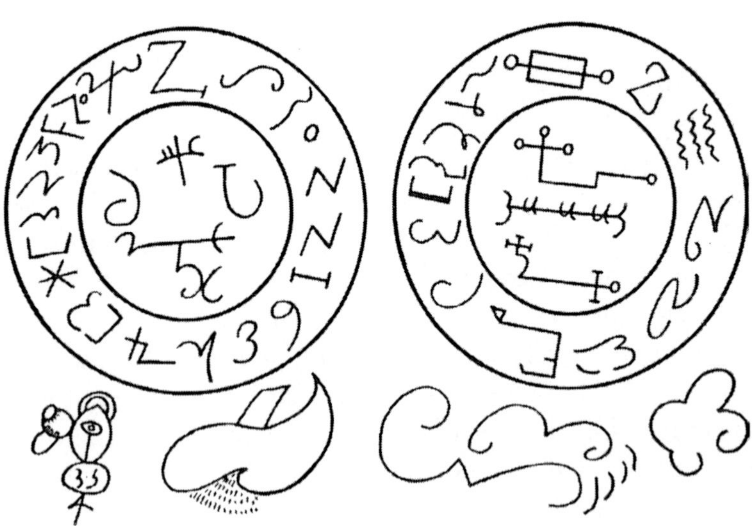

To Invoke the Spirits

It is only necessary, when you desire to invoke them, to call them by the characters, which they themselves have given. And when you wish to invoke them, call them to serve you, in the manner taught in the Third Part.

Descending to the Inferiors

The two inferiors of Astaroth are Sagatana and Nesbiros, and their characters are:

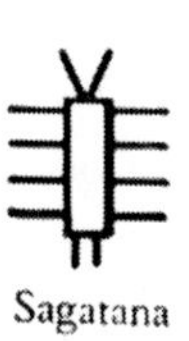

Sagatana

Nesbiros

Lucifer has two demons under him: Satanackia and Agalierap. Those of Béelzébuth are Tarchimache and Fleruty. The characters of Satanackia and Fleruty are:

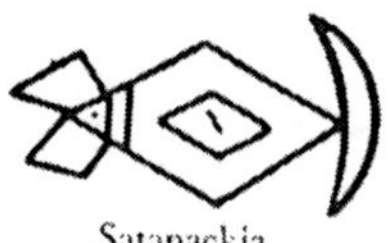

Satanackia

Fleruty

There are yet other demons, apart from these, who are under Duke Syrach. There are eighteen of these, and their names are:

Clauneck, 1; Musisin, 2; Bechaud, 3; Frimost, 4; Klepoth, 5; Khil, 6; Mersilde, 7; Clisthert, 8; Sirchade, 9; Segal, 10; Hicpacth, 11; Humots, 12; Frucissiere, 13; Guland, 14; Surgat, 15; Morail, 16; Frutimiere, 17; and Huictiigaras, 18.

These are the characters of fifteen inferior spirits:

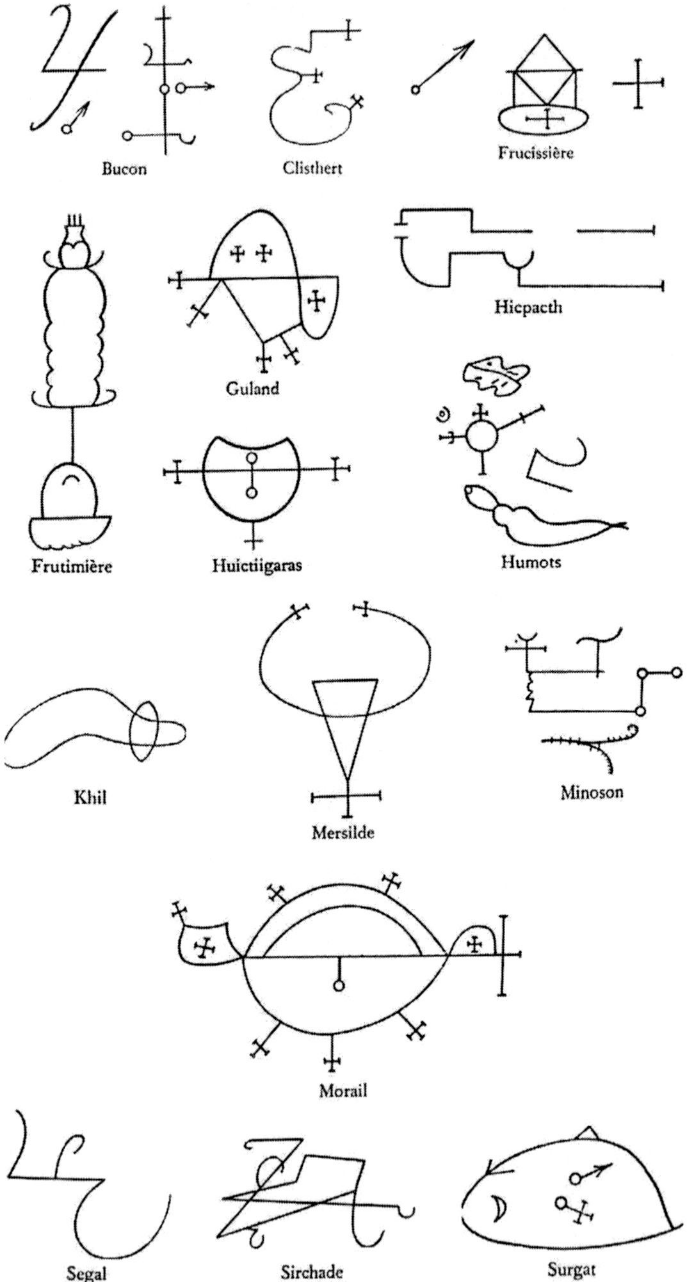

The Second Part of the SSJ [sic]

AGLA * ADONAY * JEHOVA

There are other demons, but as they have no power, we shall not speak of them. The powers of the eighteen above-mentioned ones are these:

CLAUNECK has power over riches, can cause treasures to be found. He can give great riches to he who makes a pact with him, for he is very much loved by Lucifer. It is he who causes money to be brought.

MUSISIN has power over great lords, teaches all that happens in the Republics, and the 'affairs of the Allies'.

BECHAUD has power over storms and tempests, rain and hail, and other natural forces.

FRIMOST has power over women and girls, and will help you to obtain their use.

KLEPOTH makes you see all sorts of dreams and visions.

KHIL makes great earthquakes.

MERSILDE has the power to transport anyone in an instant anywhere.

CLISTHERT allows you to have day or night, whichever you wish, when you desire either.

SIRCHADE makes you see all sorts of natural and supernatural animals.

HICPACTH will bring you a person in an instant, though he be far away.

HUMOTS can bring you any book you may desire.

SEGAL will cause all sorts of prodigies to appear.

FRUCISSIERE revives the dead.

GULAND causes all illnesses.

SURGAT opens every kind of lock.

MORAIL can make anything invisible.

FRUTIMIERE prepares all kinds of feasts for you.

HUICTIIGARAS causes sleep in the case of some, and insomnia in others.

Under Satanachia and Sataniciae are forty-five (or, according to others, fifty-four) demons. Four of these, the chiefs, are Sergutthy, Heramael, Trimasael and Sustugriel. The others are of no great consequence.

These spirits are of great advantage, and they work well and speedily, in the case that they are pleased with the operator.

Sergutthy has power over maidens and wives, when things are favourable.

Heramael teaches the art of healing, including the complete knowledge of any illness and its cure. He also makes known the virtues of plants, where they are to be found, when to pluck them, and their making into a complete cure.

Trimasael teaches chemistry and all matters of conjuring of the nature of deceit or sleight-of-hand. He also teaches the secret of the making of the Powder of Projection, by means of which the base metals may be turned into gold or silver.

Sustugriel teaches the art of magic. He gives familiar spirits that can be used for all purposes, and he gives also mandragores.

Agalierept and Tarihimal are the rulers of Elelogap, who in turn governs matters connected with water.

Nebirots rules Hael and Sergulath. The former (Hael) enables anyone to speak in any language he will, and also teaches the means whereby any type of letter may be written. He is also able to teach those things which are most secret and completely hidden.

Sergulath gives every means of speculation. In addition, he instructs as to the methods of breaking the ranks and strategy of opponents. Subject to these there are the eight most powerful subordinates:

1. PROCULO, who can cause a person to sleep for forty-eight hours, with the knowledge of the spheres of sleep.
2. HARISTUM, who can cause anyone to pass through fire without being touched by it.
3. BRULEFER, who causes a person to be beloved of women.
4. PENTAGNONY, who gives the two benefits of attaining invisibility and the love of great lords.
5. AGLASIS, who can carry anyone or anything anywhere in the world.
6. SIDRAGOSAM causes any girl to dance in the nude.
7. MINOSON is able to make anyone win at any game.
8. BUCON can cause hate and spiteful jealousy between members of the sexes.

The Third Part of the Book

This is the Invocation:

HELOY ✠ TAU ✠ VARAF ✠ PANTHON ✠ HOMNORCUM ✠
ELEMIATH ✠ SERUGEATH ✠ AGLA ✠ ON ✠
TETRAGRAMMATON ✠ CASILY.

The Invocation is to be made on Virgin Parchment, with the Character of the Demon upon it, which causes the intermediary SCYRLIN to come. For from this depend all the others, as the messenger of the others, and it can constrain them to appear in spite of themselves, as it (he) has the power of Emperor.

Orison: Preparation (Ablution of the Sorcerer)

"Lord God Adonay, who hast made man in Thine own image and resemblance out of nothing! I, poor sinner that I am, beg

Thee to deign to bless and sanctify this water, so that it may be healthy for my body and my soul, and that all foolishness should depart from it.

"Lord God, all-powerful and ineffable, and who led Thy people out of the Land of Egypt, and has enabled them to cross the Red Sea with dry feet! Accord me this, that I may be purified by this water of all my sins, so that I may appear innocent before Thee! *Amen.*"

When the operator has thus purified himself, he is to set about the making of the Instruments of the Art.

Of the Knife

It is necessary to have a knife or a lancet, of new steel, made on the day and hour of Jupiter with the Moon crescent (i.e. new). If it cannot be made, it may be bought, but this must be done at the time, as above.

Having achieved this, you will say the Orison or Conjuration following, which will serve for the knife and lancet:

Conjuration of the Instrument

"I conjure thee, O form of the Instrument, by the authority of our Father God Almighty, by the virtues of Heaven and by the Stars, by the virtue of the Angels, and the virtue of the Elements, by the virtues of stones and herbs, and of snow-storms, winds and thunder: that thou now obtain all the necessary power into thyself for the perfectioning of the achievement of those things in which we are at present concerned! And this without deception, untruth, or anything of that nature whatsoever, by God the Creator of the Sun of Angels! *Amen.*"

Then we recite the Seven Psalms, and afterwards the following words:

"DALMALEY LAMECK CADAT PANCIA VELOUS MERROE LAMIDECK CALDURECH ANERETON MITRATON: Most Pure Angels, be the guardians of these instruments, they are needed for many things."

Of the Sacrificial Knife

On the Day of Mars [Tuesday] at the New Moon, make a knife of new steel which is strong enough to cut the neck of a kid with one blow, and make a handle of wood on the same day and in the same hour, and with a graver you engrave on the handle these characters:

g233

Then asperge and fumigate it, and you have prepared an instrument for service when and where you wish.

Manner of Asperging and Fumigation

First, there is the orison which is needful on asperging, and it is thus that it is recited:

"In the name of the immortal God Asperge [N] and clean you of all foolishness and all deceit, and you will be whiter than snow. *Amen.*"

Then pour as the aspersion blessed water thereon, saying:

"In the Name of the Father and of the Son and of the Holy Spirit, *Amen.*"

These aspersions are necessary for every item of equipment; so also is the fumigation which follows.

To fumigate, it is necessary to have a cruse, in which you place coal newly kindled with a new fire, and let all be well ablaze. On this you place aromatics, and when perfuming the article in question, say the following:

"Angels of God, be our help, and may our work be accomplished by you. Zalay, Salmay, Dalmay, Angrecton, Ledrion, Amisor, Euchey, Or. Great Angels: And do thou also, O Adonay, come and give to this a virtue so that this creature may gain a shape, and by this let our work be accomplished. In the Name of the Father, and of the Son, and of the Holy Spirit. *Amen.*"

Then recite the Seven Psalms which come after *Judicium tuum Regida* and *Laudate Dominum omnes gentes.*

Of the Virgin Parchment

Virgin parchment can be made in many ways. Generally it is made of the skin of a goat or lamb, or other animal, which must be virgin.

After inscribing on the blade AGLA, and having fumigated it, the knife will serve you for all purposes.

Remember that when you make the Sacrifice in order to obtain the virgin parchment from the kid, all the instruments must be on the altar.

You make the Batôn [rod] of the Art from hazel wood that has never borne, and cut it with a single stroke on the day and in the hour of Mercury [Wednesday], at the Crescent Moon. And you engrave it with the needle, the pen or the lancet, in the following characters:

The Seal and Character of Frimost to be inscribed on the First Rod:

Then you make another baton of hazel wood, which has never borne, and which is without seed, and cut it in the day and hour of the Sun, and on this you engrave these characters:

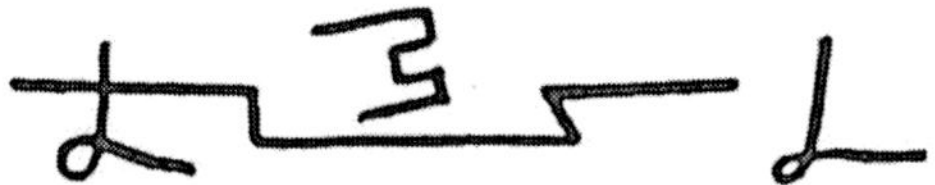

The Seal and Character of Klippoth is to be inscribed on the Second Rod.

This having been done, you say over your batôn the following orison:

Orison

"Most wise, most powerful Adonay, deign to bless, sanctify and conserve this baton so that it may have the necessary virtue, O most holy Adonay, to whom be honour and glory for all time. *Amen.*"

Of the Lancet

It is necessary to have a new lancet, conjured and prepared like the knife and sickle. Make it in the day and hour of Mercury, at the Crescent Moon.

Now follows the method of *Making the Sacrifice of the Kid*:

Take your goat and place it on a flat surface, so that the throat is uppermost, the better to cut it. Take your knife and cut the throat with a single stroke, while pronouncing the name of the Spirit which you wish to invoke.

For example, you say:

"I kill you in the name and to the honour of [N]...."

This is to be well understood, and take care that you sever the throat at first, and do not take two strokes, but see that he dies at the first.

Then you skin him with the knife, and at the skinning make this invocation:

Invocation

"Adonay, Dalmay, Lauday, Tetragrammaton, Anereton, and all you, Holy Angels of God, come and be here, and deign to infuse into this skin the power that it may be correctly conserved, so that all that is written upon it may become perfected."

After the skinning, take well-ground salt, and strew this upon the skin, which has been stretched, and let the salt cover the skin well. Before you use the salt it must have this benediction said over it:

Benediction of the Salt

"I exorcise you, O Creature of the Salt, by the God who is living, the God of all Gods, the Lord of all Lords, that all fantasies may leave you, and that you may be suitable for the virgin parchment."

When this is finished, let the skin with the salt upon it remain in the sun for a full day.

Then obtain a glazed pottery jar, and write these characters around it with the Pen of the Art:

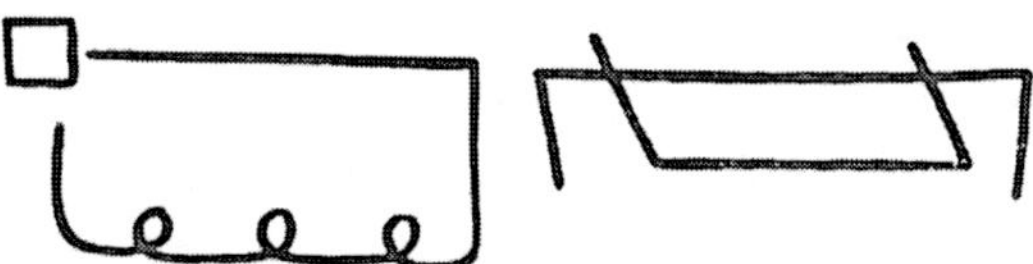

Get quicklime and slake this with exorcised water, and put these in the jar. When it is liquid place in it your goatskin, and leave it long enough for the hairs to peel off of themselves.

As soon as the hair is in such a condition as to come off with a touch, remove it from the jar and peel the hairs with a knife made from carved hazel. The knife must have had these words said over it:

"O holiest Aboezra [one version has it 'Adonay'] put into this wood the power to cleanse this skin, through thy holy name Agason. *Amen.*"

The skin, when peeled, may be stretched over a piece of new wood, and stones are to be placed on the skin, so that they hold it down. These are to be stones from a river bank. Before placing the stones, say this orison over them:

Orison of the Stones

"O Adonay, most puissant and all-powerful Lord, allow that these stones may stretch this skin, and remove from them all wickedness, so that they may possess the required power. *Amen.*"

Of the Aspersion of the Water

All water used in these experiments must be asperged, by saying this over it:

"Lord God, Father, all-powerful, my refuge and my life, help me, Holy Father, for I love you, God of Abraham, of Isaac, of Jacob, of the Angels, of the Archangels and Prophets, Creator of All. In humility, and, calling upon Thy holy Name, I supplicate that thou wilt agree to bless this water, so that it may sanctify our bodies and our souls, through Thee, most holy Adonay, Everlasting Ruler. *Amen*."

The skin is allowed to dry after this, and before quitting the spot, say over the parchment:

"Je, Agla, Jod, Hoi, He, Emmanuel! Stand guard over this parchment, in order that no spectra may take charge of it!"

When the skin is dry it may be removed from its wooden frame, blessed and fumigated, and then it is ready for use.

It is important that this must not be seen by any women, and more especially during certain times of theirs, otherwise it will lose its power. It must also be known that when you make and use this parchment, you must be clean, pure and chaste.

The operator is to say one Mass of the Nativity then, and all the instruments are to be on the Altar.

Of Aspersion

You take an asperser made with a bunch of mint, marjoram and rosemary which is secured by a thread which has been made by a virgin maiden.

The asperger is made in the day and hour of Mercury when the Moon is at its crescent.

Of the Perfumes

These are to be wood of aloes, incense and mace. As for the mace, this is all that you need for the circle, and over the perfumes is to be said the following orison:

Orison of the Aromatic Perfumes

"Deign, O Lord, to sanctify the creature of this, in order that it may be a remedy for the human race, and that it may be a remedy for our souls and bodies, through the invoking of Thy holy name! Agree that all creatures which may breathe in the vapour of this may have wealth of their bodies and souls: through the Lord who has fashioned the time eternal! *Amen.*"

Of the Pen of the Art

Take a new quill, and asperge and fumigate this in the same way as the other instruments, and when you are cutting its point, say:

"Ababaloy, Samoy, Escavor, Adonay: I have from this quill driven out all illusions, so that it may hold within it with effectiveness the power needed for all those things which are used in the Art: for both the operations and the characters and conjurations. *Amen.*"

Of the Ink-horn

You buy a new ink-horn on the day and in the hour of Mercury. At this time, too, these characters are inscribed upon it:

JOD HE VAU HE METATRON JOD KADOS ELOYM SABAOTH.

Then newly made ink is exorcised with this exorcism before being placed in the horn:

"I exorcise you, Creature of this Ink, by the Names Anston, Cerreton, Stimulator, Adonay, and by the Name of

He who created all with one word, and who can achieve all, so that you shall assist me in my work, and so that this work may be accomplished by my desire, and brought to a successful end through the agreement of God, He who rules in all things, and through all things, omnipresent and eternal. *Amen*."

Then the ink is to be blessed with this Blessing of the Ink:

"Lord God, almighty, ruler over all and for ever, Thou who dost cause to take place the greatest wonders in Thy creations, deign to grant the grace of Thy holy spirit through this ink. Bless it, and sanctify it, and impart to it a special power, that whatever we may say or do or desire may be accomplished: through Thee, Most Holy Prince, Adonay. *Amen*."

The Preparation of the Sorcerer

When the implements are ready, the operator must prepare himself. This is first done by this Preparatory Orison:

"Lord God, Adonay, who hast formed man in Thine image, I, the unworthy and sinful, beseech Thee to sanctify this water, to benefit my body and soul, cause me to be cleansed...."

As he says this the operator is to wash his face and hands with the water that he is blessing.

NOTE:

This water is to be used for washing the hands and feet, and know also – and know and know again – that it is necessary and most necessary, to abstain three days from sin: and above all mortally, however much the human frailty may be, and especially guard your chastity.

During the three days, study the book... and during this time, pray five times during the day and four times each night, with the following form:

"Astroschio,[1] Asath, a sacra Bedrimubal, Felut, Anabotos, Serabilem, Sergen, Gemen, Domos: O Lord my God, Thou who art seated higher than the Heavens, Thou who seeth even unto the depths, I pray that Thou grant unto me the things which I have in my mind and that I may be successful in them: through Thee, O Great God, the Eternal and who reigns for ever and ever. *Amen.*"

All this having been done correctly, all that remains is to follow your invocations and draw your characters, and you do as follows:

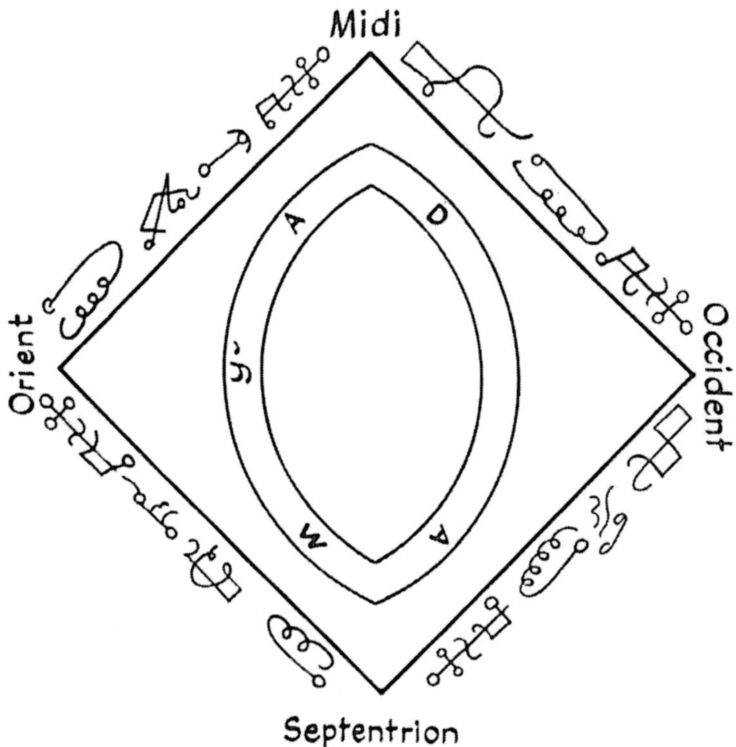

Sign and Character of Scirlin.

[1] Variation: "Astrachios, Asach, Ascala, Abedumabal, Silat, Anabotas, Jesubilin, Scingin, Geneon, Domol – "

In the day and hour of Mars [Tuesday] the Moon being at the crescent, and at the first hour of the day – which is a quarter of an hour before sunrise – you will prepare a piece of virgin parchment, which shall contain all the characters and the invocations of the Spirits which you wish to produce.

For example, in the said day and hour, you will attach to the small finger of the hand [which is the finger of Mercury] a thread spun by a virgin girl, and pierce the finger with the lancet of the Art, to get blood from it, with which you form your Scirlin characters, as is given at the commencement of this book. Then write above your invocation, which is that which follows:

Invocation to Scirlin

"Helon – Taul – Varf – Pan – Heon – Homonoreum – Clemialh – Serugeath – Agla – Tetragrammaton – Casoly."

You must write the first letter of your name where is the letter A, and that of your surname where is the letter D. The spirit Aglassis, whose character it is, is very potent to render you service, and will cause you to have power over the other spirits.

Make above the Character of the Spirit that you desire to come, and burn incense in his honour. Then make the conjuration which is addressed to the Spirit that you want to cause to appear, and burn incense in his honour.

Conjuration of Lucifer

"Lucifer, Ouyar, Chameron, Aliseon, Mandousin, Premy, Oriet, Naydrus, Esmony, Eparinesont, Estiot, Dumosson,

Danochar, Casmiel, Hayras, Fabelleronthou, Sodirno, Peatham, *Venite*, Lucifer, *Amen.*"

Conjuration for Béelzébuth

"Béelzébuth, Lucifer, Madilon, Solymo, Saroy, Theu, Ameclo, Segrael, Praredun, Adricanorom, Martino, Timo, Cameron, Phorsy, Metosite, Prumosy, Dumaso, Elivisa, Alphrois, Fubentroty, *Venite*, Béelzébuth, *Amen.*"

Conjuration for Astaroth

"Astaroth, Ador, Cameso, Valuerituf, Mareso, Lodir, Cadomir, Aluiel, Calniso, Tely, Plorim, Viordy, Cureviorbas, Cameron, Vesturiel, Vulnavij, Benez meus Calmiron, Noard, Nisa Chenibranbo Calevodium, Brazo Tabrasol, *Venite*, Astaroth, *Amen.*"

After having said seven times the conjuration addressed to superior Spirits, you will see the Spirit at once appear, to do whatever you desire.

NOTE
Dismissal of the Spirit

When you have written the conjuration on the virgin parchment, and have seen the spirit, being satisfied, you can dismiss him by saying this:

"Ite in pace ad loca vestra et pax sit inter vos redituri ad mecum vos invocavero, in nomine Patris ✠ et Filii ✠ et Spiritus Sancti ✠ *Amen.*"

Conjuration for Inferior Spirits

"Osurmy ✠ delmusan ✠ atalsloym ✠ charusihoa ✠ melany ✠ liamintho ✠ colehon ✠ paron ✠ madoin merloy ✠ bulerator ✠ donmedo ✠ hone ✠ peloym ✠ ibasil ✠ meon ✠ alymdrictels ✠ person ✠ crisolsay ✠ lemon sessle nidar horiel peunt ✠ halmon ✠ asophiel ✠ ilnostreon ✠ baniel ✠ vermias ✠ slevor ✠ noelma ✠ dorsamot ✠ lhavala ✠ omor ✠ frangam ✠ beldor ✠ dragin ✠ *Venite* N..."

In this conjuration the name of the Spirit replaces the 'N', and he will appear to you, and give you what you wish, after which you will dismiss him in the following words:

Dismissal of the Inferior Spirit

"Go in peace, [N]..., whence you came, peace be with you, and come every time I shall call you, in the Name of the Father ✠ and of the Son ✠ and of the Holy Spirit ✠ *Amen*."

Then you will burn the characters, because they will serve only once.

Another Conjuration

"I conjure thee, [N]..., by the Name of the Great Living God, Sovereign Creator of all things, that thou appear in human form, fair and agreeable, without noise or inconvenience, to answer truthfully in all the interrogations that I shall make.

"I conjure thee to do this by the power of the Holy and Sacred Names."

Orison of the Salamanders

"Immortal, eternal, ineffable and Holy Father of all things, who is carried by the revolving chariot unceasingly, of the worlds which continually revolve: dominator of the Etherian countries where there is raised the throne of Thy power: above which Thy redoubtable eyes see all, and Thy holy ears hear all – aid Thy children whom Thou hast loved since the birth of the centuries: for Thy golden and great and eternal majesty shines above the world, the sky and the stars, Thou art elevated above all, O sparkling Fire, and Thou illuminatest Thyself by Thy splendour, and there go out from Thy essence untarnishable rays of light which nourish Thy infinite spirit. That infinite spirit produces all things, and makes the mighty treasure which cannot fail, to the creation which surrounds Thee, due to the numberless forms of which she bears, and which Thou hast filled at the start.

"From this spirit comes also the origin of those most holy kings who are around Thy throne, and who compose Thy Court, O Universal Father!

"O Unique One, O Father of happy mortals and immortals!

"Thou hast created in particular the powers which are marvellously like the eternal thought, and from Thy adorable essence.

"Thou hast established them over the angels, Thou hast created a third kind of sovereign in the elements.

"Our continual exercise is to worship Thy desires. We burn with the desire to possess Thee, O Father, O Mother, the most tender of Mothers! O wonderful example of feelings and tenderness of Mothers! O Son, the flower of all sons! O Form of all forms! Soul, Spirit, Harmony and Name of all things, preserve us and we shall be blessed. *Amen*."

Pentacles, of the Rings of Solomon, son of David

I have put here the form of the Pentacle of Solomon, so that you may make the arrangements, they being of great importance:

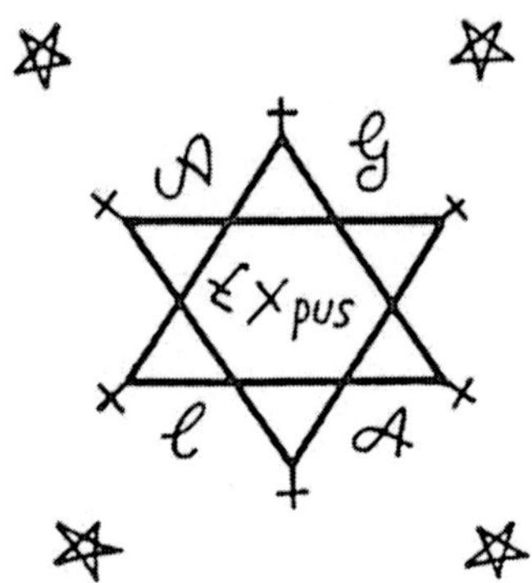

When you make your circle, before entering therein, it is to be perfumed with musk, amber, aloes wood and incense. And for the perfume which you will need for the invocations, that is incense alone.

It is to be observed that you need to have always a fire during invocations, and when you perfume, this will be in the name of the Spirit that you would invoke. When you are placing the perfume on the fire, say all the time:

"I burn this [N]..., in the name and to the honour of [N]..."

It is to be remembered that you must hold the invocation in the left hand, and in the right a rod of elder, and a ladle and a knife are to be at your feet.

When all this is ready, stand inside the circle. If you have companions with you, they are to hold a hand one of the other. When inside, trace the form of the circle with the knife of the Art. Then pick up the wands, one after the other, reciting the Fiftieth Psalm (*Misere mei...*). When the circle is complete, perfume and sprinkle it with holy water. Characters are to be written at the four corners of the circle [there are generally four pentacles, one at each point of the compass]; and the Spirit is prohibited specifically from entering into the precincts of the Circle.

Then the invocations are to be repeated seven times. When the Spirit appears, make him sign the character which you are holding in your hand, which promises that he will come whenever you may call him. Ask for what you think needed, and he will give it to you.

Dismissing the Spirit

Let him go away with these words:

"Go in peace to your own place, and peace be with you, until I shall invoke you again. In the name of the Father ✢ and of the Son ✢ and of the Holy Spirit. *Amen.*"

A Rare and Surprising Magical Secret

The Manner of Making the Mirror of Solomon, useful for all Divinations.

In the name of the Lord, *Amen.* Ye shall see in this mirror any thing which you may desire. In the name of the Lord who is blessed, in the name of the Lord. *Amen.*

Firstly, you shall abstain from actions of the flesh, and also from any sin, whether in word or action, during the period of time laid down herein. Secondly, you must perform acts of good and piety. Thirdly, take a plate of finest steel, burnished and slightly curved, and with the blood of a white pigeon write upon it, at the four corners these names: JEHOVA, ELOYM, METATRON, ADONAY.

Place the steel in a clean, white cloth. Look for the new Moon, in the first hour after the Sun has set, and when you see it, go to a window, look devoutly towards Heaven, and say:

"O Eternal, O King Eternal! God Ineffable! Thou, who hast created all things for the love of men, and by a concealed decision for the wellbeing of man, deign Thou to look on me, [N]..., who am Thy most unfit and unworthy Servant, and look upon this, which is my intention.

"Deign to send unto me Thine Angel, *Anael*, upon this same mirror; he who does command and order his companions – Thy servants – whom Thou hast formed, O Most Powerful Lord, Who hast always been, Who art, and Who shall ever be, so that in Thy Name they may work and act with equity, giving me knowledge in everything that I shall seek to know of them."

Now you are to throw down upon the burning embers a perfume. While you are doing this, say:

"In this and with this, that I pour forth before Thy Face, O God, my God, Thou who art blessed, Three in One, and in the state of exaltation most sublime, who sits above the Cherubim and Seraphim, Who will judge the earth by the fire, hear me!"

This is to be said three times. When you have done so, breathe three times upon the surface of the mirror, and say:

"Come, *Anael*, come: and let it be thy agreement to be with me willingly: in the name ✠ of the Father, the Most Puissant, in the name ✠ of the Son, Most Wise, in the Name of the Holy Spirit, the Most Living!

"Come, *Anael*, in the terrific name of JEHOVA! Come, *Anael*, by the power of the everliving ELOHIM! Come, thee, by the right arm of the mighty *Metatron!*

"Come to me, N... [say the name again over the mirror], and order thy subjects so that they may make known to me through their love, joy and peace, the things which are hidden from my eyes."

When you have finished this, raise your eyes towards Heaven and say:

"O Most Powerful Lord, who does cause all things to move in accordance with Thy Will, listen to my prayer, and may my intention be agreeable to Thee! O Lord, if it be Thy Will, deign to gaze upon this mirror and sanctify it, that Thy Servant *Anael* may come thereto with his companions, and be agreeable to me, N..., Thy poor and humble servant! O God, blessed and raised above all the spirits of Heaven, Thou who livest and reignest for all time. *Amen*."

When this is done, make the Sign of the Cross over yourself, and also on the mirror on the first day, and also on the next forty and five days. At the end of this time, the Angel Anael will appear to you, like unto a beautiful child. He will greet you, and will order his companions to obey you.

It does not always require as long as this to cause the Angel to appear, however. He may come on the fourteenth day, but this will depend upon the degree of application and fervour of the operator.

When he comes, ask him whatever you may desire, and also beg him to come and do your will whenever you shall call him.

When you want Anael to come again, after the first time, all you have to do is to perfume the mirror, and say these words: "Come, Anael, come, and let it be thy agreement" – and the rest of this prayer to Anael as we have given you above, until the Amen.

Dismissing the Spirit

When he has answered your questions, and you are satisfied with him, you must send him away by saying this:

"I thank thee, Anael, for having appeared and having fulfilled my requests. Thou mayst therefore depart in peace, and shall return when I call unto thee."

The perfume of Anael is saffron.

Divination by the Word of Uriel

To succeed in this operation, he who makes the experiment must do all things which are told herein. He is to choose a small room or place which for nine days or more has not been visited by women in an impure state.

This place must be well cleaned and consecrated, by means of consecrations and aspersions. In the middle of the room there is to be a table covered with a white cloth. On this is a new glass vial full of spring water, brought shortly before the operation, with three small tapers made of virgin wax mixed with human fat; a piece of virgin parchment, and the quill of a raven suitable for writing with; an inkpot of china full of fresh ink; a small container of metal with materials to make a fire.

You must also find a small boy of nine or ten years old, who shall be well behaved and cleanly dressed. He should be near the table.

A large new needle is taken, and one of the three tapers is mounted upon it, six inches behind the glass. The other two tapers should be positioned at the right and left of the glass, and an equal distance away.

While you are doing this, say:

"Gabamiah, Adonay, Agla, O Lord God of Powers, aid us!"

Place the virgin parchment on the right of the glass and the pen and ink on the left. Before starting, close the door and windows.

Now stir the fire, and light the wax tapers. Let the boy be on his knees, looking into the glass vial. He should be bareheaded and his hands joined.

Now the master orders the boy to stare fixedly into the vial, and speaking softly into his right ear, he says:

The Conjuration

"Uriel, Seraph, Josata, Ablati, Agla, Caila, I beg and conjure thee by the four words that God spoke with His mouth to His servant, Moses: Josta, Agla, Caila, Ablati. And by the name of the Nine Heavens in which thou livest, and also by the virginity of this child who is before thee, to appear, at once, and visibly, to reveal clearly that truth which I desire to know. And when this is done, I shall discharge thee in peace and benevolence, in the Name of the Most Holy Adonay."

When this conjuration is finished, ask the child whether he sees anything in the vial. If he answers that he sees an angel or other materialisation, the master of the operation shall say in a friendly tone:

"Blessed Spirit, welcome. I conjure thee again, in the Name of the Most Holy Adonay, to reveal to me immediately...." (And here you will ask the Spirit what you will.)

Then say to the Spirit:

"If, for any reason, thou dost not wish what thou sayest to be heard by others, I conjure thee to write the answer upon this virgin parchment, between this time and the morrow. Otherwise thou mayst reveal it to me in my sleep."

If the Spirit answers audibly, you must listen with respect. If he does not speak, after you have repeated the supplication three times, snuff the tapers, and leave the room until the following day. Return the next morning, and you will find the answer written on the virgin parchment, if it has not been revealed to you in the night.

Divination by the Egg

The operation of the Egg is to know what will happen to anyone who is present during the experiment.

One takes an egg of a black hen, laid in the daytime, breaks it, and removes the germ.

You must have a large glass, very thin and clear. Fill this with clear water, and into it put the egg-germ.

The glass is placed in the Sun at midday in summer, and the Director of the Operation will recite the prayers and conjurations of the day.

These prayers and conjurations are such as are found in the *Key of Solomon*, in which we treat amply of airy spirits.

And with the index finger, agitate the water, to make the germ turn. Leave it to rest a moment, and then look at it through the glass, not touching it. Then you will see the answer, and it should be tried on a working-day, because these are spirits that will come during the times of ordinary occupations.

If one wishes to see if a boy or a girl is a virgin, the germ will fall to the bottom; and if he (or she) is not, it will be as usual.

To See the Spirits of the Air

Take the brain of a cock, powder from the grave of a dead man (which touches the coffin), walnut oil and virgin wax.

Make all into a mixture, wrapped in virgin parchment, on which is written the words:

"GOMERT, KAILOETH," with the Character of Khil.

Burn it all, and you will see prodigious things. But this experiment should be done only by those who fear nothing.

To Make three Girls or three Gentlemen appear in your Room, After Supper

It is necessary to be three days chaste, and you will be elevated.

1. *Preparation.* On the fourth day, as soon as it is morning, clean and prepare your room, as soon as you have dressed. You must be fasting at this time. Make sure that your room will not be disturbed for the whole of the ensuing day. Note that there shall be nothing hanging, neither anything crosswise to anything else, no tapestries or clothes hanging, and no hats or cages of birds, or curtains of the bed, and so on.

   Above all, make sure that everything is clean in every way.
2. *Ceremony.* After you have supped, go secretly to your room, which has been cleaned as already described. Upon the table there is now to be set a white cloth, and three chairs at the table. In front of each place, set a wheaten roll and a glass of clear and fresh water. Now place a chair at the side of the bed, and retire, while saying this:
3. *Conjuration.* "Besticitum consolatio veni ad me vertat Creon, Creon, Creon, cantor laudem omnipotentis et non commentur. Stat superior carta bient laudem omviestra principiem da montem et inimicos meos o prostantis vobis et mihi dantes que passium fieri sincisibus."

The three people, having arrived, will sit by the fire, eating and drinking, and will thank the person who has entertained them. If you are a gentleman, three girls will come; but if you are a lady, three young men will be invoked.

Then the three will draw lots as to who is to stay with you. If the operator is a man, the girl who wins will sit in the chair which you have placed by the bed, and she will stay and be with you until midnight. At this time she will leave, with her companions, without having been dismissed.

The two others will stay by the fire, while the first entertains you.

While she is with you, you may ask her any question, about any art or science, or upon any subject at all, and she will at once give you a definite reply. You can ask the whereabouts of hidden treasure, and she will tell you as to where it is, and how and when to remove it. If the treasure is under the guardianship of infernal spirits, she will come herself, with her companions, and defend you against these fiends.

When she leaves, she will give you a ring. If you wear this on your finger, you will be fortunate at gambling. If you place it on the finger of any woman or girl, you will be able at once to obtain your will of her. Note: The window is to be left open. You can do this experiment as often as you please.

To Make a Girl come to You, however Modest she may Be

Experiment of a marvellous power of the superior intelligences. Watch for the crescent or the waning moon, and when you see it, make sure that you see also a star, between the hours of eleven and midnight. Before starting the process, do thus:

Take a virgin parchment, and write on it the name of the girl whom you desire to come. The shape of the parchment is to be as you see in the figure on the right:

On the other side of the parchment, write MELCHIAEL, BARESCHAS. Then put the parchment on the earth, with the part where the name of the person is written next to the ground. Place your right foot upon the parchment, and your left knee, bent, upon the ground.

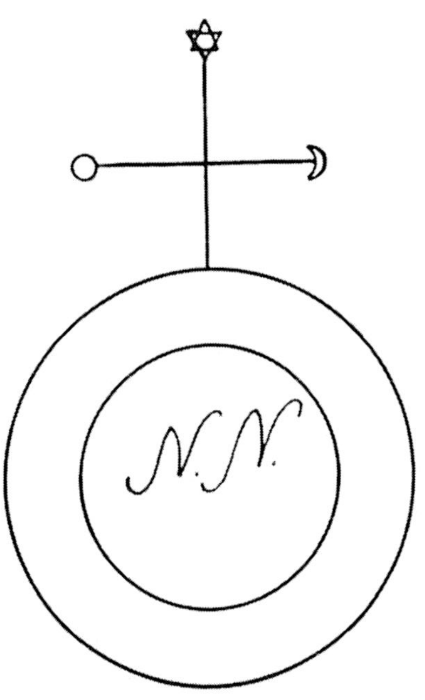

Then look for the highest star in the sky, while in this position. In your right hand hold a taper of white wax, sufficiently large to burn for one hour. Then say the following:

Conjuration

"I salute thee and conjure thee, O beautiful Moon, O most beautiful Star, O brilliant light which I have in my hand. By the air that I breathe, by the breath within me, by the earth which I am touching: I conjure thee. By all the names of the spirit princes living in you. By the ineffable Name ON, which created everything! By you, O resplendent Angel Gabriel, with the Planet Mercury, Prince, Michiael and Melchidael.

"I conjure you again, by all the Holy Names of God, so that you may send down power to oppress, torture and harass the body and soul and the five senses of N..., she whose name is written here, so that she shall come unto me, and agree to my desires, liking nobody in the world, and especially thus

N..., for so long as she shall remain unmoved by me. Let her then be tortured, made to suffer. Go, then, at once! Go, Melchidael, Baresches, Zazel, Firiel, Malcha, and all those who are with thee! I conjure you by the Great Living God to obey my will, and I, N..., promise to satisfy you."

When this conjuration has been said three times, burn the parchment with the taper. On the next day, take the parchment, put it in your left shoe, and let it stay there until the person whom you have called comes to seek you out. In the Conjuration you must say the date that she is to come, and she will not be absent.

To Make oneself Invisible

Collect seven black beans. Start the rite on a Wednesday, before sunrise. Then take the head of a dead man, and put one of the black beans in his mouth, two in his eyes and two in his ears. Then make upon his head the character which follows here.[1]

When you have done this, bury the head, with the face upwards, and for nine days, before sunrise, water it each morning with excellent brandy. On the eighth day you will find the spirit mentioned, who will say to you: "WHAT WILT THOU?"

You will reply: "I AM WATERING MY PLANT." Then the Spirit will say: "GIVE ME THE BOTTLE, I DESIRE TO WATER IT MYSELF." In answer, refuse him this, even though he will ask you again.

Then he will reach out with his hand, and will display to you that same figure which you have drawn upon the head. Now you can be sure that it is the right spirit, the spirit of the head. There is a danger that another one might try to trick

[1] This is the character of MORAIL; see page 92.

you, which would have evil consequences – and in that case your operation would not succeed.

Then you may give him the bottle, and he will water the head and leave. On the next day – which is the ninth – when you return, you will find that the beans are germinating. Take them and put them in your mouth, and look at yourself in a mirror. If you can see nothing, it is well. Test the others in the same way, either in your own mouth, or in that of a child. Those which do not confer invisibility are to be reburied with the head.

To Have Gold and Silver, or the Hand of Glory

Tear out the hair of a mare in heat, by the roots, closest to the nature, saying DRAGNE, DRAGNE, DRAGNE. Then tie them into a knot. Now go out and buy, without dispute over the price, a new pot of earthenware, which shall have a lid. Return to your house as fast as you can, fill the pot with water from a spring, until it is not quite full. Place the knotted hairs in it, cover it, and place it where neither you nor anyone else can see it, for there is danger in this.

After nine days, at the hidden hour, bring out the pot and open it, and you will find that there is a small animal like a snake therein. This will jump up. Then say: I ACCEPT THE PACT.

Do not touch the animal with your hand. Place it in a new box, which you have bought for this purpose, and that without bargaining as to price. You must feed the creature with wheat-husks alone, daily.

When you need gold or silver, place as much as you require in the box. Go to bed, with the box at the side of the bed. Sleep, if you desire, for three or four hours. Rise, then, and you will find that the money that you have placed in the box has been doubled. But what you put first into the box must be left in it.

If it is an ordinary-looking snake, you should not ask for more than one hundred francs at each time. If, however, it has a human face, you will be able to obtain a thousand francs each time.

If you want to kill the creature, place in the box instead of its daily husks, some of the flour which has been used for the consecration in the first Mass said by a priest. After eating this it will die. 'Above all, do not omit anything, because this is not intended as a joke!'

Garters for Distances

Go out of the house, fasting; march to your left until you find a ribbon-seller. Buy one ell of white ribbon. Pay what is asked, and drop a farthing (*un liard*) into the box.

Return home by the same route. Next day do the same, until you have found a seller of pens. Buy one, as you bought the ribbon. When you are locked in your own room, write with your own blood on the ribbon the characters of the third line on the plan. This is the right garter. Those of the fourth line are for the left.[1]

When this is done, go out. The third day after, take your ribbon and pen, walk to the left until you find a pastrycook or bakery. Buy a cake or bread for a halfpenny. Go to the first tavern, order a half bottle of wine, have your glass rinsed three times by the same person, break in three the cake or bread.

Put the three pieces in the glass with wine. Take the first piece and throw it under the table without looking at it, saying IRLY, FOR THEE.

1 These are presumably the planetary symbols in the concentric circles of the plan of the Grimoire.

Then take the second piece and throw it likewise, saying TERLY, FOR THEE. Write on the other side of the garter the two names of these spirits with your blood. Throw down the third piece, saying, ERLY, FOR THEE. Throw down the pen, drink the wine without eating, pay the cost and go away.

Being outside the town, take the garters, make no mistake as to which is the right and which the left. This is important. Stamp three times with the foot on the ground, pronounce the names of the spirits TERLY, ERLY, BALTAZARD, IRLY, MELCHIOR, GASPARD, LET US GO. Then make your trip.

To Make a Girl Dance in the Nude

Write on virgin parchment the Character of FRUTIMIÈRE with the blood of a bat. Then put it on a blessed stone, over which a Mass has been said. After this when you want to use it, place the character under the sill or threshold of a door which she must pass.

When she comes past, she will come in. She will undress and be completely naked, and will dance unceasingly until death, if one does not remove the character; with grimaces and contortions which will cause more pity than desire.

To See in a Vision Anything from the Past or Future

The two N N which you see in the second small circle mark the place where you put your name.[1] To know what you will, write the names in the circle on virgin parchment, before

[1] This figure is reproduced in the process entitled: 'To Make a Girl Come to You... etc.', p. 118.

sleeping, and put it under your right ear on retiring, saying the following orison:

Orison

"O Glorious Name of Great God the ever-living, to whom all things are present, I am Thy servant N.... Father Eternal, I beg You to send me Thy Holy Angels, who are written in the Circle, and that they shall show me what I want to know, by Jesus Christ our Lord. So be it."

Having completed the orison, lie down on your right side, and you will see in a dream that which you desire to know.

To Nail (an Enemy)

Go to a cemetery, remove nails from an old coffin, saying:

"Nails, I take you, so that you may serve to turn aside and cause evil to all persons whom I will. In the Name of the Father, and of the Son, and of the Holy Spirit. *Amen.*"

When you wish to use it, you must look for a footprint[1] and making the three figures of GULAND, SURGAT and MORAIL, fix the nail in the middle saying:

"*Pater noster upto in terra.*"

Hit the nail with a stone, saying:

"Cause evil to N..., until I remove thee."

Re-cover the place with a little dust, and remember it well, because one cannot remove the evil which this causes, but by removing the nail, and saying:

[1] This is a common process in several countries. The footprint is, of course, that of the person who is being cursed.

"I remove thee, so that the evil which thou hast caused to N..., shall cease. In the Name of the Father, and of the Son, and of the Holy Spirit. *Amen*."

Then take the nail out, and efface the characters: not with the same hand as you make them, but with the other. Thus it will be without danger.

END OF THE GRIMORIUM VERUM

PART II

WHITE MAGIC: SECRETS OF ALBERTUS MAGNUS

CHAPTER V

THE SECOND BOOK OF ALBERTUS MAGNUS

MAGICAL STONES
ALBERTUS MAGNUS

The Second Boke: Of the Vertues of Certaine Stones

Marvellous Operations of the Magical Stones

Now because I have spoken before of the vertues of certaine hearbs: now in this present Chapter, I will speake of certaine Stones, and of their effecte and marvellous operations.

Magnes, the lodestone
Orhatulimus
Serpiendamus
Topazion
Memphitis, lapis juxta memphium, urbem in Egipto
Abaston
Agathes
Esmundus
Eliotrophia
Calcedonius
Bagates
Onyx
Sylonites
Medoria
Adamis, diamond
Alectoria
Celonites
Cristallus
Galeritis
Echites
Tepistites
Orithes
Saunus
Hiacinthus
Saphirus

Berilus	Epistrites
Corallus	Celidonius
Istmos	Bena
Chrysolitus	Tabrices
Nichomai	Carathides
Radianus	Quirim
Unces	Luperius
Smaragdus	Lazuli
Gallasia	Iris
Draconites	

¶ *If thou wilt know whether thy wife be chaste or no*
* Take the stone which is called Magnes, in Englishe the loadestone, it is of sadde blew colour, and it is found in the sea of Inde, and sometime in the parts of Almaine, in the province which is called Caste Fraunce.
LV Lay this stone under the head of a wife. And if she be chaste, she will embrace her husband. If she be not chast[e], she will fall forth of her bed.

Second Experiment with the Lodestone
LVI Moreover, if this stone be put brayed and scattered upon coals, in foure corners of the house, they that be sleeping shall flee the house and leave all.

¶ *If thou wilt be made Invisible*
LVII * Take the stone which is called Ophethalminus, and wrap it in the leafe of the Laurell or Bay tree. And it is called Lapis Obtelmicus, whose colour is not named, for it is of many colours, and it is of such vertue, that it blindeth the sights of them that stand about. Constantinus carrying this in his hand, was made invisible therewith.

¶ *If thou wilt provoke Sorrow, Feare, Terrible Fantasies and debate*

LVIII * Take the stone which is called Oniz, whose colour is black, and that kinde is best that is full of blacke veines. It cometh from Inde unto Araby: and if it be hanged upon the necke or finger, it soone stirreth up sorrow and heavinesse in a man, and also terrors and debate, and this hath bin proved by men of late time.

¶ *If thou wilt Burne any mans hand Without Fire*

LIX * Take the stone which is called Fetipendamus [? Serpiendamus], which is of yellow colour, and if it be hanged upon the neck of any man it healeth Articum. Also, if this stone be grip[p]ed straightly, it will burne the hand, and therefore it must be touched lightly and gently.

¶ *If Thou wilt kindle the minde of any man to joy and make his wit Sharpe*

LX * Take the stone that is called Sylonites, it groweth in ye bosome of a snaile in Inde, called Corcuses, and there is divers kindes of it, as white, redde and purple colour.

Others say that it is greene and founde in the partes of Parsia. And as olde Philosophers say, if it be tasted, it giveth knowledge of certaine thinges to come. If it be put underneath thy tongue, especially in the first Moone, it hath a vertue only for an houre. Therefore beeing in the tenth moone, hath this vertue in the first or tenth houre. But there is moving in the order, because, when it is under the toong, if our thought bee of any businesse, whether it ought to be or no: if it ought to be, it is fixed stedfastly to the heart, so that it may not be plucked away. If not, the heart leapeth back from it. Also, philosophers have saide, that it healeth Ptisicos, and weake men.

¶ *If thou wilt that Seething Water come foorth anon after thou hast put it in thy Hand*

LXI * Take the stone which is called Topazion, for the Ile Topasys, or because it showeth a similitude like gold, and there be two kinds of it. One is utterly like gold, and is more precious. The other kinde is of the colour of Saffron, and of brighter colour than gold is, and this is more profitable.

It hath beene proved in our time, that if he be put into seething water, it maketh it to run over. But if thou put thy hand in it the water is quickly drawne out: and this there was one of our brethren that did it at Paris. It is good also against Emothoicam et stimaticam, or lunatike passion or greefe.

¶ *If thou wilt plucke of[f] the skin of thine, or another mans hand*

LXII * Take the stone which is called Medora, of the region Media in which people dwelling are called Medy. And there be two kinds thereof, blacke and greene. It is said of old philosophers, and also of philosophers of later times, that if the blacke be broken and resolved in hot water, if any man wash his hands therein, the skin of his hands shall be plucked off anone.

Philosophers say also, that it is good against the gout, and blindnesse of the eyes, and it nourisheth hurt or weak eyes.

¶ *If thou wilt that a man Suffer no Paine nor be Tormented*

LXIII * Take the stone which is called Memphitis, of the city, Memphis. It is a stone of such vertue as Aaron and Hermes[1] say if it be drunken and mixed with water, and given to him to drinke, which should happen to be burned, or suffer and

1 Probably Aaron Isaac, interpreter to the Emperor Manuel Comnenus. He is quoted as having used a magical book attributed to Solomon and Hermes, in the eleventh century.

torments: that drinke induceth to great unablenesse to feele; that he that suffereth feeleth neither paine nor tormenting.

¶ *If thou wilt make a Fire continually unable to be Quenched or put out*
LXIV * Take the stone which is called Abaston, and it is of the colour of Yron, and there is found very much of it in Arabis. If that stone is kindled or inflamed, it may never be put out, or quenched. Because it hath the nature of the first feathers of the Salamander, by reason of moysty fatness which nourisheth fire kindled in it.

¶ *If thou wilt overcome thine Enemies*
LXV * Take the stone which is called Adamis, in English speech a Diamond. It is of a shining colour and very hard, insomuch that it cannot be broken but by the blood of a Goat, and it groweth in Arabia, or in Cipres.
LXVI And if it be bounde to the left side it is good against enemies, venimous beastes, and cruell men, and against venim and invasion of fantasies and some call it Diamas.

¶ *If thou wilt Eschew Perils and Terrible Things, and have a Strong Heart*
LXVII * Take the stone which is called Agathes: and it is black and hath white veines. There is another of the same kind, like to white colour. And the third groweth in a certain Ile, having black vaines and that maketh to overcome perils and giveth strength to the heart, maketh a man highly pleasant, delectable and helpeth against adversaries.

¶ *If thou Desire to Obtaine any Thing from any Man*
LXVIII * Take the stone which is called Alectoria, and it is a stone of a cocke, and it is white as the Chrystall, and it is drawne out of the cocks gisar or main, after that he hath been

gelded more then four yeeres: and it is of the greatnesse of a beane.

LXIX It maketh the belly pleasant and stedfast, and put under the tongue, it quencheth thirst. And this last hath beene proved in our time and I perceived it quickely.

¶ *If thou wilt Overcome Beasts, and interpret and Expounde all Dreames and Prophecie of things to Come*

LXX * Take the stone which is called Esmundus or Atasmundus. It is of divers colours, it putteth away poison, and maketh a man to overcome his adversaries, and the gift of prophesying and the interpretation of all dreames and making a man to understand darke questions hard to be understood or assoilved.

¶ *If thou wilt have a good understanding of things that May be Felte, and that thou mayst Not be made Drunke*

LXXI * Take the stone that is called Amarictus, it is of purple colour, and the best is found in Inde, and it is good against drunkenesse, and giveth good understanding in things that be understood.

¶ *If thou wilt Overcome thine Enemies and Flee Debate*

Take the stone which is called Berilus (it is of a pale colour and may be seene through as water) beare it about with thee, and thou shalt overcome all debate, and shalt drive away the enemies, and maketh the enemy meeke. It causeth a man to be well mannered, as Aaron saith, it giveth also good understanding.

¶ *If thou wilt Forejudge, or Conjecture of Things to Come*

LXXII * Take the stone which is called Celonites, it is purple and divers other colours, and it is found in the head of a snaile.

LXXIII If any man will beare this stone under the tongue, he shall forejudge and tell of things to come. But notwithstanding it hath no vertue but shining. Primacum fuerit, accensa, & crescens monytes in Ultima oefoendente. So meaneth Aaron, in the booke of the vertues of hearbs and stones.

¶ *If thou wilt Pacifie Tempests and goe Over Flouds*
LXXIV * Take the stone which is called Corallus, corall, and some be red and some white. And it hath been proved that it stemmeth anon blood, that putteth away the foolishnesse of him that beareth it, and giveth wisdome. And this hath beene proved of certaine men in our time. And it is good against tempests and perils of flouds.

¶ *If thou wilt Kindle Fire*
LXXV * Take the Chrystall stone and put it nigh under the circle of the Sunne, that is to say against the Sunne, and put it nigh any thing that may bee burned, and incontinently the heat of the Sunne shining will set it a fire, and if it be drunke with hon[e]y it increaseth milke.

¶ *If thou wilt that the Sunne appear of Bloody Colour*
LXXVI * Take the stone which is called Eliotropia. It is greene like to the precious stone called the Emerald. And it is sprinkled with bloudy drops. The necromancers call it Gemmi Babilonica, the precious stone of Babylon, by the proper name.

But if it be anointed with the juyce of an hearb of the same name and put in a vessel full of water, it maketh the Sunne to seem of bloody colour: as if the Ecclipse were seen. The cause of this is, for it maketh all the water to bubble up into a little cloude, which making the ayre thicke, hindereth the Sunne that she cannot bee seene but as it were through a thicke colour. A little after the cloude goeth away by dropping down like dew, as it were drops of raine.

This also borne about a man maketh a man of good fame, [w]hole and of long life.

It is said of old philosophers, that a man annointed with an hearb of this name, as we have said before, excelleth with vertue, and Eliotropia is found many times in Cipresse and Inde.

¶ *If thou wilt make Water cold that Seetheth on the Fire*

LXXVII * Take the stone which is called Epidractes, which put in water against the eye of the sun, putteth forth fiery beames of the Sun.

It is said of old and new philosophers, if it be put in seething water, the bubbling up and seething will soone cease; and a little after, it will waxe colde and it is a shining and ruddie stone.

¶ *If thou wilt Eschew Illusions and Fantasies and Overcome All Causes or Matters*

LXXVIII * Take the stone which is called Calcedonius, and it is of pale browne colour, and somewhat darke; if this bee pierced and hanged about the necke, with the stone which is called Sinerip, it is good against all fantasticall illusions, and it maketh to overcome all causes or matters in suite, and keepeth the body against thy adversaries.

¶ *If thou wilt be Pleasant*

LXXIX * Take the stone which is called Celidonius, of which there is some that is blacke, and some somewhat red, and it is drawn out of the bellies of swallows. If that which is somewhat red be wrapped in a linnen cloth, or in a calves hide, and borne under the left arm hole, is good against madnesse, and all sicknesses and diseases and the sleeping or forgetting malladies and contra epidimiam, which is a scab that runneth through the whole bodie.

Euar saith, that this stone maketh a man eloquent, acceptable and pleasant. The black stone is good against the businesse begun to an end. And if it be wrapped in the leaves of Celidon, it is said that it maketh the sight dull. And they should be drawne out in the moneth of August, and two stones are found oftentimes in one swallow.

¶ *If thou wilt be Victorious against thy Adversaries*

LXXX * Take ye stone, which is called Bagates, and it is of divers colours. The ancient philosophers saye that it hath been proved in the prince Alcides, which how long he did have it, he had alwayes victory. And it is a stone of diverse colours, like the skin of a kid.

¶ *If thou wilt Know before any Thing to Come*

LXXXI * Take the stone which is called Bena, which is like a Beastes tooth, and put it under thy tongue. And as Aaron and the old philosophers say, as long as thou doest hold it thou mayest conjecture and tell of things to come, and thou shalt not erre in any wise for judging.

¶ *If thou wilt that thy garment cannot be burned*

LXXXII* Take the stone which is called Histmos, which as Isodorus saith is like to Saffron, and it is found in a part of Spaine. This stone bloweth like a paire of bellowes, by reason of the windiness in it. It is found nigh the Gades of Hercules, that is two I[s]les, by the further parts of Spaine beyond Garnade; and if this stone be set in a garment it can be burned in no wise, but shineth like fire. And some men affirme that the white carbuncle stone is of this kinde.

¶ *If thou wilt have Favour and Honour*

LXXXIII * Take the stone which is called Tabrices, and it is like to the Chrystall stone. The ancient Philosophers, as Euar and Aaron say of it that it giveth eloquence, favour and honour and it is said, moreover, that it healeth every dropsie.

¶ *If thou wilt drive away Fantasies and Foolishnesse*

LXXXIV * Take the stone which is called Crysolitus, and it is of the same vertue with Attemicus, as Aaron and Euar say, in the booke of the natures of hearbs and stones. This stone set in gold, and borne, driveth away follishnesse, and expelleth fantasies. It is affirmed to give wisedome, and it is good against feare.

¶ *If thou wilt Judge the Opinions and Thoughts of Others*

LXXXV * Take the stone which is called Caratides, and it is of black colour; let one hold it in his mouth, and it maketh him that beareth it, merry and in favour, and well esteemed with all men.

¶ *If thou wilt have Victory and Amity*

LXXXVI * Take the stone which is called Nichomay, and it is the same that is called Alabaster, and it is a kinde of marble, and it is white and shininge. And oyntiments are made of it to the buryenge of the dead.

¶ *If thou wilt that a Man sleeping shal Tel thee what he hath done*

LXXXVII * Take the stone called Quirim, this stone found in the neste of the lapwing or blacke plover.

¶ *If thou wilt Obtain Anything of a Man*

LXXXVIII * Take the stone which is called Radianus, and it is blacke, shining through, which when the head of a cocke is given to Emotes or Pisimeres to eat, it is found a long time after, in the head of the cocke. And the same stone is also called Tonatides.

¶ *If thou wilt make that Neither Dogs, nor Hunters, may hurt any beast which they hunt*
LXXXIX * Put before them the stone which is called Luperius, and it will runne soone to the stone. This stone is found in Lybia, and all beastes run to it as to their defender. It letteth that neither dogs nor hunters may hurt them.

¶ *If thou wilt Burne a Mans Hand without Fire*
XC * Take the stone which is called Unces, which we called before *princi penapti*, which is fixe, and it is as fire. You may straine hard this stone, it burneth soone his hand, like as if it were burned with a materiall fire, which is a marevellous thing.

¶ *If thou wilt Cure Melancholy or a Fever Quartaine in any Man*
XCI * Take the stone which is called Lapis Lazuly: it is like the colour of the heaven; and there is within it little bodies of gold: and it is sure and proved that it cureth melancholy and the fever quartaine.

¶ *If thou wilt make any Mans Wit Sharpe and Quick, and Augment his Riches, and also Prophesie Things to Come*
XCII * Take the stone which is called Smaragdus, in English an Emerald, and it is very cleare, shining through and plain, but that of a yellow colour is better. It is taken out of the nests of gripes and griffons. It doth both comfort and save, and being borne it maketh a man to understand well; and giveth to him a good memory, augmenteth the riches of him that beareth it, and if any man that hold it under his tongue he shall prophesie anon.

¶ *If thou wilt make a Rainbow to Appear*
XCIII * Take the stone which is called Iris* and it is white like to a Christall, foure-square or having hornes. If this stone be put in the beames of the sunne, by turning back it maketh a rain bowe soone to appeare on the wall.

¶ *If thou wilt make a stone that will never be made hot*
XCIV * Take the stone which is called Gallasia, it hath the figure of the haile, and the colour and hardnesse of the diamond.

If this stone be put in a very great fire it will never be hot. And the cause is, for it hath the holes so straight together, that the heat may not enter in the body of the stone.

Also Aaron and Euar say, that this stone borne, mitigateth lecherie and other hot passions.

¶ *If thou wilt know whether thy Wife lyeth with any other Married Man*
XCV * Take the stone called Galeritis, which is the same that is called Catabres, and it is found in Lybia, Britannia, the most noble I[s]le of the world (wherein is contained both countries, England and Scotland). It is of double colour: black, and the colour of saffron, and it is found gray coloured, turning to palenesse. It healeth the dropsie, and it bindeth the bellies that are loose. And as Avicenna saith, that if the stone be broken and washed, or be given to a woman to be washed, if she be not a virgin, she will shed her water, if she be a virgin the contrary.

¶ *If thou wilt Overcome thine Enemies*
XCVI * Take the stone which is called Draconites, from the dragons head. And if the stone bee drawne out from him alive it is good against all poysons, and he that beareth it in his left arme, shall overcome all his enemies.

¶ *If thou wilt Engender Love between Any Two*

XCVII * Take the stone which is called Echites, and it is called of some Aquileus, because the Eagles put these in their nests. It is of purple colour, and it is found nigh the bankes of the Ocean Sea and sometime in Persia; and it alwaies containeth another stone in it which soundeth in it, when it is named.

It is said of ancient Philosophers, that this stone, hanged upon the left shoulder, gathereth love between the husband and wife. It is profitable to women great with childe, it letteth untimely birth, it mitigateth the peril of making afraid, and it is said to be good to them that have the fling skins; and as the men of Chaldee say and affirme, that if there be any poyson in thy meates if the aforesaid stone be put in, it letteth that meat be swallowed downe, and if it be taken out, meate is soone swallowed downe. And I did see that laste was examined sensible of one of our brethren.

¶ *If thou wilt make a Man Sure*

XCVIII * Take the stone that is called Tepistites. It is found in the sea; and it is said in the Booke of Alchorath that if it be borne before the heart, it maketh a man sure, and restraineth all seditions and discords. It is said also that it mitigateth the fleyes with long hinder legs, which burneth corne with touching of it and devoureth the residue, foules cloudes, haile, and such as have power of the fruits of the earth. And it hath beene proved of Philosophers of late time, and of certaine of our brethren, that, it being put against the Beame of the Sunne putteth forth fiery beames. Also, if this stone be put in seething water, the seething wil soon cease and the water will be cold a little after.

¶ *If thou wilt that Strangers walk Sure*

XCIX * Take the stone which is called Hiacinthus, in English a Jacinth, it is of many colours. The Green is best, and it hath redde veines, and should be set in silver. It is said in certaine Lectures, that there is two kindes of it, of the water, and of the Saphire. The Jacinth of the water is yellow and white. The Jacinth of the Saphire is very shining yellow, having no watrishnes, and this is better. And it is written of this in lectures of Philosophers, that it being borne on the finger or necke, maketh strangers sure and acceptable, to their ghests. And it provoketh sleepe for the colouresse of it, and the Jacinth of Saphire hath property this.

¶ *If thou wilt be saved from Divers Chances and Pestilent Bittes*

C * Take the stone which is called Orithes, of which there be three kinds; one blacke, another greene, and the third – of the which one part is rough, and the other plain; and the colour of it is like the colour of a plate of iron, but the greene hath white spots. This stone borne, preserveth from divers chances and perils of death.

¶ *If thou wilt Make Peace*

CI * Take the stone which is called Saphire, which cometh from the East into India, and that of yellow colour is the best; which is not very bright. It maketh peace and concord, also it makes the mind pure and devout to God. Further, it strengtheneth the minde in good things, and keepeth a man from too much inward heate.

¶ *If thou wilt Cure a Virgin*

CII * Take the stone which is called Saunus, from the I[s]le Sauna. It doth make firme or consolidate the minde of the bearer of it; and being bound to the hand of a woman travelling with childe, it hindereth the birth, and keepeth it still in the wombe. Therefore in any such occasion it is forbidden, that this stone touche a woman.

¶ *Purity to be Observed in these magical operations*
CIII Thou shalt finde many other things in the booke of mines, of Aaron and Euar. The manner of doing things, consisteth in this, that the bearer of any of these things, be a cleane person, but especially in his bodie.[1]

*EXPLICIT

Isodorus seemeth to say, that hicania hath in his head a stone of most noble vertue, and is of white colour, which brayed, given to them that have the strangulation, to drinke, it loseth perfectly the vrine and shortly healeth; it putteth away the fever quartane. Also it taketh away a white spot or pearle in the eye. Also if a woman with childe beare it on her, she looseth not her birth: moreover, the flesh of them that is sodden and eaten is good for them that have an exulceration or sore in the lungs, with a consumption of all the body, and spitting of blood. Also the powder of the beasts, with rinde or barke of trees, and some graines of Pepper, is profitable against the Emerodes and growing out of flesh about the buttockes. Likewise they being raw, brayed with rindes or barke or trees, break ripe impostumes.

1 Edition of 1617; Edition of 1525, *sic*: "The manner of doynge these thinges, consisteth in this, that ye bearer for a good effecte, be clean from all pollution, or defylynge of the bodye."

CHAPTER VI

THE MAGICAL USES OF CERTAIN HERBS

(THE SECRETS OF ALBERTUS MAGNUS)

OF THE VIRTUES OF HERBS THE SECRETS OF ALBERTUS MAGNUS

The First Booke: Of the Vertues of Hearbes

Magic not unlawful

ARISTOTLE, THE PRINCE of Philosophers, saith in many places, that every science is of the kinde of good things: But notwithstanding, the operation sometimes is good and sometime evill: as the science is changed unto a good or to an evill end, to that which it mayketh. Of the which saying, two things are concluded: the first is that the science of Magick is not evill, for by the knowledge of it, evill may bee eschewed, and good by meanes thereof may be followed.

The second thing is also concluded, for so much as the effect is so praised and so happily esteemed for the end, and also the end of science is dispraised, when it is not ordained to good or to vertue. It followeth then that every science or facultie, as operation is sometime good and sometime evill.

Therefore, because the science of Magick is a good knowledge (as it is presupposed) and is somewhat evill in beholding of causes and natural things, as I have considered and perceived in very many ancient authors: yea and ALBERT my selfe have found out the truth in many things and I suppose or imagine the trueth to be in some part of the Booke of Chirander, and also the Booke of Alchorac.

First, therefore, I wil declare of certayne herbes, secondlye, of certayne stones, and the vertues of them.

POWERS OF THE SIXTEEN MAGICAL PLANTS

The sixteen magical plants given by Albertus, with his version of their Latin and English names[1] are as follows:

1. Eliotropia	*Marygolde*
2. Urtica	*Nettle*
3. Virga Pastoris	*Wilde Teasell*
4. Celidonia	*Celindine*
5. Provinca	*Periwinkle*
6. Mepeta	*Calaminte, Peniroyale*
7. Lingua canis	*Hounds toung*
8. Jusquianus	*Henbane*
9. Lillium	*Lillie*
10. Usicus Querci	*Missell toe*

[1] These herbs are probably those better known under the following names: (1) Marygold; (2) Nettle (*Urtica: Urticacae*); (3) Teasel (*Dipsacus*); (4) Celandine (prob. *Chelidonium*, prob. not 'Lesser Celandine'); (5) Periwinkle, one of the *Apocynaceae*; (6) Pennyroyal (Mint family: *M. Pulegium*); (7) Hound's-Tongue (*Cynoglossum*); (8) Henbane (*Hyoscyamus*); (9) Lily; (10) Mistletoe; (11) probably Centaurea, rather than Centaury (Erythraea); (12) Sage; (13) Verbena; (14) Smallage; (15) Rose; (16) probably Snakeweed (*Polygonium bistorta*).

11. Centaures	*Centory*
12. Salvia	*Sage*
13. Verbena	*Vervain*
14. Milisopholos	*Smallage*
15. Rosa	*Rose*
16. Serpentina	*Snakes Grasse*

(All these forenamed hearbs shalt thou find in their severall places, with their wonderfull operation, and markings, but yet if thou dost not observe the times and seasons, wherein their should be ministred and put in practise, all thy labour is of none effect.)[1]

(1) The firste herbe is called with the men of Chaldea, Elios, with the Greekes Matuchiol, with the Latynes, Eliotropium, with Englysh men, Marygolde, whose interpretation is of Elion, that is, the Son [Sun], and Tropos, that is, alteration, or change, because it is turned according to the Sun. The vertue of this herbe is marvellous for if it be gathered, the Sunne being in the Sign Leo in August, and wrapped in the leafe of a Lawrell, or may tree, and a wolfs tooth added thereto, no man shall be able to have one word to speake against the bearer thereof, but words of peace: if anything bee stollen, and the bearer of the things before named, lay them under his head in the night, he shall see the theefe and all his conditions.

The Marygold in a process to discover immorality

I. Moreover, if the aforesaid hearbe bee put in any Church, where women be, which have broken matrimonie on their

[1] Paragraph in parentheses apears only in the edition of 1617, and does not figure in the *Boke of Secrets* of 1525 or 1565.

part: they shall never be able to goe forth of the Church, except it be put away. And this last point hath been proved, and is very true.

(2) The second hearbe is named of the Chaldae Roibra, of the Greeks Olieribos, of the Latins and Frenchmen Urtica, of English men a Nettle.

Nettle and Yarrow as a Charm to allay all Fear

II. He that holdeth this hearbe in his hand, with an hearb called milfoile, or Yarrow, or Nosbleed, is sure from all feare, and fantasie or vision.

Method of Attracting Fishes

III. And if it be put with the juyce of HOUSELEEKE, and the bearers had been anointed with it, and the residue put in water, if he enter the water where fishes are, they will gather together in his hands, adding thereto Ad piscellum. And if his hand be drawn forth, they will leap again to their own places, where they were before.

Of an Experiment with Wild Teasell

(3) The third hearb is named of the Chaldees Lorumboror, of the Greeks Allamor, of the Latins Verga Pastoris, of the Englishe men Wilde Teasell.

IV. Take this hearb, and temper it with the juice of mandrake, and give it to a bird, or to any other beast. And it shall be great with a yong one in the owne kinde, and shall bring forth the birth in the owne kinde, of the which yong one.

Of Creating Discord through the same Herb

V. If the gum toothe be taken and dipped in the meat or drinke, every one that shall drinke thereof, shall begin anon battell, and when they would put it away, give to him the juice of Velarian, and peace shal be among them as before.

Of a Talisman for Victory

(4) The fourth hearb is named Aquillaris, of the Chaldees; it springeth in the time in which the Eagles build their nests. It is named by the Greeks Vallias, of the Latins Celidonia, and of the Englishe men Celindine. This hearb springeth in the time which Swallows and also the Eagles make their nests.
VI. If any man shal have this hearb with the heart of a Mole he shal overcome all his enemies, and all matters in suite, and shal put away all debate.

To know if a sick man will die or not

VII. And if the before named hearb bee put upon the head of a sicke man, if he shal die he shal sing with a loude voice, if not, he shal weape.

Of The Fifth Herb, and a Love-Charm

(5) VIII. The fyfte hearb named of the Chaldeea is Iterisi, of the Greeks Vorax, of the Latines Provinca or Provinsa, of

Englishe men Periwinkle, when it is beaten into powder with wormes of the earth wrapped about it, and with an hearb called Semperuina, in English Houseleeke, it induceth love between man and wife, if it be used in their meats.

Other uses of this Herb

IX. And if it shall be put in the mouth of the beast called the Bugill, he shal breake anyone in the midst. And this was proved of late time. If the said confection be put in the fire it shal be turned anone into blue colour.

Experiment with the Sixth Herb

(6) The Sixt hearb is named of the Chaldeis Blieth, of the Greeks Ketus, of the Latines Mepeta, of English men Calminte, otherwise Peniroyale.

X. Take this hearb and mixe it with the stone, found in the nest of the bird called a Lapwing or Black Plover, and rubbe the belly of any beast and it shal be with birth, and have a yong one, very blacke in the own kind. And if it be put to their nostrils, they shal fall to the ground anone as dead, but a little space after they shal be healed.

XI. Also if the aforesaid confection be put in a vessel of bees, the bees shal never fly away, but they shal gather together there. And if the bees be drowned and look as they were dead, if they be put in the aforesaide confection, they shal recover their life after a litel time, as by the space of one houre, for it is proportionated to the quality lost.

And for a sure proof, if drowned flies be put in warme ashes, they will recover life after a litel space.

Of Experiments of Power over Dogs

(7) The seventh hearb is named of the Chaldes Algeil, of the Greeks Orum, of the Latines Lingua Canis, of English men Hounds Toung.

XII. Put thou this hearb with the hart of a yong frog, and her matrice, and put them where you wilt, and after a litel time all the dogs of the whole towne will be gathered together. And if thou shalt have the afore named hearb under the foremost toe, all the dogs shal keepe silence, and have no power also to barke.

XIII. If thou put the aforesaid thing in the necke of any dog (so that he may not touch it with his mouth) he shal be turned almost round about like a turning wheele until he fal onto the ground as dead, and this hath been proved in our time.

Three strange powers of Henbane

(8) The eighte hearb is named of the Chaldees Mansela, of the Greeks Ventosin, of the Latins Iusquianus, of the English men Henban.

XIV. Take thou this hearb, and mixe it cum regalis [and] hermodatalis, put them in the meate of a mad dogge, and hee will die an one.

XV. And if thou put the juice of it with the aforesaid thinge in a silver cup it shal be broken very small.

XVI. Also if thou shalt mixe the aforesaid thing with the blood of a yong Hare, and keepe it in the skin of a Hare, all the Hares will bee gathered there until it be removed.

Spontaneous Generation and Insomnia produced

(9) The ninth hearb is named of the Chaldees Ango, of the Greeks Amala, of the Latines Lillium, of the English men a lillie.

XVII. If thou wilt gather this hearb (ye sun being in the Signe of the Lyon) and mixe it with the juice of the laurel or Bay tree and afterward then put that juice under the dung of cattel a certaine time, it shal be turned into wormes, of the which, if powder be made, and put about the necke of any man or in his cloathes, he shal never sleepe, nor be able to sleepe untill it be away.

Many more things may bee done with the vertue and juice of this aforesaid hearb.

Lily-spell for inducing fever and loosing milk

XVIII. And if thou put the aforesaid thing under the dung of cattell, and anoint any man with the wormes breeding thereof, he shal be brought anon unto a fever.

XIX. And if the aforesaid thing be put in any vessell where there is cows milk, and be covered with the skin of any cow of one colour, all the kine shall loose their milke.

Mistletoe Spells

(10) The tenth hearb is called of the Chaldees Luperai, of the Greeks Assisena, of the Latins Usicus Querci, of English men Missell toe. And it groweth in trees, being holed through.

To Open All Locks

XX. This hearb with a certaine other hearbe, which is named Martegon, that is Silphion or Laserpitium, as it is written in the Almans language, it openeth all lockes.

Other Spells of the Mistletoe

XXI. And if the aforesaid things mixed together, be put in ye mouth of any man, that thinketh any thing, if it should happen, it is set on his hart, if not, it leapeth from his hart. If the aforesaid thing be hanged up to a tree with the wing of a swallow, there the birdes shal gather together within the space of five miles.

And this last was proved in my time.

Of the Marvellous Power of the Eleventh Herb

(11) The eleventh hearb is named of the Chaldees Hiphilon, of the Greeks Digelon, of the Latines Centaurus, of the English men Centory, which saith, that this hearbe hath a marvellous vertue.

XXII. For if it be joined with the blood of a female lap wing or blacke Plover, and put with oile in a lampe, all they that compass it about shal beleeve themselves to be witches: so that his head is in heaven and his feete on the earth.

And if the aforesaid thing bee put in the fire when the stars shine, it shal appeare that the starres run one against another, and fight. And if the aforesaid plaster bee put to the nostrils of any man, he shall fly away sharpely, through feare that he shal have, and this hath been proved.

Spell to Cause a Man to Lose his Senses for Fifteen Days

(12) The twelfe hearb is named of the Chaldees Coloris, or Colericon, of the Greeks Caramor, of the Latines commonly Salvie, of the English men Sage.
XXIII. This hearb being purified under dung of cattell, in a glasen vessel, bringeth forth a certaine worme or bird, having a taile after the fashion of a bird, called a black mack or Dufell, with whose blood, if any man be touched on the brest, he shal loose his sence or feeling the space of fifteene dayes and more.

Causing a Rainbow, and Thunder

XXIV. And if the aforesaid serpent bee burned, and the ashes of it bee put in the fire, anon there shal be a rainbowe, with a horrible thunder.

Of the Healing Power of the Thirteenth Herb

(13) XXV. The thirteen hearb is named of the Chaldees Olphantas, of the Greeks Hilirion, of the Latines Verbena, of the English men Vervin. This hearb (as witches say) gathered, the Sun being in the Signe of the Ram, and put with graine or corne of piony of one yere old, heals them that are sicke of the falling sickness.

Death-Spell of the Verbena Worms

XXVI. And if it be put in a safe ground, after 8 weekes, wormes shal be ingendered: which if they shal touch any man he shal die anon.

Attracting Doves, Colouring the Sun, Causing Strife

XXVII. If the aforesaid thing be put in a dove or culver house, all the doves or culvers shal there gather together. And if the powder of them be put in the sunne, it maketh the Sun seeme blew. If the powder be put in a place where men swel or lie between two lovers, anon there is made strife between them.

Of the Fourteenth Magical Herb

(14) The fourteenth hearb is named of the Chaldees Celayos, of the Greeks Casini, of the Latines Milisopholos, of English men Smallage. Of the which hearb Master Floridus maketh invention.

Smallage producing worms and victory

XXVIII. This hearbe being gathered greene and taken with the juice of the cypress tree, of one yeare put in gruell, maketh the gruell to appeare full of wormes, and maketh the bearer to be gentle and gracious, and to vanquish his adversaries.
XXIX. And if the aforesaid hearbe bee bounden to an oxes neck, he will follow thee whether soever thou wilt goe.

Of the Fifteenth Magical Herb

(15) The fifteenth hearb is named of the Chaldees Clerisa, of the Greeks Haphimus, of the Latines Rosa, of English men a Rose. And it is an hearb, whose flower is very well knowne.

To make a Tree Sterile with the Rose-Spell

XXX. Take the graine or come of it, and the corne of mustard seed, and the foot of a weasle: hang all these in a tree, and it will never beare fruit after.

Other Spells of the Rose

XXXI. And if the foresaid thing be put about a net, fishes wil gather together there. And if magaris shal be dead and put in the aforesaid commixtion half a day, it shal recover the life although it be not forthwith yet gotten. And if the aforesaid powder be mixed with oyle of the olive tree, and quick brimstone, and the house anoynted with it, when the Sunne shineth it will seeme all in a flame.

Engendering Red and Green Serpents

(16) XXXII. The sixteenth hearb is called of the Chaldees Caturlin, of the Greeks Pentaphyllon, of the Latines Serpentina, in English Snakes grasse. This hearb is well enough known with us: this hearb put in the ground with the leafe called three leafe grasse, engendereth red and greene serpents, of which, if powder be made, and put in a burning lampe, there shal appear abundance of serpents. And if it be put together under the head of any man, from thenceforth he shal not dreame of himselfe.

Of the Manner of Working, and Observances

XXXIII. The manner of working all these aforenamed things, that the effect may be good in their planets, is in their houses, and dayes, and great regard had to the observation of their due times.

OF THE VIRTUES AND USES OF THE HERBS OF THE PLANETS

XXXIV. There be seven hearbs that have great vertue, after the mind of Alexander the Emperor, and these have their chief vertues of the influence of the Planets.

And therefore every one of them taketh their vertue from the higher naturall power.

(1) The Herb of Saturn

XXXV. The first is the herbe of the Planet Saturnius, which is called Assodilius. Assodilly, the juice of it, is good against the paine of the reines, and legs. Let all them that suffer paine of the bladder eate it, the root of it being a little boild.

XXXVI. Likewise, if men possessed with evill spirits, or made men beare it, in a cleane napkin, they bee delivered from their disease: and it suffereth not a divell in the house. If children that breed their teeth beare it about them, they shal breed them without paine.

XXXVII. It is good that a man beare with him a root of it in the night, for he shal not feare, nor yet be hurt of other.

(2) The Herb of the Sun

The second is the hearb of the Sun, which is called Poligonia, or Coraligiola. This hearb taketh name of the

Sunne: for it engendered greatly, and so this hearb worketh many wayes.

XXXVIII. Others call this hearb Alchone, which is the house of the Sun: This hearb healeth the passions and griefes of the hart and stomach. He that toucheth this hearb hath a vertue of his signe or planet. If any man drink the juyce of it, it maketh him to do often the act of generation. And if any man beare the roote thereof, it helpeth the grief of the eies. And if he beare it with him before he have any griefe, there shal come to him no griefe of his eyes. It helpeth them also that be vexed with the phrensie, if they beare it with them in their breast.

XXXIX. It helpeth them also that are diseased with an inposture in the lungs, and maketh them to have a good breath, and it availeth also to the fire of melancholious blood.

(3) The Herb of the Moon

XL. The third is the hearb of the Moone, which is called Chynostates. The juyce of it pergeth the paine of the stomach and breastplates: the vesture of it declareth that it is the hearb of the moone.

XLI. The froute of this hearb purgeth great spleenes and healeth them, because this hearbe increaseth and decreaseth as doth the Moone. It is good against the sickness of the eyes, and maketh a sharp sight. It is good against the blood of the eyes. If thou put the roote of it breyed upon ye eye, it will make the eye marvailous cleere, because the light of the eyes Propinquitum miston, is of the substance of the moone. It is also good to them, that have an ill stomacke, or which cannot digest their meates by drinking juyce thereof, moreover it is good for them that have ye swine pockes.

(4) The Herb of Mars

XLII. The fourth hearb is called Arnoglossa, plantaine. The roote of this hearbe is marvellous good against the paine in the head: because the Signe of the Ram is supposed to be the house of the planet Mars, which is the head of the whole world. It is good also against evill customs of a mans stones and rottennesse or filthy biles, because his house is the signe Scorpio, and because a part of it holdeth sparma, that is, the seed which cometh against the stones: whereof of all living theings be engendered and formed.

XLIII. Also the juyce of it is good to them that be sicke of the perrillous Flixe, with excoration or rasping of the bowels, containual torments, and some blood issuing forth, and more it purgeth them that do take a drinke thereof, from the sicknesse of the fire of blood or emerhods, and of the disease of the stomacke.

(5) The Herb of Mercury

The fift is of the hearb of the planete Mercurius, which is named Pentaphilon, in English Cinquefoile, or the five leaved hearbe, of others Pentadactuilus (pentactuilus) of others Sepe declinans, of certayn Calspedola (capadolo[1]).

XLIV. The roote of this hearb braied and made in a plaster, healeth wounds and hardenes.

XLV. Moreover, it putteth away quickly the disease called the swines pockes, if the juyce of it be drunken with water. It also healeth the passions or greapes of the breast if the juyce be drunken. It also putteth away the toothach. And if the juyce of it be holden in the mouth, it healeth the greefes of

[1] Versions in parentheses are from the late edition: that of 1617.

the mouth: and if a man beare it with him, it will be to him a help.

Obtaining the Favour of Princes

XLVI. Moreover, if any man wil aske any thing of a king or prince, it giveth abundance of eloquence if he have it with him, and he shall obtaine any thing he desireth.
XLVII. It is also good to have the juyce of it, for the grefe of the stone, and the sicknes which letteth a man that he cannot pisse.

(6) The Herb of Jupiter

The sixt is the hearb of the planet Jupiter, and it is named Acharon of certaine Jusquianus, Henbane.
XLVIII. The root of it put upon botches, healeth them, and keepeth the place from inflammation of blood. If any man shall beare it before the greefe come upon him, he shall never have botch.
XLIX. The root of it also is profitable against the gout in the feet, when it is brayed and put upon the place that suffereth the paine or grief. And it worketh by vertue of those signes which have feet, and looke upon the feet: and if the juyce of it be drunken with hony, or with wine and hon[e]y sodden together, it is profitable against the griefes of the liver and all the passions thereof, because Jupiter ruleth the liver.
L. Likewise, it is profitable to them that would do often the act of generation, and to them that desire to be loved of women if they beare it with them, for it maketh the bearers pleasant and delectable.

(7) The Herb of Venus

The seventh is the hearb of the planet Venus, and is called Pisterion, of some Hierobotane, *id est*, Sterbo columbaria et Verbena, Vervin.

LI. The root of this hearb put upon the neck healeth the swine pockes, apostumus behinde the eares, and botches of the neck, and such as cannot keepe their water. It healeth cuts also, and swelling of the evill, or fundament, proceeding of an inflammation which groweth in the fundament, and the Emorhods.

LII. If the juyce of it be drunke with hon[e]y and water sodden it dissolveth those things which are about the lungs and lights.

LIII. It is also of great strength in veneriall pastimes. If any man put it in his house or vineyard, or in the ground, he shal have great store of increase.

Moreover the root of it is good for all those which will plant vineyards or trees. If infants beare this hearb, they shall be glad and joyous.

The Gathering of the Plants

LIV. Yet this is to be marked, that these hearbs be gathered from the three and twentieth day of the Moone, until the thirtieth day beginning the Signe Mercurius by the space of a whole house. And in gathering make mention of the passion or greefe, and the name of the thing for the which thou dost gather it, and the selfe hearb. Notwithstanding, lay the hearb upon wheat or Barley, and use it afterwards unto thy uses.

CHAPTER VII

ANIMALS IN MAGIC

THE VERTUES OF CERTAIN BEASTS

The Thyrde Boke of Albertus Magnus

OF THE VERTUES OF CERTAINE BEASTS

¶ Inasmuch as it hath beene spoken in the booke before of certaine effects, caused by the vertue of certaine stones, and their merveilous vertus or operation: now we will speake in this Chapter of certaine effects, caused of certaine beasts.

Aquila	An Eagle
Casso	—[1]
Bubo	A Shrike Owle
Hircus	A goat Bucke
Camelus	A Camel
Lepus	A Hare
Expetiolus	—[1]
Leo	A Lion

[1] No English equivalent given.

Foca	A Porpaise
Anguilla	An Eele
Mustela	A Wesel
Upupa	A Lapwing or Plover[1]
Pellicanus	A Pellican
Cornus	A Crow
Milnus	A Kite or gleid
Turtur	A Turtle
Talpa	A Mole
Merula	A black mack or owsel

¶ XCIII. AQUILA, the Eagle, is a bird very well known of the men of Chaldee. It is called vorax, and of the Greeks Rimbicus. Aaron and Euar say, that it hath a marveilous nature or vertue. For if the braine of it bee turned into powder, and mixed with the juice of Hemlocke, they that eat it shall take themselves by the haire, and shall not leave their hold, so long as they beare that they have received. The cause of this effect is, for that the braine is very colde insomuch that it engendereth fantasticall vertue, shutting of the powers by smoke.

¶ XCIV. CASSO is a beast that is knowne very well. It is called Rapa amongst the Chaldees, and of the Greeks Orgalo. Aaron sayeth of this: if the feete of it be borne of any man, he shall desire alwaies to go forth. Also he that beareth the feet of it shall alwayes overcome, and shall be feared of his enemies. And he saith that his right eye, wrapped in a wolves skin, maketh a man pleasant, acceptable and gentle. And if meate be made of the aforesaid things, or powder [of it] given to any man in meat, the giver shall be greatly loved of him that receiveth it. This last was proved in our time.

[1] "The Lapwing... This bird by a great mistake hath been generally taken to be the upupa [hoopoe] of the Antients, which is now by all acknowledged to be the Hoopo [and not the Lapwing]" – Ray: *Dict. Triling.*, 1675.

¶ XCV. Bubo, a Shrike Owle, is a bird very well known, which is called Magis by the Chaldees, Hisopus of the Greeks: there be marvellous vertues of this foule.

XCVI. For if the heart and right foot of it be put upon a man sleeping, he will tell thee what soever thou shall ask of him. And this hath been proved of late time among our brethren.

XCVII. And if any man put this under his armhole, no Dog will barke at him, but keepe silence. And if these things aforesaid, joyned together, with a wing, if it be hanged to a tree, birds will gather together to that tree.

¶ XCVIII. Hircus, the Goat bucke is a beast well enough known, it is called of the Chaldees Erbichi, of the Greeks Massia.

XCIX. If the blood of it be taken warme with vinegar, and the juyce of Fennill, and sodden together with a glasse, it maketh the glasse soft as downe, and it may be cast against a wall, and not broken.

C. And if the aforesaid confection be put in a vessel, and the face of any man be anointed therewith, marveilous and horrible things shall appeare, and it shall seeme to him that he must die. And if the aforesaid thing be put in the fire, and there be any man that hath the falling sicknesse, by putting to the loadstone, he falleth suddenly to the ground as dead. And if the water of Eeles be given to him to drinke, he shall be cured quickly.

¶ CI. Camelus, the Camell, is a beast known well enough. It is called of the Chaldees, Ciboi, of the Greeks Iphim.

CII. If the blood of it be put in the skin of the beast called Stellio, and then set on any mans head, which is like a lizard, having on his backe spots like stars, it shall seeme that he is a Giant, and that his head is in heaven.

¶ CIII. And it is said in the booke of Alchorath, of Mercurie, that if a lanterne anointed with the blood of it be lighted it shall seem that men standing about, have camels heads, so that there be no outward light of another candle.

¶ CIV. Lepus, the Hare is a beast very much known; of the Chaldees it is called Veterillium, and of the Greeks Gulosa. The vertue of it is shewed to be marvellous, for Euar and Aaron said that the feet of it joined together with a stone or with the head of a black owsel, moveth a man to hardinesse, so that he feare not death.

CV. If it be bound to his left arme, he may go whither he will and he shal return safe without perill. And if it be given to a dog to eat, with the heart of a wesell, from thence forth shall he not cry out although he should be killed.

¶ CVI. Experiolus is a beast well enough knowne. If the clove of it be buried and consolidated, and bee given in meate to any horse, he wil not eat for the space of three dayes: and if the aforesaid thing be put to a little turpentine it wil be cleare; and secondly, it shall be made as a cloude in blood, and if it be cast into a little water a while, an horrible thunder shall be made.

¶ CVII. Leo, a Lyon, is a beast well knowne; he is called of the Chaldees, Balamus, of the Greeks, Beruth. If thongs of leather be made of the skin of him, and a man gird himselfe with all, he neede not feare his enemies. And if any man will eate of the flesh of him, he shall be cured from the fever quartan. And if any part of his eyes be put under a man's arm hole, all beasts shall fly away, bowing down their heads to their bellies.

¶ CVIII. Foca, a Porpaise, is a fish well knowne, of the Chaldees it is called Daulumber, of the Greeks Labor: this fish is of divers natures. If the tung of it be taken and put with a little of the heart of it in water, for a surety fishes will gather there together. And if thou wilt beare it under thy arme hole, no man shall be able to get victory against thee, for thou shalt have a gentle and pleasant judge.

¶ CIX. ANQUILLA, an Eele, it is a fish sufficiently knowne. The vertues of it is marvellous, as Euar and Aaron says. For if it die for fault of water, the heart remaining [w]hole, and strong vinegar taken and mixed with the blood of the foule, called in Latin Vultur (which some call in English a Gripe, and some a Raven), and put under dung in any place, they shall all how many soever they be, recover their life, as they had before. And if the worme of this eele be drawne out, and put in the aforesaid confection the space of one moneth, the worme shall be changed into a very blacke eele, of which, if any man eate he shall die.

CX. MUSTELLA the wesell is a beast sufficiently known. If the heart of this beast be eaten yet quaking, it maketh a man to know things to come. And if any dog eat of the heart with the eyes and tongue of it he soone shall loose his voice.

CXI. UPUPA the Lapwing or Black Plover, is a bird sufficiently known. Of the Chaldees it is called Bordicta; of the Greeks, Isoa.

The eyes of it borne, make a man grosse or greate, and if the eyes of it be borne before a mans breast, all his enemies shal be pacified. If thou shalt have the head of it in thy purse, thou canst not be deceived of any merchant. This hath been proved of our brethren.

CXII. PELLICANUS, the Pellican, is a bird well known. It is called of the Chaldees Voltri, and of the Greeks Iphalari.

The vertue of it is marvellous. If young birds be killed and their heart be taken and put warme in the mouth of the young birds, they wil againe soone receive life as before.

If it be hanged up to the necke of any bird, it shal flie all wayes, untill it fall dead. And if the right foot of it be put under any hot thing after three moneths somewhat shal be engendered quicke [i.e. alive], and shal moove itselfe of the humor and heat, which the bird hath. And Hermes in the book of Alchorath, and Plinius doth witnesse this.

CXIII. Cornus, called of some a Raven, and of others a Crow. The vertue of this foule is marvellous, as Euar and Aaron rehearse. If her egges be sodden, and put againe in the next, the Raven goeth soone to the red sea, in a certaine I[s]le, where Aldoricus or Alodrius is buried. And she bringeth a stone wherewith she toucheth her egges, and all the egges be as rawe [again].

CXIV. It is a marvellous thing to stire up sodden egges. If this stone be put in a ring, and the leafe of the Lawrell tree under it, and if a man be bound in chains, or a doore shut, be touched therewith, he that is bond shall be loosed, and the doore shall be opened.

And if this stone be put in a mans mouth, it giveth him understanding of [?the 'speech' of] all birdes. The stone is of India; because it is found in India, after certaine wise men say, and sometime in the Red Sea. It is of divers colours, and maketh a man to forget all wrath, as we have said above in the same stone.

CXV. Milnus, a Kite or Gleide, is a birde common amongst us. Of the Chaldees it is called Bifcus, of the Greeks Melos. If the head of it be taken, and borne before a man's breast, it giveth him love and favour of all men and women. If it be hanged to the necke of a hen, she shall cease to run, until it be put away. And if a cocks combe be anointed with the blood of it, hee will crowe from thenceforth. There is a certaine stone found in the knees of this bird, if it be looked craftily, which if it be put in the meat of two enemies, they shall be made friends, and there shal be made very great friendship among them.

CXVI. Turtur, a Turtle, is a birde very well knowne. It is called Merlon of the Chaldees, of the Greeks Pilax. If the heart of this foule be borne in a Wolves skin, he that weareth it shal never have an appetite to commit lechery from henceforth. If the heart of it be burned, and put above the egges of any foul, there can never young birds be engendered of them from thenceforth. If the feet of a foule be hanged to a tree it shall not beare from thenceforth.

And if an hairy place, or an horse be anointed with the blood of it, and with water wherein a Mole was sodden, the black hairs will fall of[f].

CXVII. TALPAS, a Mole, is a beast very well knowne. The vertue of this beaste is marvellous, as it is rehearsed of the Philosophers. If the foot of it be wrapped in the leafe of a Lawrell tree, and bee put in the mouth of an horse, hee will flie for feare. And if it be put in the next of any foule, there shall never come forth young birds of there eggs. And if thou wilt drive away Moles, put it in a pot, and quicke brimstone kindled, and all the other Moles shall come together there. And the water of that decoction maketh a blacke horse white.

CXVIII. MERULA, a blacke macke or Owsel, is a foule very well knowne, and the vertue of it is marvellous. For if the feathers of the right wing of it be hanged up in the midst of an house, with a redde leafe, which is never occupied, no man shall be able to sleepe in that house, untill it be put away. Moreover if the hart of it be put under the head of a man sleeping, if you aske him anything, he shall tell all he hath done with a high voyce.

CXIX. The manner of doing these aforesaid things, that the effect may bee good and profitable, is that it be done under a favourable planet, as Jupiter and Venus, as is in their dayes and houres.

CXX. If any man therefore will doe these things truely, without doubt he shall find truth and very great effect and vertue, in the aforesaid things as I have proved and seen oftentimes together with our brethren in our time.

CXXI. Therefore let a man consider here, which shall find plenty of those aforesaid things, that he possesseth a Lordship of vertues. For if they be done in their contraries, as a good effect in a malicious signe, his vertue and effect should be hindered by his contrary, thereby good and true things growe to be despised.

We see by daily experience, very many people are deceived in true things which, if they had knowne, and kept [to] the qualities and signes – or the right measure of times and seasons – they should have gained their will and effect, in the aforesaid things.

CXXII. Isidorus seemeth to say, that the ashes of a great frog, borne at a woman's girdle, restraineth greatly the comming of a womans naturall purgation.

CXXIII. And in a probation, if it be bound about a hennes necke, there shal come forth no blood of her, or of any other beast.

CXXIV. Also if it be tempered with water, and the head or any other place be anointed with it, heare [hair] will no more grow there.

CXXV. If any mane beare a dogs heart on his left side, all dogs shall hold their peace, and not barke at him.

CXXVI. If any man will binde the right eye of an wolfe on his right sleeve, neither men nor Dogs may hurt him.

HERE are ended some secrets of
ALBERTUS MAGNUS of Colone
upon natures, vertues &
effects of certaine
Herbes, Stones &
Beastes.

And here fol[l]oweth in what hour every planet hath his dominion.[1]

[1] This chapter constitutes Chapter XIX, p. 331.

CHAPTER VIII

A BOOK OF SPELLS

THE MARVELS OF THE WORLD

Heere beginneth the Boke Of the Mervayles of The World, set forth by Albertus Magnus

I. After it was knowne of Philosophers, that all kinds of things move and incline to the senses, because an active and rationable vertue is in them, which they guide, and move as well to themselves as to others, as fire moveth to fire, etc.

Characteristics project their power

II. Also Avicenna said: When a thing standeth long in salt, it is salt, and if any thing stand in a stinking place, it is made stinking; and if any thing standeth with a bold man, it is made bold, and if it stand with a fearefull man, it is made fearefull. III. And if a beast companyeth with men, it is made tractable and familiar. And generally it is verified of them by reason and divers experience, that every nature moveth to his kinde, and this verifying is known in the first qualities – and likewise in the second – and the same chanceth in the third. And there is nothing in all disposition and quality, which moveth to itself according to his whole power.

And this was the root, and the second beginning of the works and secrets and turne thou not away the eyes of thy minde. After that, this was grafted in the mindes of the Philosophers.

Two kinds of Characteristic

IV. Then they found the disposition of naturell things. For they knew surely is grafted in it, in other some, great boldnesse, in some great wrath, in some great feare, in some barennesse is ingendered; in some is one vertue, or another ingendered, either after the owne kinde (as boldnesse is naturall to a Lyon) or *Fecundum in dividium*, as boldnes is in a harlot, not by a mans kind, but *per individium*, there are by this great marvels and secrets able to be wrought.

V. And they that understand not the marvellousnesse, and how that might be, dispise and cast away all things in which is the labour and wit of Philosophers: whose intent was to their owne praise in their posterity, that they might by their writing, make things called false, be holden in great estimation.

VI. It is not bidden to of people that every like helpeth and strengthens his like, and loveth, moveth, and imbraceth it.

Like affects Like

VII. And Philosophers have said, and verified, that the liver helpeth the liver, in their writings; and every member helpeth his like. And the turners of one metall into another called

Alchemists know, that by manifest truth, how like nature secretly entreth and rejoyceth his like. And every Science hath now verified that in like. And note this diligently, for marvellous workes shall be seene upon this.[1]

Natural Enmities

VIII. Now it is affirmed and put in all mens minds, that every naturall kinde, and that every particular and generall nature hath naturall amitie and enmitie towards other. And every kinde hath some horrible enemy, and destroying thing, to be feared. Likewise something rejoycing exceedingly, making glad, and agreeing by nature, as the sheepe doth feare the wolf, and it knoweth not only him alive but also dead. Not only by sight, but also by taste; and the Hare feareth the dog, and the Mouse Catte, and all the four footed beastes feare the Lion, and all flying birds the Eagle, and all beaste feare man: and this is grafted to every one by nature, and some have this, *secundum individium*, and at a certaine time.

Matter contains and retains Power

IX. And it is the certifying of all philosophers that they which have others in their life, hate their Parents, and altogether after they die. For a skinne of a sheep is consumed of the skinne of the Wolfe, and a timbrell, tabor or drum made of the skin of a Wolfe, causeth that which is made of a sheeps

[1] A combination of the alchemistical theory with the magical belief in 'sympathy'.

skin, not to be heard,[1] and so it is in all others. And note this for a great secret.

Human Character and its Projection

X. And, it is manifest to all men, that a man is the ende of all naturall things, and that all naturall things are by him, and he overcometh all things. And naturall things have naturall obedience grafted in them to man, and that man is full of marveilousnesse, so that in him are all conditions, that is intemperance in hot and cold, temperate in every thing that it will, and in him be the vertues of all things, and all secret arts worketh in mans body itselfe and every marvelous thing cometh forth of him, but a man hath not all these things at one time, but in divers times and *diversis individuis*, and in him is found the effecte of all things.

Thou shalt note how much reason may see and comprehend and how much thou mayest prove by the experience, and so understand that which is against man.

Ignorance the reason for Derision

XI. There is no man but doth know that everything is full of marvellous operations, and that knowest not which is the greatest operation, til thou hast proved it. But every man dispiseth the things whereof he knoweth nothing, and that hath done no pleasure to him. And every thing hath of hot and cold, that is proper to him. And fire is not more marvellous than water, but they are divers and after another manner.

[1] This idea connects with sympathetic magic and *mana* and *agasa* (invisible force).

And Pepper is not more marvellous than Henbane, but after another manner. And he that believeth that marvellousnesse of things cometh from hotte and cold, cannot but say that there is a thing to be marvelled in every thing, seeing that every thing hath both the hot and cold that is convenient to it.

Star influences in Magic

XII. And hee that beeleeveth that the marvellousnesse of things be in stars of which al things like their marvellous and hid properties, may know that every thing hath his proper figure celestiall, agreeing to them, of which also commeth marvellousnesse in working. For every thing which beginneth, beginneth under a determinate ascendant and celestiall influence, and getteth a proper effect, or vertue of suffering or working a marvellous thing. And he that beleiveth of the marvellousnesse of things that come by amity and enmity, as buying and selling cannot be denied so to come, and thus universal everything is ful of marvellous things, after every way of searching the natures of them. And after that the Philosophers knew this, they began to prove and say what is in things.

Qualifications needed to be able to Verify Magic

XIII. Plato saith in *Libro regimenti* that he that is not expert in Logick of which the understanding is made ready, lifted uppe nimbly or light and speedy; and he that is not cunning in naturell science, in which are declared marvellous things, both hot and cold, and in which the property of every thing in itselfe is shewed; and which is not cunning in the science of Astrology, and in the sights and figures of stars, of which every one of which be high, hath a vertue and property – cannot understand nor verifie al things, which Philosophers have written; nor can certifie all things which shall appeare to mans sences. And he shal goe with heavinesse of mind, for in those things is a marvellousnesse of all things, which are seene.

XIV. A pure Astrologian beleeveth that all marvellousness of things and that the root of experience, and of all things which bee apparent when they be put together, were from a celestiall figure which every thing getteth in the houre of his killing or generation.

And hee hath verified it in everything that he hath proved, hee findeth that the concourse of things, is according to the course of the starres. And, victory, joy, heavinesse, dependeth thereof, and is juged by it. And therefore he commanded all things to be done in certaine dayes, in certaine houses, in certaine conjunctions, and seperations, in certaine ascentions, and their wit could not attaine to all the knowledge of Philosophers.

Combination of certain elements to produce Magical Potency

XV. A great part of Philosophers or Phisytions, have believed that al marvellousness of experience, and marvels, came from naturall things, when they be brought to light, by hot and colde, drie and moist, and they shewed these four qualities and put them to bee the rootes of all marvellous things. And mixtion of them is required to every marvellous thing. They verified that in their workes; and when they found experiences of Philosophers they might not verifie those things by hot and colde, but rather by his contrary.

XVI. It causeth them to marvell continually, and to be foxy and to deny that often times, although they see it.

Therefore Plato said for a good cause that he which is not very cunning in logicke and wise in the vertues of naturall things likewise the aspects of the starres, shall not see the causes of marvellous things, nor know them, nor participate of the treasures of the Philosophers.

XVII. Therefore I know that every thing hath that which is his owne of heat and colde, of which it maketh another thing effectuall by accident, directly and indirectly, and it hath all his vertues of the starres, and the figure of his generation, which it worketh in mortality, construction and greeting with other.

Students must Believe and Trust

XVIII. And notwithstanding everything hath his owne naturall vertues, by which every thing is a beginning of a marvellous effect. Therefore seeing that nature moveth to his owne like, it may be imagined of the marvellousness of effects, everything that thou wilt.

XIX. And thou shalt verifie all things which thou shalt heare, both of Phisicke and all other naturall sciences, after a divers way of thy thought and wit. And I shall shew thee manifestly, that thou mayest helpe thy selfe, and prepare thee to receive those things which I will tell to thee: gathered and collected of Philosophers and divers ancient authors.

XX. Therefore have thou this thing in thy minde, that an hot thing, as much as it is by it selfe helpeth in colde passions, and it is an experience in them, and agreeth not with hotte things, but by accident or indirectly, and again the which falleth out or comes by accident may deceive thee in the first

qualities; for oftentimes a hot thing healeth not likenesse, that is accident or indirectly.
XXI. Therefore if thou wilt have experience: First it becometh thee to know of those things, whether they be hot or colde. And after that note what is the disposition and naturall properties of it, whether it is boldnesse or fearfulnesse, or honestie or barreness. For what nature everything hath, he is like to such in the things in which he is associate.

Examples: Bravery

XXII. As the Lion is a beast unfearfull and hath a naturall boldnesse, chiefly in his forehead and heart. And therefore he that taketh in his fellow shippe the eye or heart of a Lyon, or the skin which is betweene his eyes, goeth bold and not fearful, and bringeth fearfulnesse to all beasts. And generally there is in a Lion vertue to give a boldnesse and magnanimity. Likewise in a harlot boldness is exstremitate. And therefore Philosophers say if a man put on a common harlots smocke, or looke in the glasse, or have it with him, in which he beholdeth her herselfe, he goeth bolde and unfearfull.
XXIII. Likewise, there is a great boldnesse in a Cocke, in so much that Philosophers say, that the Lyon is astonished when he seeth him. And therefore they say, if any man beare any thing of his, he goeth boldly.
XXIV. And generally every beast which hath boldnes extremity by nature or chance.

Infertility

XXV. *Si ex eo construcietur huijusmodi*, it then giveth to it boldnesse. Likewise if it be a barren beast, by nature or some

accident following it, that it moveth some to barrenesse. And therefore Philosophers have written that the Mule for as much as he is bitterly barraine of his property, and whosoever it be, maketh men and women barren when some part of him is sotiate to woman.
XXVI. And likewise doth he that was born before the naturall time, and a gelded man: because barrenesse is grafted in all these, and they are like to a man in this, which doth associate to himselfe these inward things.

Love

XVII. Likewise they which will moove love, look what beast loveth most greatly, and specially in that hour in which is most stirred up in love: because there is then greater strength in it in moving love.[1] They take a part of the beast in which carnall appetite is stronger (as in the heart, the stones and the mother or matrice).
XXVIII. And, because the swallow loveth greatly, Philosophers say, therefore they choose her greatly to stirre up love.

Likewise the dove and the sparrow are holden to be of this kind, specially when they are delighted in love or carnel appetite: for then they provoke and bring in love without resistance.

[1] This is the magical theory of 'emotion-concentration': not mere sympathetic magic. It may be defined thus: "When any emotion is concentrated and at a pitch higher than normal, this becomes a force which can be used by those who know how to associate it with some object."

Eloquence

XXIX. Likewise, when they will to make a man to be a babler, or of much speach, they put nigh to him a part of a dogges tung or hart. But when they will make a man eloquent or delectable, they associate to him a nightingale. And to speake universally whatsoever vertue or naturall propertie they see in any naturall thing after an excesse, they thought to make like to moove or incline any thing disposed to that same.
XXX. For they knew surely that it might more helpe than hurt, inasmuch as it hath grafted in it, of their nature. And all vertue moveth to such as it is, according to the power of it.

And so must thou understand to be in marvellous things, of which thou shalt heare. And this is said to introduce thy mind.

Secrets and Experience

XXXI. The author liber regimenti saith[1] that there be certaine things manifest to the sences in which we know no reason. And certain bee manifest by reason: in which we perceive *nullum censum nec sensationem.* And in the first kind of things we must believe no man, but experience; and reason is to be proved by experience not to be denied.
XXXII. And in the second kind of things feeling is not to be looked for, because it may not be felt. Therefore certaine things must be beleeved onely by experience, without reason: for they be hid from men.
XXXIII. Certaine are to be beleeved onely by reason, and because they lack sences, for although we know not a manifest reason wherefore the lodestone draweth to it yron,

[1] *Sic.*

notwithstanding experience doth manifest it so, that no man may deny it. Like as this is marvellous, which only experience doth certifie, so should a man suppose in other things.

Causes of marvels are many

XXXIV. And hee should not deny any marvellous thing although he hath no reason, but that he rather ought to prove by experience: for the cause of marvellous things are hid and so divers causes going before, that mans understanding – after Plato – may not apprehend them.
XXXV. Therefore the lodestone draweth iron to it, and a certain other stone draweth glasse. So marvellous things are declared of philosophers to be in things by experience, which no man ought to deny. And that is not proved after the fashion of Philosophers which found that the Philosophers say: that the Palme is a tree, and it hath the male and female, therefore when the female is nigh the male thou seest that the female doth bow downe to the male, and the leafe and the branches of it are made so soft, and bow downe to the male.
XXXVI. Therefore when they see it, they bind ropes from the male to the female. Reddit ergo erecta, super se ipsam quasi adepta fit Masculo per continuationem fumis Virtutem masculi.

Strange Discoveries now Commonplace facts

XXXVII. Notwithstanding many of the ancient authors have shewed marvellous things, received now of common people, and taken for a trueth.

Therefore I shal shew to thee certaine things that thou mayst stablish thy mind upon them, and to know it for a certaine truth, which reason cannot stablish by seeing: because the aforesaid helpe in them. And it is that by sonne of Messias said in the *Booke of the Beastes*: If a woman great with child, put the apparell of a man, and a man put it on after her, before he wash it, if he have the fever quartaine, it will depart from him.

XXXVIII. And it is said in the *Booke of Beastes*, that the Lisard fleeth the privy members of a man; and in another place it is said Si carnem: if an old man be buried in a dove or culver house, or bee put where doves or culvers inhabit or nest, it be multiplied, until it be full of them.

Death in a Glance

XXXIX. In the Booke *De ciriaca* of Gallen, it is said that the serpent which is called Regulus in Latin, a Cockatrice in English, is somewhat white, upon whose head there be three haires, and when any man seeth them, he dieth soone. And then any man or any other living thing heareth his whistling, he dyeth.

And every beast that eateth of it being dead dyeth also.

XL. And Aristotle said: where there is Summer six months, and Winter other six; there is a flood wherein Adders are found, whose property is, they never see themselves but they die: but when they be dead, they hurt not. And Aristotle put craftily in the mind of Alexander that he should take a great glasse, and go towards them there. And when they did behold themselves in the glasse they died.

Avicenna's opinion of Aristotle's Snake story

XLI. This saying of Aristotle was not believed of some men. For Avicenna said against Aristotle: if any man did see it, he dyed. Wherefore there is no truth in his speech. And they said, if any man would take the milke of a woman, giving suck to her own daughter, of two yeere old, and let it be put in a glasen vessell, or hanged up in a dove or culver house, when they goe in or out doves will abide and be multiplied there: untill they be innumerable.

And said, when the mouth of a dead man is put upon him which complaineth of his belly, his belly is healed.

Spell of Alexander

XLII. And Alexander said: when any thing is taken out of the navel of an infant which commeth forth of it being cut, and be put under the stone of a ring of silver or gold, then the passion or griefe of the cholicke commeth not in anywise to him that beareth it.

XLIII. And Gallen saith: when the leaves of Sorrel be beaten, they loose the belly. And when the seed of it be drunken, it looseth the belly.

And it is said that the roote of Sorrel hanged on him that hath the swine pockes helpeth him.

And philosophers say, when thou wilt that a beast returne to his lodgings, anoint his forhead with Sepe Squilla, and it will returne.

Taming Animals by Magical means

XLIV. And Aristotle said in the *Booke of Beastes*: if any man put wrought ware upon the homes of a cows calfe, it will goe with him wheresoever he will without labor.

And if any man anoint the homes of kine with ware and oyle, or pitch, the paine of their feet goeth away.

And if any shall anoint the tungs of oxen with any tallow, they neither taste[e] nor eat meat, but they shall die for hunger, except it be willed away with salt and vinegar.

And if any man anoint the nether parts of a Cocke with oyle, he neither wil nor may tread a henne.

If thou desire that a Cocke grow not, anoint his head and forehead with oyle.

XLV. It is said in the booke of *Archigenis* Quando cum ilia, of the haires hanged upon him that suffereth the chollicke, it profiteth him.

And Aristotle saide, the Emeraudes goeth away from him, which sitteth upon the skin of a Lyon.

XLVI. And if the dung of a Hare be broken unto powder, and cast abroad upon a place of Emotes, or Pismires, then the Pismires leave the other place.

XLVII. Philosophers say, if the head of a Goat is hanged upon him which suffereth swine pockes, he is healed by it.

Love-Charm

XLVIII. If thou wilt that a woman bee not visious nor desire men, take the private members of a Woolfe, and the haires which doe grow on the cheekes or eyebrowes of him, and the haires which bee under his beard, and burne it all, and give it to her to drinke, when she knoweth not, and she shal desire no other man.

XLIX. And it is said, when a woman desireth not her husband: then let him take a little of the tallow of a bucke Goat – meane between little and great – let him anoint his privy members with it, and do the act of generation. She shall love him, and shall not doe the act of generation afterwards with any other.

Against Poison

L. And it is said, that when the snaile is poysoned, it eateth the herb called Organy, and is healed. And therefore they know that the hearb called organy, hath lien under poyson. Also it is said when the Wesell is poisoned of a serpent, it eateth rew, and they know by this that rew is contrary to the venim of serpents.

LI. And a moule put under the pricked of Scorpions, delivereth a man; because shee is contrary and feareth not him.

LII. Philosophers have invented that if any woman be barren when there is put to her a thing that maketh a woman barren, she can in no wise be fruitfull.

LIII. And it is said that when a sponge is cast in wine mixed with water, and after drawne forth strained and wringed, the water commeth forth of it, and the wine remaineth.

Charm against a cough

LIV. Tabereces said: If a stone be hanged upon a Sponge, on the necke of a childe, which cougheth with a vehement or great cough, his cough is mittigated and restrained.

LV. And being put on the head of an asse, or into his fundament, *Scarabeus* – that is a flie with a blacke shell – that breedeth in cowsheards and is blacke, called a beetle, cutteth him, and he turneth, untill it be drawn from him.

LVI. It is said also, that if any stone be bounden to the taile of an asse, he will not bray nor rore.

LVII. And it is said if you make a ring of a rod of a fresh Mirre tree, and put on thy ring finger, it mitigateth or extincteth the impostume under the armholes.

LVIII. In the booke of Aristotle, it is said that the root of white Henban, when it is hanged upon a man suffering of the Cholicke, it is profitable to him.
LIX. And when salt peter is put in a vessel and vinegar upon it, it will boile or seeth mightily without any fire.
LX. Belbinus said, when thou takest the white of an egge and Alom, and anointeth a cloth with it, and washest it of[f] with water of the sea being drie, it letteth the fire to burne.

Spell to Prevent the hands burning with a Red-Hot Iron

LXI. Another said: when redde Arsenicum is taken, broken and confected, or made with juice of the hearbe called Housleeke, and the gal[l] of a bul[l], and a man anointeth his hands with it, and after taketh hot iron, it burneth not them.

Likewise if there be taken Ex magne and alum lamenti and strong vinegar and great malowes or holihockes, and then bray them well together, and anoint thy hands therewith, fire hurteth them not.[1]

Illusion

LXII. When thou wilt that they which bee in a palaice seeme without heads, take smert brinstone, with oyle, and put it in

[1] This seems to be a recipe to be used against the fire ordeal. Witches and sorcerers in the earlier days of the Inquisition were expected to carry red-hot metal bars in their bare hands without harm in order to prove their innocence. The theory was that a miracle would vouchsafe their innocence, if they had been unjustly accused.

a lampe, and make light with it, and put it in the middest of men; and thou shalt see a marvellous thing.
LXIII. And Belbinus said againe, hee that shall put an hearbe called Purselain upon his head, shall not see dreame nor vision at any time.

Animals and Spells

LXIV. And Aristotle saith, that mares when they smell the smocke of a lampe put out, they bring forth their birth, before it is perfite; and likewise this chanceth to certaine women with child.

If thou wilt know when a woman telleth thee a Lie

LXV. Take the tongue of Sea Pie, and conveigh it cunningle into the bosome of her.

Improving the Memory

LXVI. And if the heart, eye or braine of a Lapwing or black plover be hanged upon a mans necke, it is profitable against forgetfulness and sharpeneth mans understanding.

If a woman may not conceive

LXVII. Take an Harts horne, turned into powder, and let it be mixed with a cows gall; let a woman keepe it about her... and she shall conceive.

Teething

LXVIII. The tooth of a fole or colt of one yere old, put around the necke of a child, maketh his teeth to breed without paine.

Madness

LXIX. The tooth of a mare being put upon the head of a man being mad, delivereth him from his fury.

Against mice

LXX. The hoofe of an horse perfumed in a house driveth away mice. The same chanceth also by the hoofe of a Mule.

That the hot water come out of a Caldron

LXXI. Take a blaunch that is terra francisca, with pitch cast it in water and it shall come forth all.

That Fire may come forth of Water

LXXII. Take a shell of an egge, and put it in the quicke brimstone and lime, and shut the hole and put it in the water, and it kindleth.

Plaguing a man with Flies

LXXIII. And they say if any man be anointed with the milke of an asse, all the flies in the house will gather to him.

To write letters or Bills, which be not Reade but in the Night

LXXIV. Take the gall of a snaile, or milk of a sow, and put in the fire, or with water of a worme shining late.

Making a 'Topacious' Stone

LXXV. If ye mingle together many whites of hennes egges, a moneth after they are made glasse, as hard as stone: and of this being after this fashion is made a sophisticall precious stone, called topacious, if it be conjoynted before with Saffron or red earth.

Against Drinking

LXXVI. Likewise, if the fome which is found about the stones of a Hart or a horse, or asse being weary, be mixed with wine, and the wine be given to any man to drinke, hee shall abhore wine for a moneth.

LXXVII. And, if any man shall have many Eeles in a wine vessell and they bee suffered to die in it, if any man drinke of it, hee shall abhore wine, and by chance forever.

Spell of the Pot

LXXVIII. And it is said, if a rope be taken, with which a theefe is or has been hanged up with, and a little chaffe, which a whirle-wind lifteth up to the ayre, and let them be put in a pot and set among other pottes, that pot shall breake all the other pots.

Bewitching bread

LXXIX. Also take thou a little of the aforesaid rope, and put it on any instrument, with which the bread is put in the oven. When he that should put it in the oven should put it in, he shal not be able to put it in: but it shall leape out againe immediately.

That men may seeme without heads

XC. Take an Adders skin, auri pigmentum, and greene pitch of Reuponticum, and the wax of new Bees, and the fat or grease of an asse, and breake them all, and put them in a dull seething pot ful of water, and make it to seeth at a slow fire, and after let it waxe cold, and make a tapor.[1] And every man that shall see light of it, shall seeme headlesse.

That men may seeme to have the Visage or countenance of a Dog

XCI. Take the fat out of the ear of a dog, and anoint with it a little new silke, and put it in a new lampe or greene glasse, and put the lampe among men, and they shall see the visage of a dog.

That men may seeme to have Three Heads

XCII. Take the hair of a dead asse, and make a rope, and dry it. Take the marrow of the principall bone of his right shoulder. Mixe it with virgin waxe and anoint the cord, and

1 Taper.

put it upon the thresholds of the house. They that come into the house shall seeme to have three heads. They that be in the house shall seeme asses to them that enter in.

If thou wilt that a mans head seeme an asse head

XCIII. Take up the covering of an asse and anoint the man on his head.

If thou will that a chicken or other thing leape in the dish

XCIV. Take quicksilver and the powder calemite, and put it in a glasse bottle well stoppered. And put it within a hot thing. For seeing quicksilver is hot, it moveth itselfe, and maketh it to leape or dance.

If thou wilt see that other men cannot

XCV. Take the gall of a male cat, and the fat of an hen all white, and mixe them together, and anoint thy eyes, and thou shalt see it that others cannot see.

If thou wilt understand the voyces of birds

XCVI. Associate with two fellowes in the twenty-eighth day of October, and goe into a certaine wood with dogges as to hunt. And cary home with thee the beast which thou shalt find first. Prepare it with the heart of a foxe, and thou shalt understand the voice of birds and beasts. And if thou wilt also that any other understand, kisse him, and he shall understand.

If thou wilt loose bonds

XCVII. Goe into the wood, and looke where the Pie hath her neste with her birds, and when thou shalt be there clime up the tree and bind about the hole of it whatever thou wilt.

For when she seeth thee, she goeth for a certain hearb which she will put to the binding, and it will breake. And that hearb falleth to the ground upon a cloath – which thou shouldst put under the tree – and be then present, and take it.

Invisibility

XCVIII. In the nest of the lapwing or black plover is a certaine stone, which is of divers colours. Beare it with thee, and thou shalt be invisible.

That a Woman may confesse what she has Done

XCIX. Take a water frog quicke, take away her Tong[ue], and put it into the water, and put the tong unto a part of the hart of the woman sleeping. Then aske what thou wilt, she shall say the truth.

To put any man in Fear in his Sleep

C. Put under his head the skin of an ape.

Delusions

CI. A perfume whereby every man shall seeme to all that be in the house in the forme of elephants or horses:

Take a spice which is called Alchacengi, and bray it mixed with fat of a Dolphin fish, and make thereof graines, as of pomecitron. After, perfume some of them upon a fire of crows dung, which is milked. And let not a place bee in the house, from which smoke come forth.

But let yate and the milke be in the lodging of all seem as they were great men in the shape of horses and Elephants, and it is a very marvellous thing.

CII. *Another Perfume*, which when thou makest, thou seest outwardly green men and men of many shapes, and infinite marvels, which are not discerned for their multitudes:

Take Timar – that is, Vermillion – and the stone Lazalus, and Peniroyall of the mountaines, and beat it all to powder, and sift it. Mix it with the fat of a Dolphin fish, horse or Elephant, and make graines or cornes after the fashion of rice, and drie them in a shadow. Perfume it with what thou wilt, and it shall be done what is said.

A Perfume to See in our sleepe, what is good and what is Ill

CIII. Take the blood of an asse congealed, and the fat Lupi cerivi, and sweet incense or gum called storax, and also storar, and of some called stirar. Gather it all up together by equall weights, and let them be mixed and graines or cornes bee made thereof: and let the house bee perfumed with them. Thou shalt see him in thy sleepe, that shall shew to thee all things.

Magical Tapers

CIV. The Manner of making a match or candle, or candle weeke, which being kindled, thou shalt see men in what shape thou wilt.

Take the eyes of a shrike owle, and the eyes of a fish which is called Assures, and the eyes of a fish which is called a Libinicis, and the gall of wolves.

Break them with thy hands, and mixe they all together, and put them in a vessell or glasse. Then, when thou wilt worke it, take the fat of any beaste thou wilt, that this may be made in the shape of it; melt it and mixe it perfitely with that medicine, and anoint the match candle weeke, or whatsoever thou wilt with it.

After, kindle it in the midst of the house, and the men shall seeme in the shape of that beast whose fat thou didst take.

Another match or candle weeke, that men may seeme in the Shape of Angels:

CV. Take the eyes of a fish, and the eyes of filoe – that is, of a breaker of bones – and break them with thy hands; and make them soft and put them in a vessell of glasse, vii days. After, put some oile in them, and lighten it in a greene lampe, and put it before men which be in the house. They shall see themselves in the shape of Angels by the light of the fire.

Another match, or weeke of a candle, making men appeare with blacke faces:

CVI. Take a blacke lampe and powre in it oyle of the elder or alder tree or quick silver, a part of them that bee in letting blood, and in that blood oyle of the elder or alder tree (some saith of the Bur tree) and quicksilver.

A marvellous Lampe, in which appeareth a thing of terrible quantity, having in the hand a rod, and feareth a man:

CVII. Take a greene Frog, and strike of[f] the head of it upon a green cloth, and make it wet with the oyle of a

Burre tree or elder tree, and put it in the weeke and light it in the greene lampe. Then shalt thou perceive a blacke man standing, betweene whose heads there shall be a lampe and a marvellous thing.

Another weeke, which being kindled, and water put there on, waxeth strong; and if oyle, it goeth out:

CVIII. Take lime which water hath not touched, and put it with a weight, equal to it, of waxe and the halfe of it of the oyle of balme and Napta Citrina: with equall to it of brimstone and make a weeke of it, and drop downe like dew upon it water: and it shall be kindled; and drop down oyle upon it, and it shal be put out.

Another week which, being kindled, all things seeme white as silver:

CIX. Take a lizard, and cut away the taile of it, and take that which commeth out, for it is like quicke silver. After, take a weeke and make it wet with oyle, and put it in a new lampe, and kindle it: and the house shall seem bright and white, or gilded with silver.

A weeke which being lighted, women cease not to dance and play, as they were mad for joy:

CX. Take the blood of a hare and the blood of a certaine foule which is called *solon*, and is like a turtle Dove, and the blood of the turtle male, equal to the half of it.

Then put it in a weeke, and lighten it in the midst of the house in which are singers and wenches, and a marvellous thing shall be proved.

If thou wilt seeme all inflamed from thy head to thy feet, and yet not hurt

CXI. Take white great mallows, or Hollyhocke, mixe them with the whites of egges, and anoint thy body with it, and let it be until it be dried up. And after anoint thee with alom, and afterward cast on it small brimstone, beaten into powder: for the fire is enflamed on it, and hurteth not. And if thou make upon the palme of thy hand, thou shalt be able to hold the fire without hurt.

If thou wilt See Deep into Water, read books by night

CXII. Anoint thy face with the blood of the Keremouse or Bat: and thou shalt doe as I say.

... A Lantern... of which he that seeth it shal be afraid

CXIII. Make a weeke of white linnen cloth, and put in the hollowness of it the slough of a serpent and grosse salt, and fill it with oile olive, and give it to whom thou wilt: but as soone as he lighteth it, he shall tremble and be sore afraid.

Here endeth the Secrets of ALBERTUS MAGNUS.

PART III

THE ART OF COMMANDING SPIRITS

CHAPTER IX

THE BOOK OF THE *Art Almadel*

THE MAGICAL TALISMAN

The Book of The Art Almadel of Solomon

The *Art Almadel* consists of the Fourth Book of the work attributed to Solomon, king of Israel, entitled the *Lemegeton*. As in the case of the other sorcerers' handbooks, the magician was expected to possess a copy written on virgin parchment with his own hand. Several copies exist in manuscript form in the larger research libraries of Oxford, London and Paris.

In spite of a very thorough search I have been unable to locate a printed copy of the *Almadel* as such. In the cases where extracts have been published, it would appear that these are taken from less complete sources than, for example, the seventeenth-century handwritten codex numbered Sloane 2731, in the British Museum. Some forty years ago, it is true, there was some account of the *Almadel* published by a British writer.[1] Unfortunately, this was not a verbatim transcript. Stranger still, although attributed to the same original source (Sloane 2731), the published version differed considerably from the original. It must be concluded that

[1] Waite: *Book of Ceremonial Magic*, London, 1911, pp. 21, 72 etc.

what is represented as copied from this early *Lemegeton* has, in fact, been derived from a secondary source.

In order to remedy this defect, as well as to fill the gap in knowledge of this important text, I am therefore reproducing the entire original text here.

Briefly, it may be said that the *Art Almadel* is a complete process of Ritual Magic by means of which a spirit is made to appear and obey the magician. This is accomplished with the actual Almadel – a talisman of wax – plus a certain seal made from precious metal, and a knowledge of the names and powers of certain Angels.

It is a ritual of what is conventionally known as 'white magic': both because it does not involve the use of blasphemy, the conjuring of demons and the like – and because the operator is specifically warned that it may not be used for unlawful purposes. In origin and probably in conception, the process is Jewish. Unlike many other rites which became popular in the Middle Ages, there are no Christian interpolations.

The sequence of the ritual is thus: the operator must obtain wax, and certain coloured dyes. With these he makes the Almadel talisman and candles. Then he makes the seal, in gold or silver. He must have powdered mastic,[1] which will serve as his incense, and robes in the colours of the 'choir' or 'altitude' of spirits whom he is to invoke. Virgin parchment, a vessel to contain the incense, and live coals complete the equipment.

The operator first makes the Almadel, then the seal. After this he calls the appropriate angel or angels at the time and on the day of their rulership: information which is supplied to him in the book.

[1] Mastic – *Pistacia Lentiscus*, a form of the pistachio-nut tree. In the British Isles this shrub is grown on sheltered walls.

After the invocation (which is read from the parchment), the angel is supposed to manifest itself, and a dialogue ensues.

The angel is saluted and praised, and finally begged to aid the magician: which he agrees to do. In the case of any difficulty in materialisation of the spirit, the candles are touched with the metal seal, whereupon he obeys and appears.

The actual text is as follows:[1]

Here beginneth the... Art Almadel of Solomon

By this art Solomon attained great wisdom from the chief angels that govern the four Altitudes of the World: for you must observe that there are four Altitudes which represent the four Altitudes of the West, East, North and South: the which is divided into 12 parts; that is, every part 3. And the Angels of every of these parts hath their particular virtues and powers, as shall be showed in the following matter.

Making the Talisman

Make this Almadel of pure white wax;[2] but the others must be coloured suitable to the Altitudes. It is to be 4 inches square, and 6 inches over every way, and in every corner a hole, and write betwixt and every hole with a new pen those words and names of God following. But this is to be done in the clay and hour of Sol [the Sun]. Write upon the first part towards the East, ADONAIJ, HELOMI, PINE. And upon the second towards

1 Minor adjustments in punctuation have been made, to facilitate reading.
2 White wax is used for calling spirits of the 'Eastern Altitude'.

the South part HELION, HELOI, HELI. And upon the West part JOD, HOD, AGLA. And [on] the Fourth part which is North write TETRAGRAMMATON, SHADAI, JAH.

And betwixt the first and the other parts make the pentacle of Solomon thus:

and betwixt the first quarter write this word ANABONA, and in the middle of the Almadel make a Sexangle figure, and in the middle of it a triangle, wherein must be written these names of God HELL, HELION, ADONAIJ,[1] and this last have round about the six-angled figure, as here it is made for an example [see below]:

The making of the Candles

And of the same wax there must be made four candles. And they must be of the same colour as the Almadel is of. Divide your wax into three parts: one to make the Almadel of, and the other two parts to make the candles of. And let there come forth from everyone of them a foot made of the same wax to support the Almadel.

[1] The diagram reproduced by Waite (*op. cit.*) does not agree with this manuscript, and omits the names HELL, HELION, ADONAIJ, as well as differing in other ways from the original.

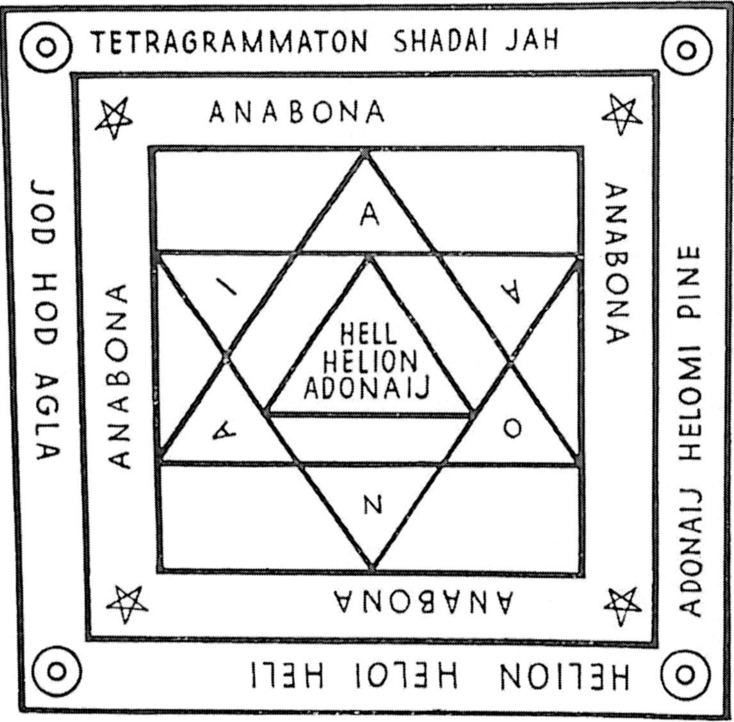

The Almadel

The making of the Seal

This being done, in the next place you are to make a seal of pure gold or silver (but gold is best) whereon must be engraved those three names HELION, HELLUION, ADONAIJ.

The First Altitude of Angels and their Calling

And note that the First Altitude is called *Chora Orientis*, or the East Altitude. And to make an experiment in this Chora it is to be done in the day and hour of the Sun.[1] And the power and office of those angels is to make all things fruitful, and increase both animals and vegetables in creation and generation, advancing the birth of children, and making barren women fruitful.

And their names are these, viz: ALIMIEL, GABRIEL, BARACHIEL, LEBES, HELISON.

And note you must not pray for any angel but those that belong to the Altitude you have a desire to call forth.

And when you operate set the four candles upon four candlesticks, but be careful you do not light them before you begin to operate.

Then lay the Almadel between the four candles upon a waxen foot that comes from the candles, and lay the golden seal upon the Almadel, and having the invocation ready written upon virgin parchment, light the candles and read the invocation.

Appearance of the Angel

And when he appeareth he appeareth in the form of an angel carrying in his hand a banner or flag having the picture of a white cross upon it, his body being wrapped round with a fair cloud, and his face very fair and bright, and a crown of rose flowers upon his head.

He ascends first upon the superscription on the Almadel, as it were a mist or fog.

Then must the exorcist have ready a vessel or earth of the same colour as the Almadel is of, and the other of his

[1] Days and hours of the Planets are given in Chapters XIX and XX, pp. 331-49.

furniture, it being in the form of a basin, and put thereinto a few hot ashes or coals, but not too much lest it should melt the wax of the Almadel. And put therein three little grains of mastick in powder so that it may fume and the smell go upwards through the holes of the Almadel when it is under it.

And as soon as the Angel smelleth it he beginneth to speak with a low voice, asking what your desire is, and what you have called the princes and governors of this Altitude for. Then you must answer him, saying:

> "*I desire that all my requests may be granted and what I pray for may be accomplished: for your office maketh it appear and declareth that such is to be fulfilled by you, if it please God*" – adding further the particulars of your request, praying with humility for what is lawful and just: and that thou shall obtain from him.

But if he do not appear presently, then you must obtain the golden seal, and make with it three or four marks upon the candles, by which means the Angel will presently appear as aforesaid.

And when the Angel departeth he will fill the whole place with a sweet and pleasant smell, which will be smelled for a long time.

And note the golden seal will serve and is used in all the operations of all four Altitudes.

The colour of the Altitude belonging to the first Altitude, or Chora, is lily-white; the second Chora a perfect red rose colour; the third Chora is to be a green mixed with a white silver colour; the fourth Chora is to be black mixed with a little green or a sad colour.

Of the Second Chora or Altitude

Note that the other three Altitudes, with their Signs and Princes [can exert] power over goods and riches, and can make any man rich or poor.[1]

And as the first Chora gives increase and maketh fruitful, so these give decrease and barrenness. And if any have a desire to operate in any of these three following Choras or Altitudes, they must do it in *die Solis* [Sunday] in the manner above showed.

Times of Operation and prohibitions

But do not pray for anything that is against God and His laws, but what God giveth according to the custom or course of nature: that you may desire and obtain.

All the furniture to be used is to be of the same colour the Almadel is of.[2]

Princes of the Second Altitude

And the princes of the second Chora are named, viz: APHIRIZA, GENON, GERON, ARMON, GEREIMON. And when you operate

[1] This passage apparently does not exist in Waite's original; because he says that the offices ('powers') of the angels of the third and fourth Altitudes are not stated. We see, however, from our text, that the third, fourth and second 'Choras' 'can exert power over goods and riches, and can make any man rich or poor' (cf. Waite, *op. cit.*, p. 74).

[2] 'Furniture' here stands for the accessories or items used in the process: robes, wax, etc.

kneel before the Almadel, with clothes of the same colour, in a closet hung with the same colours also; for the holy apparition will be of the same colours.

And when he appeareth, put an earthen vessel under the Almadel, with fire or hot ashes and three grains of mastick to perfume as aforesaid.

And when the Angel smelleth it he turneth his face towards you, asking the exorcist with a low voice why he hath called the princes of this Chora or Altitude. Then you must answer as before:

> "*I desire that my requests may be granted, and the contents thereof may be accomplished: for your office maketh [it] appear and declareth that such is to be done by you, if it please God.*"

And you must not be fearful, but speak humbly, saying:

> "*I recommend myself wholly to your office, and I pray unto you, Prince of this Altitude, that I may enjoy and obtain all things according to my wishes and desires.*"

And you may further express your mind in all particulars in your prayer, and do the like in the two other Choras following.

The Angel of the second Altitude appeareth in the form of a young child with clothes of a satin, and of a red rose colour, having a crown of red gilly flowers upon his head. His face looketh upwards to heaven and is of a red colour, and is compassed round about with a bright splendour as the beams of the sun. Before he departeth he speaketh unto the exorcist saying, "I am your friend and brother."

And illuminateth the air round about with his splendour, and leaveth a pleasant smell which will last a long time upon their heads.

Of the Third Chora or Altitude

In this Chora you must do in all things as you was [*sic*] before directed in the other two.

The angels in this Altitude are named, viz:

> ELIPHANIASAI, GELOMIROS, GEDOBONAI, TARANAVA & ELOMINA.

They appear in the form of little children or little women dressed in green and silver colours very delightful to behold, and a crown of baye leaf with white and colours upon their heads. And they seem to look a little downwards with their faces. And they speak as the others do to the exorcist, and leave a mighty sweet perfume behind them.

Of the Fourth Chora or Altitude

In this Chora you must do as before in the others, and the Angels in this Chora are called BARCAHIEL, GEDIEL, GEDIEL,[1] DELIEL and CAPITIEL.

They appear in the form of little men or boys, with clothes of a black colour mixed with a dark green; and in their hands they hold a bird which is naked; and their heads compassed round about with a bright shining of divers colours.

1 Some versions lack this name.

They leave a sweet smell behind them, but differ from the others something.

The Times to Invoke the Angels

Note that there is twelve Princes, beside those in the four Altitudes: and they distribute their offices amongst themselves, every one ruling thirty days every year.

Now it will be in vain to call any of the Angels unless it be those that govern them. For every Chora or altitude hath its limited time, according to the twelve signs of the Zodiac; and in that Sign the Sun is in that or those Angels that belong to that Sign hath the government. As, for example: suppose that I would call the 2 first or the 5 that belong to the first Chora.

Then choose the first Sunday in March, after the Sun hath entered Aries: and then I make an experiment.[1] And so do the like, if you will, the next Sunday after again.

And if you will call the two second that belong to the first Chora, that Sunday after the Sun enters Taurus in April.[2] But if you will call the last of the 5, then you must take those Sundays that are in May after the Sun has entered Gemini,[3] to make your experiment in.

Do the like in the other Altitudes, for they have all one way of working. But the Altitudes have names formed severally in the substance of the heavens, even a character. For when the Angels hear the names of God that is attributed to them, they hear it by virtue of that character.

Therefore it is in vain to call any angel or spirit unless he knows what name to call him by.

1 i.e., the first Sunday after March 22nd.

2 Sun enters Taurus, April 21st.

3 Sun enters Gemini, May 22nd, each year.

Therefore observe the form of this conjuration or invocation following:

Invocation to call Angels or Spirits

"O thou great, blessed and glorious Angel of God [NAMING THE ANGEL], who rulest and is the chief governing Angel in the [NUMBER OF ALTITUDE] Chora or Altitude. I am the servant of the Highest, the same your God Adonaij, Helomi, and Pine, whom you do obey, and is your distributor and disposer of all things both in heaven earth and hell, do invocate, conjure and entreat you [NAME OF ANGEL] that thou forthwith appear in the virtue and power of the same God, Adonaij, Helomi and Pine; and I do command thee by him whom ye do obey, and is set over you as King in the divine power of God, that you forthwith descend from thy orders or place of abode to come unto me, and show thyself visibly here before me in this crystal stone [*sic*], in thy own proper shape and glory, speaking with a voice intelligible to my understanding.

"O thou mighty and powerful Angel [NAME OF ANGEL], who art by the power of God ordained to govern all animals, vegetables and minerals, and to cause them and all creatures of God to spring increase and bring forth according to their kinds and natures: I, the servant of the Most High God whom you obey, do entreat and humbly beseech thee to come from your celestial mansion, and shew unto me all things I shall desire of you, so far as in office you may or can or is capable to perform, if God permit to the same.

"O thou servant of mercy [NAME], I do humbly entreat and beseech thee by these holy and blessed names of your God ADONAIJ, HELLOMI, PINE.

"And I do also constrain you in and by this powerful name ANABONA, that you forthwith appear visibly and plainly in your own proper shape and glory in and through this crystal stone, that I may visibly see you, and audibly hear you speak unto me, and that I may have thy blessed and glorious angelic assistance, familiar friendship and constant society, community and instruction, both now and at all times, to inform and rightly instruct me in my ignorance and depraved intellect, judgement and understanding, and to assist me both herein and in all other truths also, through the Almighty Adonaij, King of Kings, the giver of all good gifts that his bountiful and fatherly mercy be graciously pleased to bestow upon me.

"Therefore, O thou blessed Angel [NAME], be friendly unto me, so far as God shall give you power and presence, to appear, that I may sing with his holy Angels.

"O Mappa Laman, Hallelujah. *Amen.*"

Greeting to the Spirit

When he appears, give him or them kind entertainment; and then ask what is just and lawful, and that which is proper and suitable to his office. And you shall obtain it.

So endeth the 4th book called the Almadel of Solomon the King.

CHAPTER X

THE *Lemegeton* OF SOLOMON

THE BOOK OF THE SPIRITS

Raising the Spirits of the Lemegeton

Famous among sorcerers as the Book of the Spirits,[1] the grimoire known as the *Lemegeton* was the source of many 'authoritative' Black Books of the seventeenth and eighteenth centuries. By means of it, spirits were raised, made to submit to the magician, sent to find treasure, kill and maim, procure wisdom and honour – the whole gamut of human desires was catered for by this work attributed to Solomon the King, and called his *Little Key*.

Readers of the *Arabian Nights* will be aware that a horde of powerful genies were cajoled into a brazen vessel by Solomon,[2] and cast into the sea. It is at this point that the *Lemegeton* takes up the story. In Babylonian times, we are told in the Preface, this dangerous vase was discovered, and thought to hold a great treasure. When it was opened, alas, the devils were released, and are still at liberty. Two of the most famous of occult authors – Weirus the demonologist and Cornelius Agrippa – have made lavish use of this work:

1 Not to be confused with the *Liber Spirituum*, which is described in Part V, Chap. XV, p. 311.

2 Chapter XI gives Solomon's supposed method of raising these demons.

and its possession was a *sine qua non* for every responsible magician. There is only one small detail here: that the sorcerer must himself copy it out in his own writing, into a book made of virgin parchment, before it would be of use in the conjuration of spirits. Nevertheless, even printed copies are so scarce today that they cannot be bought; manuscripts are known in some of the larger libraries of Paris and London.

The Magician's Ring, according to the *Lemegeton*

As with other rituals, it is held that the genies of the *Little Key* are to be invoked with the proper ceremony of the magical circle and invocations. In addition to this, however, the signs of the spirits must be known, and inscribed within the circle, or the genie will not make his appearance.

In addition to information concerning the names and ranks of the demons, the *Lemegeton* gives valuable information as to the aspect (sometimes horrible) in which any particular spirit will appear, and the times for invoking them, with the metals properly to be used in the making of the talismans which contain their signs.

There are seventy-two aristocratic genies named in this curious work. Of these, eighteen are kings – numbering within their ranks several recognisable as Babylonian and Semitic demons: Baal, Asmoday and Belial among them.

Astaroth – the love and war god of the ancient Semites – is numbered among the dukes, of whom there are no fewer than twenty-six. In addition there are to be remarked fifteen marquises, twelve presidents and five earls. Several of them have aliases and alternative names, according to different versions. This may be due to the fact that some occultists maintain that the true names of demons are never known to men: they merely give a name by which they are to be called, and this name may vary according to the invocant. Their names and powers are tabulated in Appendix I.

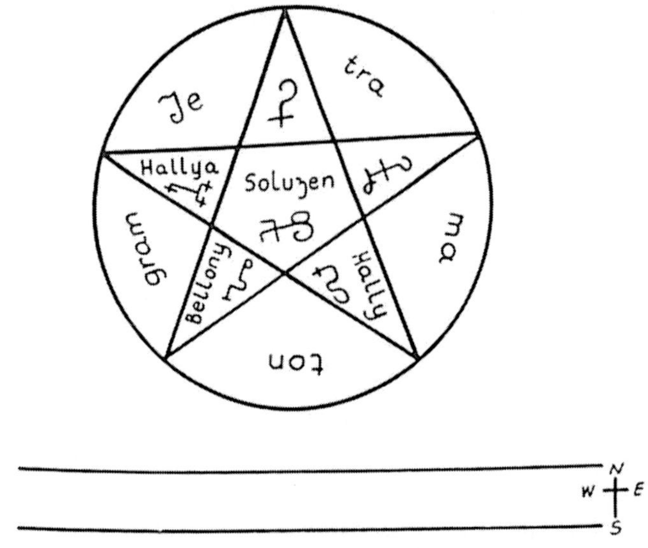

The Pentagram of Solomon, from the *Lemegeton*

The *Lemegeton* is nothing if not class-conscious, and thus the full detailing of the abominable hierarchy is carried out within its pages, almost to the point of boredom. For this reason the present author has to some extent edited and condensed the essential matter, in order to make it more readable.

These powers, then, are conjured by the magician in order to do his bidding. Assuming that the master already has a knowledge of the making of the magical circle, there are few variations from the traditional requirements. A circle is drawn, with a triangle outside its precincts, for the spirit to occupy while negotiations with the operator are being carried out. The circle itself is the conventional double one, with four eight-pointed stars within its inner arc, each composed of two interlinked equilateral triangles: the 'Shield of David'.

The actual 'Pentacle' – the Pentagram of Solomon – must be made of virgin calfskin,[1] and carried by the magician. Actually, it usually is said to be worn on one side of the front of the robe. This pentagram, be it noted, is not the same as the Seal of Solomon, which must also be drawn with a virgin black cock's blood on virgin parchment. It will be recalled by all wizards that ritual purity (in this case extending to one month before the operation) is essential.

The Seal is made when the Moon is rising in Virgo, and only on a Saturday or Tuesday night. Naturally the incense for this is alum, cedar wood, aloes and resinous gum.

The other equipment of the operator is also familiar to magicians: a white robe of linen, a cap of the same colour, the sword, wand and belt made of lionskin. Oil is also carried, for anointing the face, and consecrated water for bathing.

The actual ceremony of evocation is similar in many ways to that laid down in the *True Grimoire*, as detailed elsewhere in this book. The difference is that the process at present under consideration contains only Jewish words and phrases, and does not involve Christian (therefore presumably later) formulas.

When the magician has assembled his materials he is to robe himself with the white cloak (some writers say that it

[1] Compare Chapter I.

should resemble that of a priest), and repeat the well-known prayer:

> "Thou shalt purge me with Hyssop, O Lord..."

– the prayer of David for sanctification, contained in Psalm li of the Old Testament.

Then comes the oration of enrobement:

> "Through the symbolism of this garment I take on the protection of safety, in the power of the All-Highest ANOOR, AMACOR, AMIDES, THEODONIAS, ANITOR. O ADONAI, cause that my desire shall be accomplished, by virtue of Thy power. To Thee is praise and honour for ever and ever. *Amen.*"

Then follows a pause for concentration upon the object of the ritual and the name and powers of the spirit being invoked. When this has been completed, the exhortation to the spirit begins:

"O Spirit [NAMING THE SPIRIT] I conjure thee, empowered with the strength of the Greatest Power, and I order thee by BARALAMENSIS, by BALDACHIENSIS, by PAUMACHIE, APOLORESEDES, and by the most powerful Princes Genio, Liachide: the Ministers of the Tartar Seat, commanding Princes of the Throne of Apologia, in the ninth place!

"I conjure thee, O Spirit [NAMING THE SPIRIT], by He whose Word created, by the Strong and Highest Names of ADONAI, EL, ELOHIM, ELOHE, SABAOTH, ELION, ESCHERCE, JAH, TETRAGRAMMATON, SHADDAI – Appear immediately here so that I may see thee, in front of this Circle, in a pleasant and human body, without any unpleasantness!

"Come at once, from any part of the world; come pleasantly, come now, come and answer my questions, for thou art called in the Name of the Everlasting, Living and Real God, HELIOREM.

"Likewise I conjure thee by the name under which thou knowest thy God, and by the name of the prince and king who rules over thee.

"I conjure thee to come at once and to fulfil my desires, by the powerful Name of Him who is obeyed by all, by the Name TETRAGRAMMATON, JEHOVA, the names which overcome everything, whether of this world or any other: come, speak to me clearly, without duplicity; come, in the Name of ADONAI SABAOTH; come, linger not. ADONAI SHADAI, the King of all Kings, commands thee!"

This powerful conjuration should, we are told, take effect at once. If, however, the spirit named does not manifest himself during the recitation, it is to be repeated once or twice more.

By this time the spirit should be in occupation of the triangle set aside for him. If he is not there, he is to be called again, in the terrible words of the Second Conjuration (which will be found, together with the Third Conjuration, in Appendices I and II to this book) and failing his coming then, the Third Conjuration is to be used. There is a possibility that the spirit's non-arrival may be due to the fact that he is working somewhere else. Thus he is to be called through the King who rules over him, to release him. This form is included in Appendix III, and should be repeated twice or three times.

There is now only one other possibility, if the desired evocation does not take place following the calling of the King: the spirit must be chained down in Hell, and unable to release himself. This, however, is no obstacle to a determined exorcist. A form of cursing – the Curse of Chains – is now intoned,[1] and the following rite performed:

[1] Appendix V.

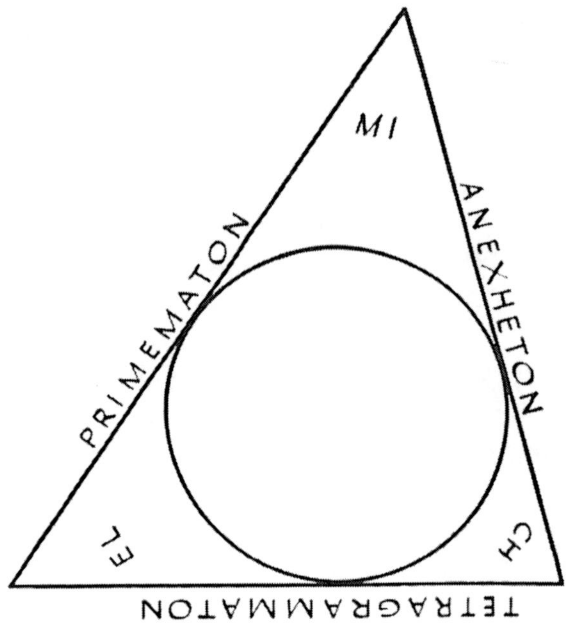

The Triangle of Solomon, into which spirits are conjured (from the *Lemegeton*)

The seal of the spirit is written on a piece of consecrated parchment, placed in a black box with noxious fumigants such as sulphur, asafoetida and the like, and the box wound with iron wire. Taking the sword, the magician impales the box thereon, and holds it over the charcoal fire, with these fateful words:

"I conjure thee, Fire, in the Name of Him who made thee, and by all the created creatures of the world to torture and burn, to torment this spirit [NAMING THE SPIRIT] for ever and ever."

Then the 'Invocation to a Rebellious Spirit' is recited with great vehemence,[1] when he should appear. If he does not come, the 'Second Invocation to a Rebellious Spirit' is used.[2]

1 Appendix IV.

2 Appendix VI.

The Grimoire continues that the spirit must then come, as soon as the box is placed on the charcoal fire. Then he must be allowed to see the Pentacle of Solomon, which was previously covered with a piece of linen, and he is addressed thus:

"See, Spirit, the Pentacle of Solomon, which I have brought. See the penalty of disobedience. See the magician, who is named Octinimoes. He is here, carrying out the rite of conjuration, empowered by God, without fear. Make, O Spirit, answer to my questions and obey me, in the Name of thy Master, and in the Name of Lord Bathal, moving to Abrac, Abeor, moving to Beror."

Having heard this, the spirit will submit himself and ask what it is that he desired of him.[1] Seeing that he is now repentant, he is to be addressed 'fairly and with good humour', and welcomed thus:

"Welcome, Spirit, welcome to my presence. Thou wert invoked in the Name of Him who has created heaven, and earth and hell, and obeyed through this power.

"I hereby bind thee, so that thou shalt remain here, visible and friendly, and within the confines of that triangle, while I still require thee, and leave not without the Licence to Depart and then not without having completed all my requests."

Then the sorcerer is to treat with the spirit, and command him to do what he will, within the competence of the spirit, and afterwards give him the Licence to Depart. It is

[1] J. A. C. Collin de Plancy, in his *Dictionnaire Infernal* (Paris, 1823), substitutes simply the single 'Great Universal Conjuration' for the long-drawn-out methods of this text. It runs as follows:

"I (NAME OF OPERATOR) conjure thee, Spirit (NAME OF SPIRIT), in the Name of the Great Living God, to appear to me in this form (FORM TO BE MENTIONED); otherwise St Michael the invisible, the Archangel, will cast thee into the deepest of all the Pits of Hell. Come thou, then (NAME OF SPIRIT), come thou, come and do my will!"

emphasised by occultist writers that this Licence must never be omitted, or else grave evil may befall the operator.

This is the Licence, in one of its many forms:

"O Spirit [NAMING THE SPIRIT] now that thou hast correctly and diligently completed my tasks and answered my questions, thou mayst leave. Leave, then, without harm to any, man or beast. Leave, then, and be at my disposal whenever I shall call thee again. Leave now, in peace and quiet, I adjure thee! May there be peace between thee and me for ever. *Amen*."

Then all that the Magician has to do is to wait for a short time, until the spirit has disappeared, and he may then leave and repair to his own home. During this time he is to say prayers and give thanks for the successful completion of the rite.

All these ceremonies, of course, presuppose that the operator is in possession of the secrets which actually cause the spirit to appear. He must, for example, know the times and places at which they can be called, as well as the metals of which their talismans are made.

Kings and Princes are conjured between the ninth and twelfth hours; their seals are, appropriately enough, wrought in gold. Silver is the metal for the Marquises, who are called between the third and ninth hours, and also if needed between sunrise and sunset. Dukes may be called only between sunrise and noon, and their talismans consist of their seals engraved upon copper. The metals of Prelates are of tin or silver, and they appear during the daylight hours. Cavaliers come between the fourth hour and sunset, or between dawn and sunrise. They are called with a talisman of lead. Presidents and Earls may be invoked in daylight: the former with seals of 'fixed mercury', the latter with a silver-copper alloy. The entire hierarchy is under the four Kings of the points of the compass: ZIMINAR, King of the North, GAAP, King of the

South, CORSON, King of the West, and AMAYMON, King of the East. These latter are the Kings called to release reluctant spirits.

Another document gives variations in the names of the monarchs. There are four Emperors: in the North, DEMORIEL, to the South, CASPIEL, to the West, AMENODIEL, and the Emperor of the East, CARNEFIEL. These, in turn, rule the four Kings: the King of the North, RASIEL, King of the South, PAMERSIEL, the King of the West, MALGARAS, and the King of the East, BARNIEL.

This manuscript of the *Lemegeton* states that they are to be invoked in order that they bring their surbordinate spirits within the control of the magician. They are dangerous, and can be controlled only if the operator shields his face with his magical ring.

Kings and Emperors are to be conjured into a magical crystal, as are individual spirits. This is done by engraving a certain design upon a metal table-top, and mounting upon this a crystal ball with a diameter of four inches.

Then the seal of the spirit is taken and fixed to the breast of the magician, and this conjuration is spoken seven times:

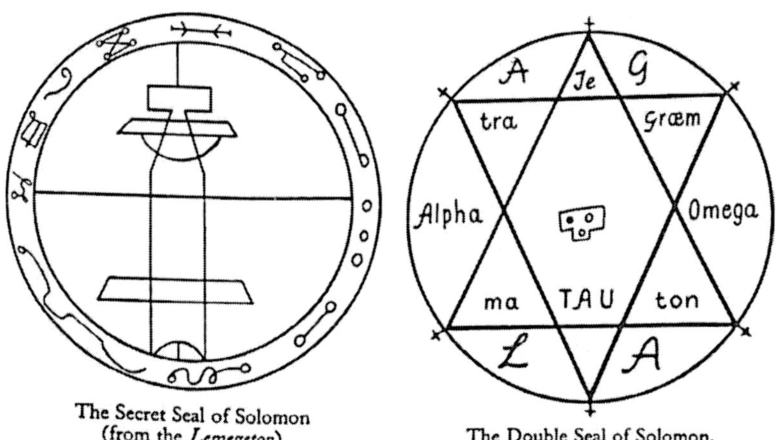

The Secret Seal of Solomon (from the *Lemegeton*).

The Double Seal of Solomon.

"I conjure thee, thou mighty and potent spirit (NAME AND RANK), who ruleth as (RANK) in the dominion of the (NORTH, &C, according to the rulership of the King, &c, invoked)."

The Seventy-two Spirits of Solomon

Four things are needed for the successful evocation and commanding of Solomonic spirits: knowledge of their names, functions, seals – and the conjurations. I have, therefore, condensed and arranged the list given by the *Lemegeton* which contains the data about the spirits, and present it here in alphabetical order:

AGARES is a Duke whose power is in the East (towards

Agares

which direction he is always to be invoked). He appears in the form of a distinguished sage, riding upon a crocodile, and carrying a hawk. His functions are to bring back those who have run away, to stop movement such as running away itself. In addition, he provides the gift of knowledge of all tongues, and can, when asked, cause earthquakes and reduce important men to a status of having nothing.

AINI is a powerful Duke, shaped like a man with three

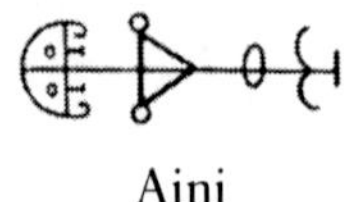

Aini

heads: one of a snake, the second like a man, the third of a cat. His mount is a viper; in his hand he bears fire, and spreads destruction by means of it. His function is to teach cleverness, and he can also answer questions of things which are not known.

ALLOCEN is another strong Duke, comes riding; on

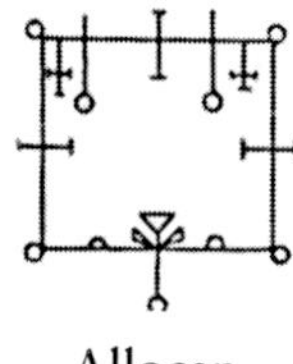

Allocen

horseback, attired as a warrior, though his visage is that of a red, fearsome lion. He speaks loudly and with a rough voice, his eyes flashing like fire.

ALLOCER is another name for ALLOCEN, used in some versions of the *Lemegeton*, and by various demonologists. He is also known in other works as ALLOIEN.

AMDUSCIAS is another Duke. His shape is that of a unicorn; though when requested he will assume human form. He can make music play from a hidden orchestra. Among his powers are to cause trees to fall, and to grant familiar spirits to the magician.

Amduscias

Amon

AMON is an exceedingly important and powerful Marquis in this hierarchy of Hades. His shape on arrival is that of a wolf, with a serpent's head or tail. It is necessary to command him to change into human form: which he does, but the transformation may not be complete, and it is said that he sometimes has a huge bird's head surmounting normal human shoulders. His functions include the reconciliation of enemies, the causing of love, and telling what is to happen in the future, and what has already come to pass.

Amy is a powerful President, whose favourite form when

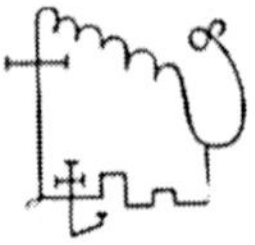

Amy

he appears is that of a flame. Like the other spirits, he will change to human shape when ordered. His specialities are science, and magicians may learn astrology from him in the twinkling of an eye. Any hidden treasure that is guarded by a spirit can be obtained through him. He will also provide the invocant with a useful familiar spirit.

Andras, a Marquis, favours an angel's body with the head

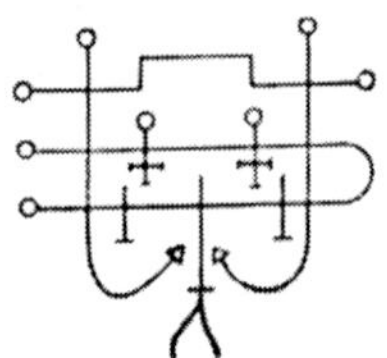

Andras

of a raven. He rides upon a large wolf, and in his hand gleams a terrible sword. He is entirely destructive, and is so dangerous that he may kill the magician himself.

Andrealphus, another Marquis, is normally seen as a

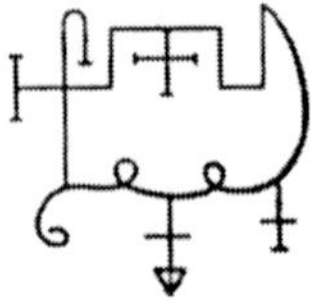

Andrealphus

beautiful peacock. His specialities are to teach mathematics – especially geometry – and to transform people into birds. The

Grimoire remarks that he will first arrive with a 'terrible noise'; but settles down when told to assume human form.

ANDROMALIUS is both a Duke and an Earl; thus,

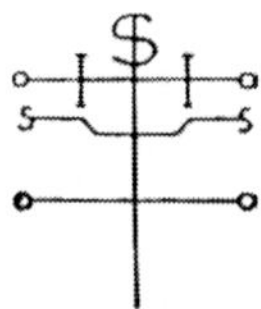

Andromalius

presumably, he can be conjured under the conditions obtaining for either rank of spirit. His normal appearance is human, and in his hand there is a snake. The magician may get treasures from him, recover any stolen article, and get to the bottom of all intrigue and plotting.

ASMODAY is a King with three heads: the first is that of a

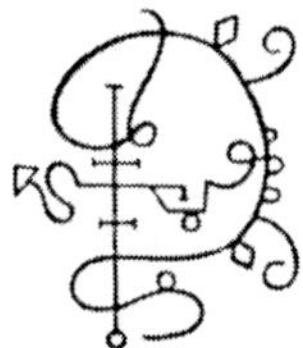

Asmoday

ram, the second is that of a bull, the last of human shape. Riding a dragon, he carries in his hand a mighty spear. Magicians were cautioned to summon him with the head uncovered, and some even hold that the master must stand in his presence. His powers are varied, ranging from the teaching of arithmetic to conferring invisibility, producing lost treasures and teaching the making of things. He is also obliging enough to answer any question put to him.[1]

[1] The demonographer Collin de Plancy quotes Jewish sources as identifying Asmodeus with Samael.

ASTAROTH is another demon who appears in the form of an

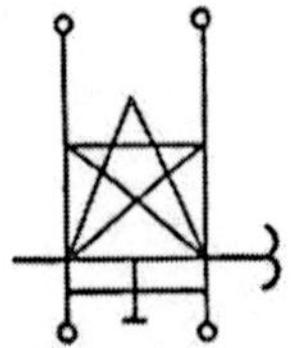

Astaroth

angel. Opinion is divided as to whether it is a good or bad angel, but an angel he is, that much is agreed. He is an important Duke, and is mounted upon a dragon, with a snake in his right hand. He will tell the sorcerer all of the past, the present and the future. He will also teach every secret and science.

AYM is another version of AINI, and appears in both forms in several manuscripts.

AYPEOS is an alias of IPOS, whose details are given later, and whose further name is rendered by certain magical writers as AYPOROS.

BAAL. This is the name of one of the most powerful of all

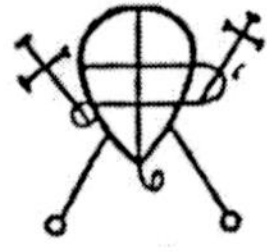

Baal

Kings of demons. He may present himself as a man with a human head or that of a cat or toad. Occasionally he is seen with all at once. Speaking in a hoarse voice, he gives knowledge of all kinds, and tells the means to obtain invisibility.

BALAM is the name of a frightful King, who appears with

Balam

three heads: one human, and two of different animals. Like several other spirits, his voice is hoarse, and he rides a bear and carries a hawk at his wrist. Those who lack wit might well invoke him, for he gives it to those who ask him. In addition he knows and will tell the secret of invisibility, and gives answers concerning the future and the present and past.

BARBATOS is a Count and Duke, dressed as a hunter. He

Barbatos

never comes alone, but is invariably escorted by troops and kings. His time to appear falls only under the astrological sign of Sagittarius.[1] The knowledge given by him includes the finding of treasure, the past, present and future, and the method of bringing people together in amity. He commands thirty infernal legions.

BATHIN is a mounted Duke, riding a horse. He seems

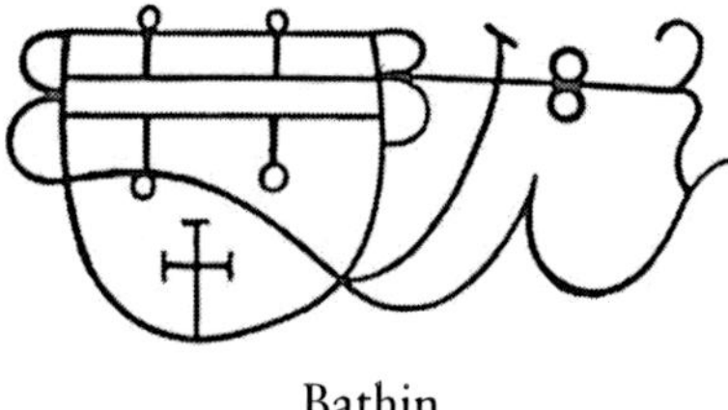

Bathin

human except perhaps for the serpent's tail which he wears. His specialities are to cause a person to be transported from one place to another as quick as light. He also knows – and will tell – of the virtues of stones and herbs. He has been mentioned by some as BATHYM.

BEAL is simply another name for BERITH, used by certain demonologists.

1 Nov. 23rd to Dec. 22nd.

BELETH is a King of some importance, who does not come

Beleth

without considerable reluctance. Even then he is not alone, but is accompanied by some sort of band or orchestra. He may be most angry, and has to be commanded to enter the triangle by the magician, who is armed with the magical Wand. In doing this, demonographers say, the Wand must be directed towards the southeast.

Protection against his temper may be obtained by wearing a ring of silver on the middle finger of the left hand, and used to shield the face. One wonders why he should be invoked at such risk, when all he can do is to produce love between the sexes: especially considering that this is a function of twelve of the other spirits.

BELIAL. This wicked entity of the Bible is not only a King

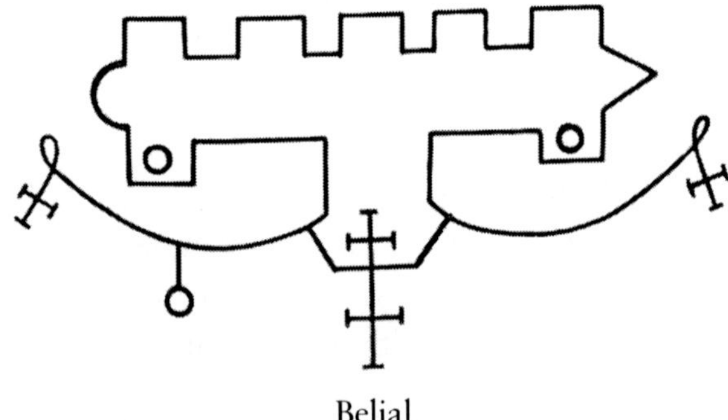

Belial

of the Lower Hierarchy, but was actually created immediately after Lucifer himself. Some trace of the fact that he was good before he fell from grace is contained in the mode of his appearance when invoked by sorcerers. He comes, we are told, like a beautiful angel, drawn in a fiery chariot. Even his tones when spoken to are well modulated. Some demonographers maintain that his greatest fault is that he deceives all, including the operator, unless continually faced with the Divine Name. His chief uses to a magician are as a helper towards promotion and one who made men receive favour. Unlike most of the other spirits, he expects that sacrifices should be offered to him.[1]

BERITH is the name of a soldier-Duke, who comes wearing

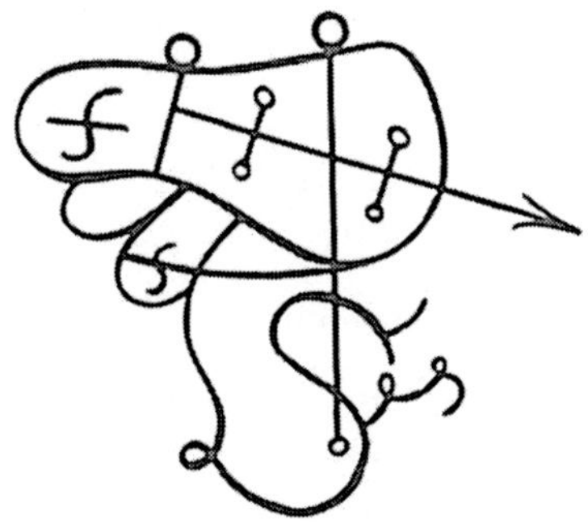

Berith

a crown of gold, mounted upon a red horse, with uniform of the same colour. He is one of the less trustworthy spirits, and magicians warn against his duplicity. Like several other Solomonic demons, he can tell of the past, present and the future. He can cause men to rise to high places and honours. Not the least among his abilities is to transmute any metal into gold at will.

BIFRONS. This Earl appears as a monster, and remains such

Bifrons

1 Such sacrifices to spirits are described in the *Key of Solomon*.

until told to transform his terrible appearance into something more human. Among the subjects which he can teach without any difficulty are astrology and mathematics, the knowledge of magical herbs and stones. Those who desire to perform magic with corpses call him, especially to transfer the body from one place to another.

BOFI is merely the name used by some writers to describe Berith, who has been mentioned above. He has another alias, too, that of BOLFRY, according to certain exponents of the Black Art.

BOTIS is the next great 'President and Earl'. The manner of

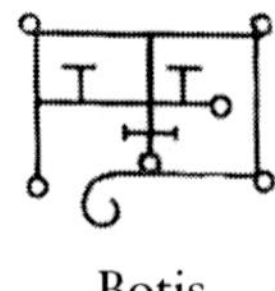

Botis

his first appearance to the exorcist is in the shape of an extremely distasteful serpent. When he has turned himself into human form, he still retains traces of his demoniac nature through a set of large teeth, and a pair of horns sprouting from the head. In addition to this, he is armed with a formidable sword. Botis is called to give answers as to things past, present and future, and to cause reconciliations.

BUER, another spirit – and President – who will come only

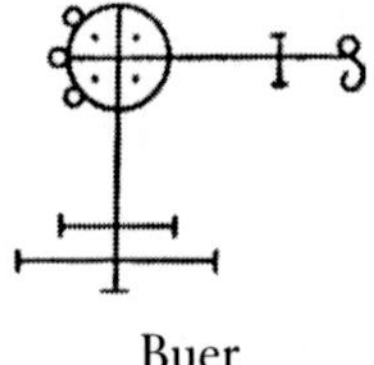

Buer

when the Sun is in the zodiacal sign of Sagittarius. Those seeking familiars, the curing of disease by magical means, or a knowledge of philosophy and logic call him. His appearance is that of a starfish.

BUNE is a Duke and at the same time another spirit sporting

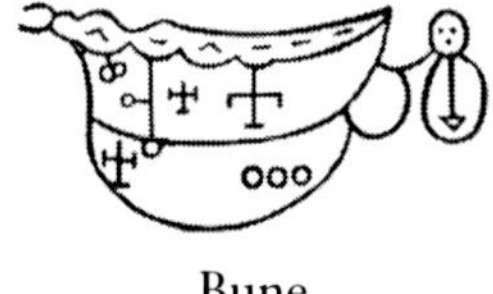

Bune

three heads: only one of these is human, the others being of a griffin and a dog. Wisdom and facility of speech, bewitchment of graves by demons, the acquisition of wealth: these are the powers attributed to Bune.

BYLETH is an alias of BELETH.

CAACRINOLAAS is a variation of GLASYALABOLAS, who is noted below; CAASIMOLA being another of his pseudonyms.

CAIM. Comes in the shape of a thrush. He is an important

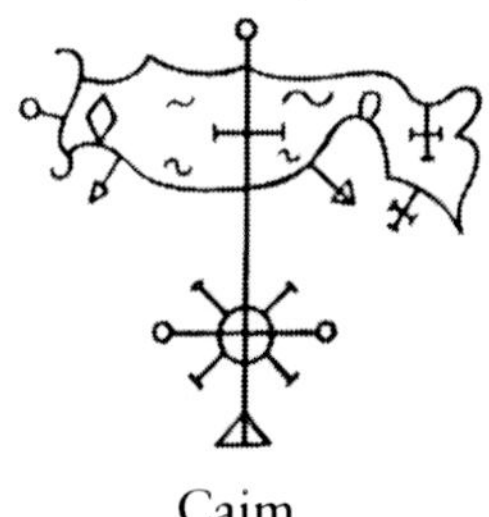

Caim

President in the infernal hosts. When a question is asked of him, the answer appears in flaming coals. To him is attributed the knowledge of the language of the birds – one of the attributes of King Solomon whom he is said once to have served. He also knows – and will teach, if requested – the tongues of other creatures: of dogs and cattle, and even the meaning of the murmurings of waves. Apart from this, a magician may learn of him secrets of the future.

CERBERUS is another version of NABERIUS.

CHAX (see SHAX).

CIMERIES, another Marquis: another brave soldier. He

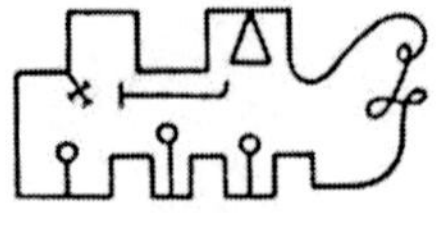

Cimeries

rides upon a black horse, and among his powers is to make a man soldierly. Literature is also learned from him, as are the location of buried treasures, anything lost, and anything appertaining to his domain of Africa.

CURSON (variation of PURSON).

DANTALIAN. This strong Duke when conjured appears with

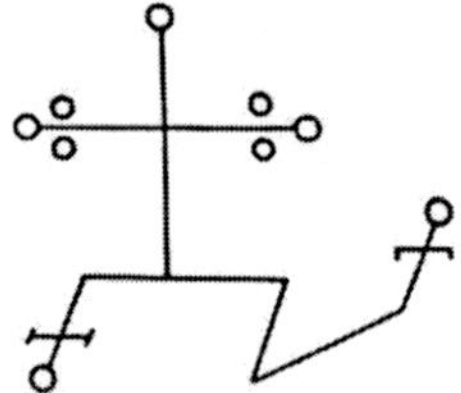

Dantalian

a multitude of male and female faces, and carrying a book. He is invoked in order to produce a vision of another person, to give news of secrets and even the innermost thoughts of men; to teach any art or science: and to influence the minds of men against their will – and without their knowledge.

DECARABIA. Those who invoke this Marquis should not be

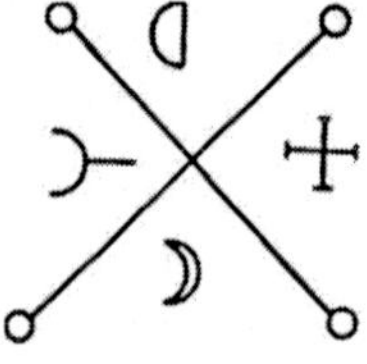

Decarabia

at all surprised to see him appear in the inanimate form of a star within a pentagram. He can, of course, assume human form if ordered. Magicians desiring familiar spirits disguised as birds should apply to him, it is stated. Knowledge of the powers inherent in plants and stones is also to be gained from Decarabia.

ELIGOR is another military spirit: a Duke, appearing like a

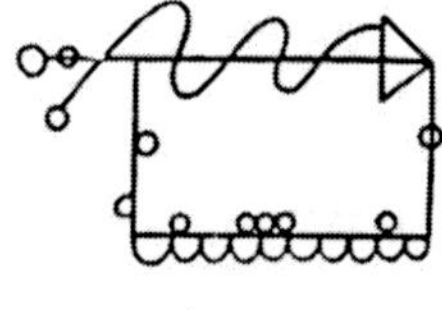

Eligor

knight, with accoutrements. The main favours bestowed by him are the knowledge of hidden treasure, favour at courts, creating love or attraction. In addition to these things he will start wars and cause armies to be collected.

FLAUROS appears like a leopard. Even when constrained

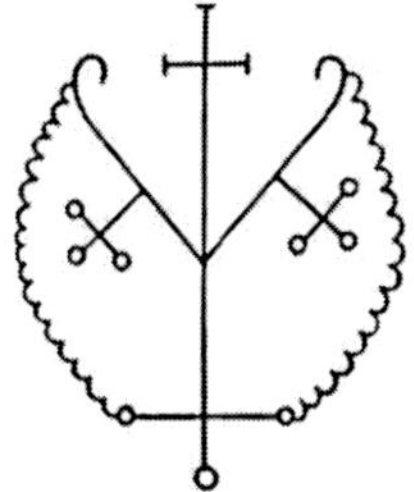

Flauros

to appear in more human shape, he still has a disturbing aspect. He is an important Duke. His aid is invoked against other spirits, and he will protect the magician against them. Sorcerers are cautioned that anything that this spirit may say outside the triangle will probably be false. Like many another Solomonic spirit, he knows all things of every tense, and will tell them. He is destructive inasmuch as he will annihilate the enemies of the magician if he is asked, and this by fire.

FOCALOR, also a Duke; his general form is that of a man

Focalor Foras

with wings. His powers extend over the seas. If asked he will cause death by drowning, sink ships, cause winds to blow.

FORAII – alias of MORAX, *q.v.*

FORAS is a President, and has the usual appearance of a man. FORCAS is another version of his name. Logic and allied subjects are taught by him, as is the lore of the magical virtue inherent in stones and plants. He can confer the power of invisibility, and will also make the invocant wise, witty and possessed of treasures. FORAS will also restore lost property.

FORFAX. Another name for MORAX, *q.v.*

FORNEUS has the appearance of a monster from the sea. He will, of course, become human for the time being if asked. He has the ability to teach the operator all arts and sciences. In addition to this, one may learn from him all languages. Those who desire the love of their enemies are counselled by occult writers to call upon him.

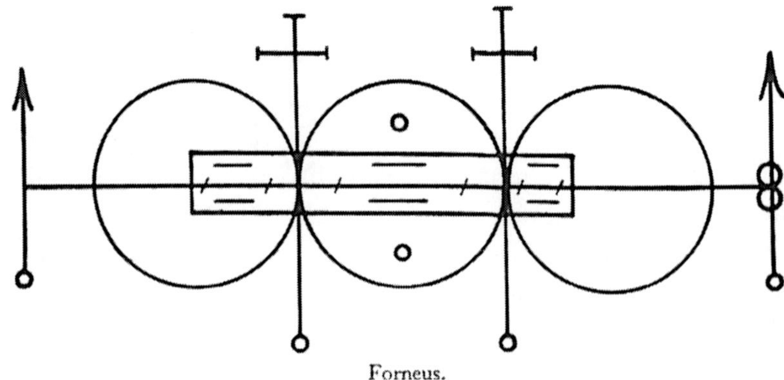

Forneus.

FURCAS looks like an old man, and anything but a benevolent one. He rides a horse and carries a spear. He is a Duke, and can teach philosophy and a variety of other sciences.

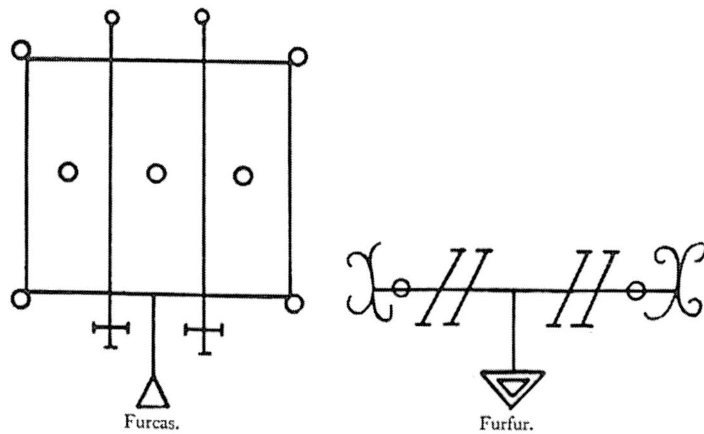

Furcas. Furfur.

FURFUR is an Earl, the commander of twenty-six infernal legions, and seems to be in the shape of a type of deer, winged and breathing fire. He is decorated with the tail of a serpent. He bestows marital love, causes thunder and lightning, and reveals secrets.

GAAP is the somewhat unflattering name of one who is not

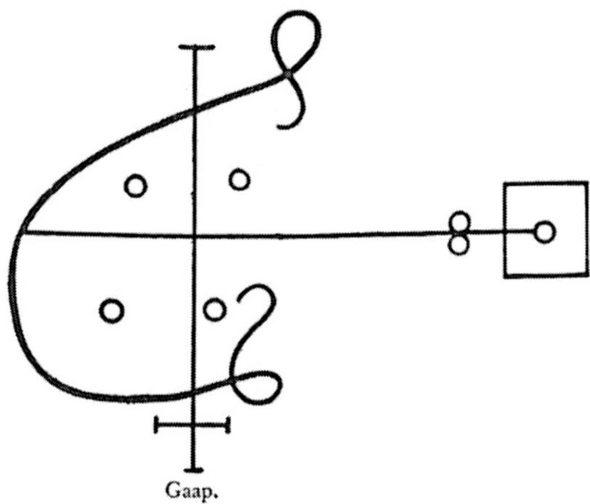

Gaap.

only a Prince but a President as well. He is attended by four kings, and assumes a human body when conjured. His specialities are causing love or hate, telling the future or unknown things from the past or present. In addition, he can arrange for a person to be transported where he will instantaneously, and even deprives other sorcerers of their familiars in favour of he who currently calls him.

GAMYGYN is a Marquis, who comes in the shape of a horse

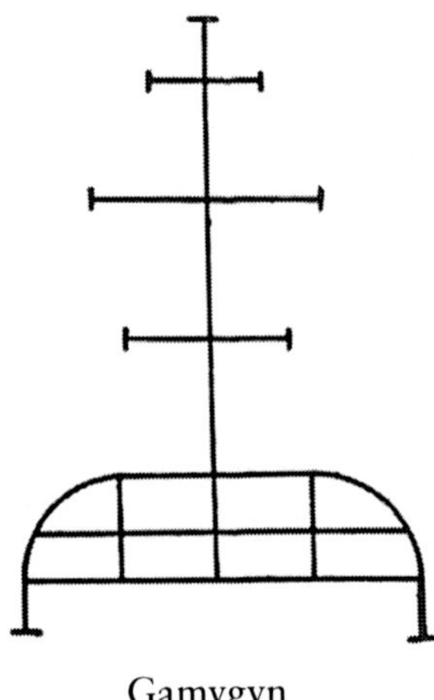

Gamygyn

or donkey. He is credited with being able to bring back for interrogation the souls of those who are dead, even if they are in the Nether Regions. For this reason he was invoked for necromantic purposes. Like many another spirit, he is a teacher of science.

GLASYALABOLAS is a powerful President, whose importance

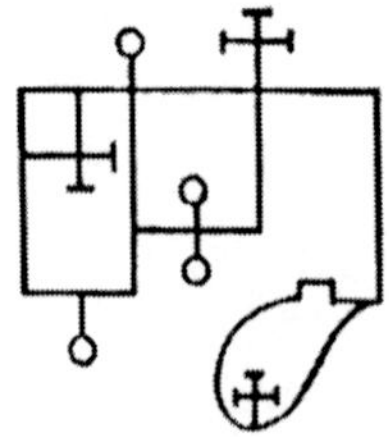

Glasyalabolas

is belied by his appearance as a winged dog. In addition to teaching all sciences, he causes murder, makes men invisible, and knows all about the past, present and future.

GOAP (see GAAP).

GOMORY. This Duke is the only spirit of this series who

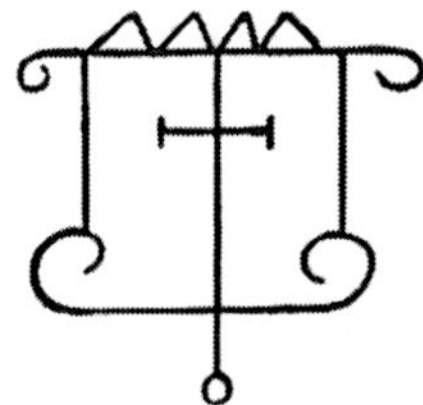

Gomory

appears in the form of a woman. She is beautiful, wearing a crown of gold, and causes the sorcerer to be loved of women and young maids. Those who wish to know the past, present or future may call her. Similarly she knows of hidden gold.

GUSAYN, variation on the name of GUSION, *q.v.*

GUSION, another Duke, who has the power to grant

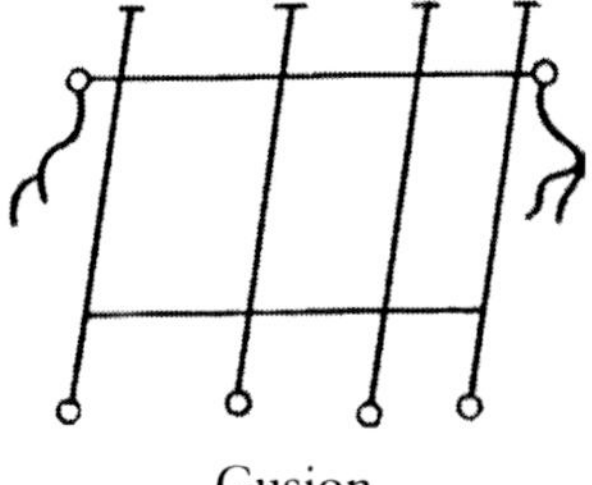

Gusion

position and honour, to tell all of the past, present or future, and to make those who are inimical friendly.

HABORYM is another name of AINI, *supra.*

HAGENTI; a bull with wings is the normal appearance of

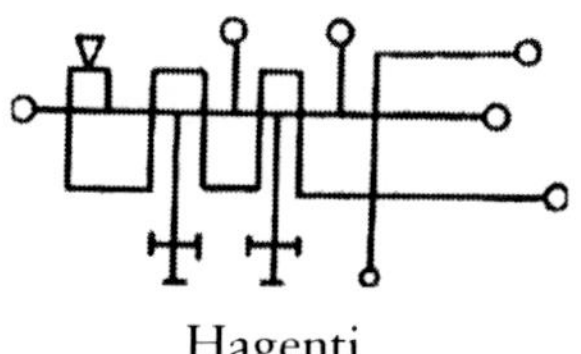

Hagenti

this mighty President of the demons. His speciality is transmutation of metals into gold – and wine into water.

HALPAS, an Earl, manifesting himself as a dove. He is

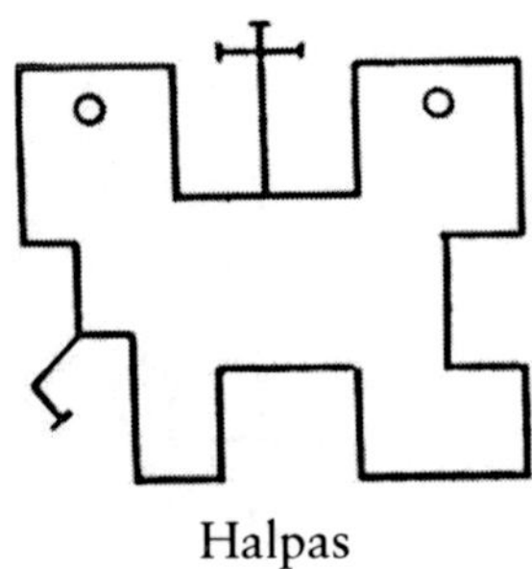

Halpas

destructive and warlike: causes wars and punishes sinners with the sword.

IPES is a variant on the name of the next spirit.

IPOS, who is both Prince and Earl. He may have the form of an angel or a lion, or a combination of both. In either case he is stated to be repulsive. Those who stand in need of wit or who are not brave call him. He also has knowledge of what is past, and what to come.

LERAJIE, a Marquis. He carries a quiver and bow, and

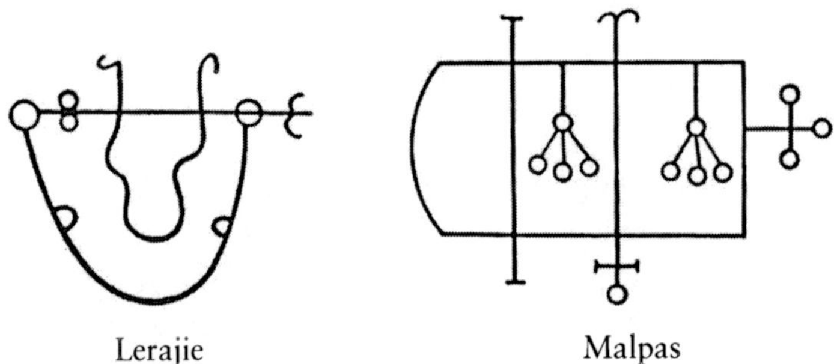

Lerajie Malpas

wears a green habit. His main operations are to cause wounds to delay healing. In addition, Lerajie will start battles when commanded by the magician.

MALAPHAR – see VALEFOR, *infra*, whose alias this is.

MALPAS is a President first seen in the form of a black bird. He is a spirit who can cause anything to be made by supernatural means. There is a widespread story in the Middle East that this type of demon helped Solomon to build many things. He is deceitful, however.

MARCHOSIAS, a Marquis. His form is that of a wolf, winged

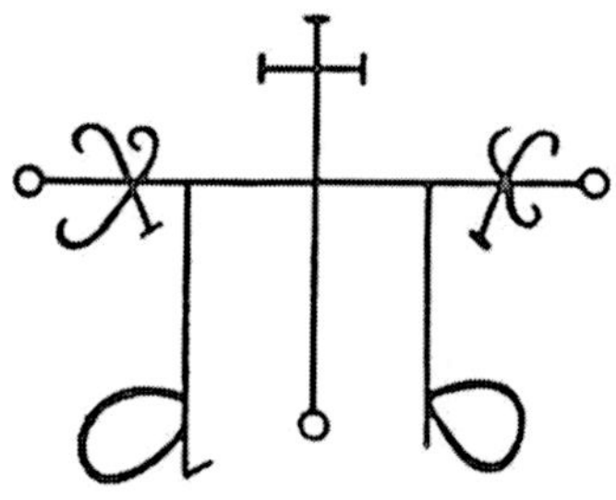

Marchosias

and breathing fire. He gives help in battles, and will provide answers to any questions that may be addressed to him.

MARTHIM – another name of BATHIN, *q.v.*

MORAX combines the offices of Earl and President, and

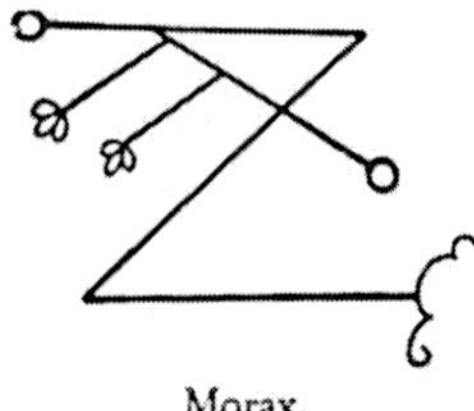

Morax.

is most powerful in the infernal hierarchy. The nearest that he can get to human shape is a normal body with a bull's head. He gives instruction in the magical uses of stones and herbs, teaches astrology and sciences. If asked, he will provide the magician with one or more familiar spirits to attend him.

MURMUR is a military Duke and Earl. He rides a griffin,

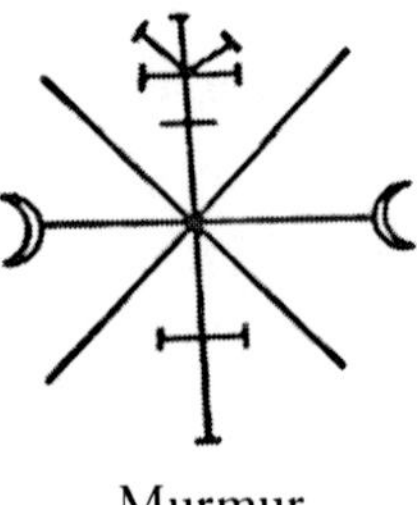

Murmur

wears a crown denoting his ducal status, and speaks with a harsh, grating voice. He will be accompanied upon evocation, says the text, by two heralds or courtiers, and a fanfare of cornets. Naturally, he will be wearing soldierly garb.

Murmur is chiefly to be invoked to teach philosophy, and to cause the souls of those long dead to appear before the circle; he can compel the said souls to answer truthfully any question that the sorcerer may put to them. He is also said to be one of those spirits who will be reinstated to a post similar to that which he held before his fall from grace – and hence, it is supposed, he is not wholly bad.

NABERIUS has a voice as unpromising as that of Murmur,

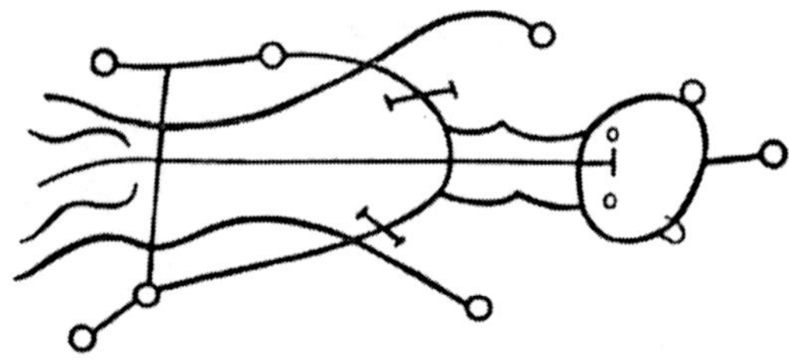

Naberius

and his usual form of appearance when invoked is that of a cock which seems 'unable to stand still'.[1] Naberius is a

[1] He may have three heads, and be birdlike.

proud and honoured Marquis, who not only teaches such things as logic and rhetoric, but can also ensure that a person retrieves any lost favours or honours which he formerly possessed.

ORIAS is a powerful Marquis, and comes as a lion, riding a

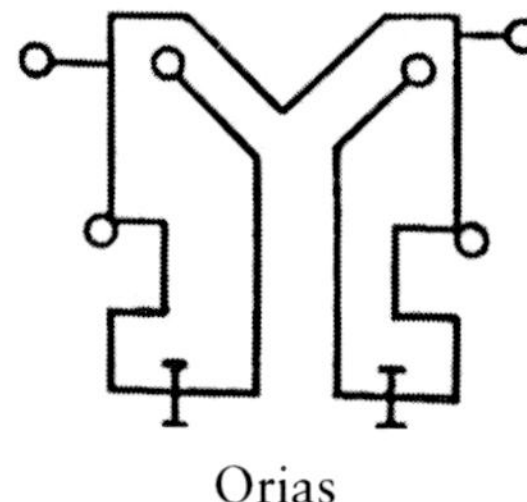

Orias

great horse. His tail is like that of a snake, and in his hands he bears two more serpents. Those who desire to learn astrology without the tiresome need to study merely apply to him: and they know the science 'in a flash'. He can also change men into any shape, and in addition has the very valuable power of causing even enemies to favour the exorcist. A direct appeal to him will result in a place of honour being accorded to his invocant.

OSE is another President, who favours the form of a large

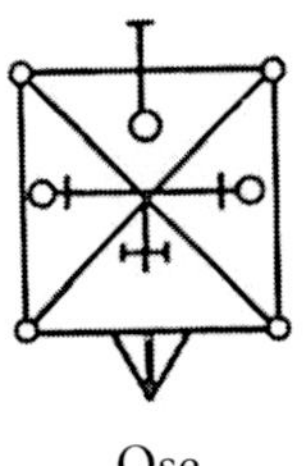

Ose

and graceful leopard. Like the previous spirit, he is able to transform people into whatever form they will. He causes delusions and insanity if required. Those who have been changed by him may not know it, and continue to behave as they normally do, in spite of their altered appearance.

Things which are secret and hidden – especially hidden knowledge – will be revealed by him, as well as the more prosaic knowledge of all sciences and arts.

PAIMON has the rank of King, and directly under the Supreme Devil. Those who know his Seal and call him in accordance with the ritual of this *Lemegeton*, we are informed, can gain any honour from him. He confers the power to dominate all men, will produce useful familiar spirits to serve the magician, can teach at once all the arts and sciences.

Paimon comes like a king before the circle, riding a camel, and with a numerous court in attendance. The sorcerer is cautioned in some texts not to fear his terrible voice, which is alarmingly loud.

Paimon

Phoenix.

PHOENIX has a pleasant appearance (that of a bird) and an equally delightful voice (like a child), but some hold that he is not to be trusted at all. Others maintain that this Marquis obeys the magician's every order. His speciality is poetry and letters.

PIRSOYN – variant of GUISON, *q.v., supra.*

PROCEL is a powerful Duke, who comes to the circle in

Procel

angelic shape. His powers are somewhat mixed: for instance, he can cause the impression that there is thunder and torrents of rain, if requested; he will teach sciences and especially mathematics. Those who seek any of these obligements and wish to know any secret at all, should call upon him, say the demonologists. He has one other name, which is given as PUCEL.

PURSON, a King, commanding hidden treasures. His lesser

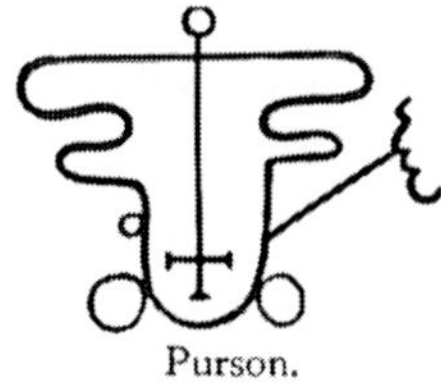

Purson.

accomplishments are to say what is past, present or future, to grant the aid of familiar spirits, and to tell anything at all that can be known, when he is asked. His appearance may be rather against him. He looks like a man, very huge, and his head is that of a lion. Being a King, he arrives with a court and musicians, astride a bear, with a snake in his hand.

RAUM, sometimes called RAYM. This Earl comes like a

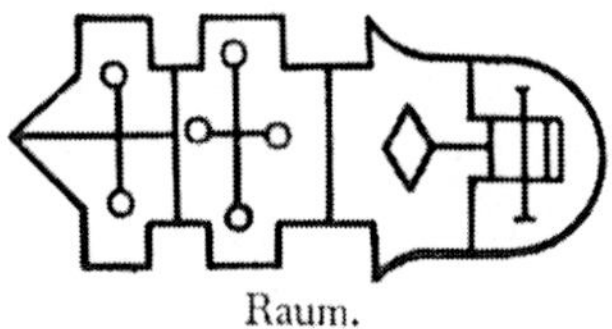

Raum.

blackbird at first. Those who wish to create love can call upon him. He will reconcile enemies, too, and destroy cities and even demolish a reputation.

Like many other spirits, he will tell of the past, present and future whatever is desired of him. Those in need of money can have it stolen by Raum, and brought to them. In fact, he very much resembles many of the genii whose exploits are related in oriental tales.

RONEVE is another name of RONOBE, *q.v.*

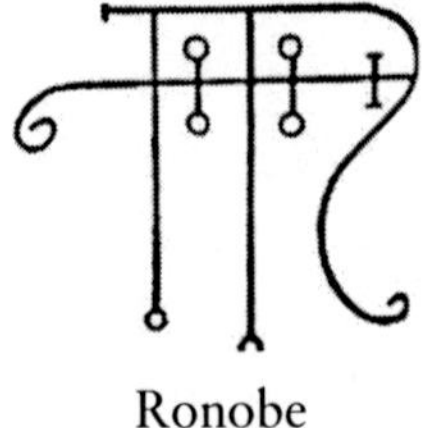

Ronobe

RONOBE: A Marquis and Earl, teaches languages, gives favour of friends and enemies alike.

SABNACK is another spirit who appears as a warrior, again

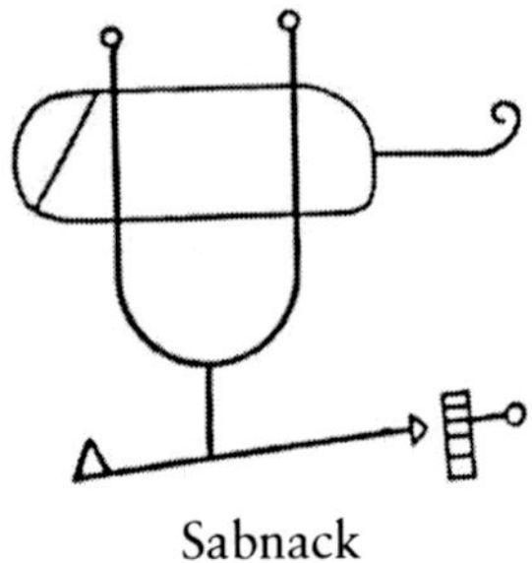

Sabnack

with the head of a lion, and on horseback. This Marquis of the Demons is in control of fortifications and military camps, and also presides over wounds, which he can cause to become incurable. Some writers have called him SABURAC.

SALEOS is a Duke, another soldier, and his territory is

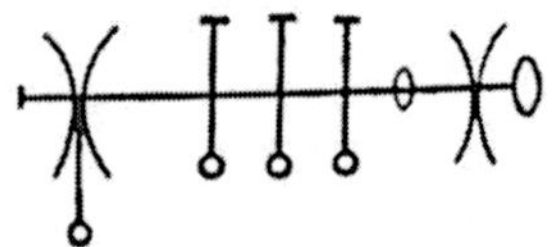

Saleos

exclusively that of causing love between the sexes when asked.

Scox, alias SHAX, has the form of a bird, large or small, and

Shax

is a Marquis. Used for diabolical purposes, he will steal money and bring it to the magician, will cause any person to become deaf, dumb or blind. He will produce a familiar spirit for the sorcerer, and can find things which are lost or hidden.

SEERE is the name of a powerful Prince, whose greatest

Seere

power is that he can cause anything to happen in the twinkling of an eye. Like most of the other spirits, he can be used for good or evil processes. He appears as a man with long hair, upon a winged steed.

SEPAR, another name of Vepar.

SOLAS is a potent Prince, whose usual form is that of a

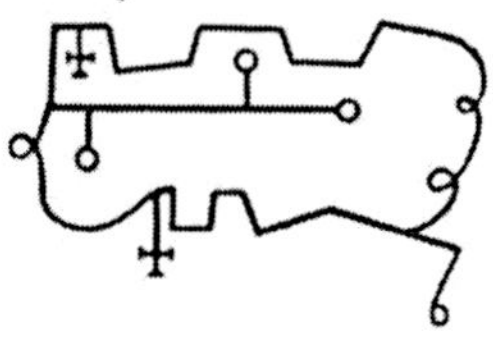

Solas

black raven. Like the other spirits, he will change upon request into more or less human shape. He is learned in star-lore, and everything touching the magical powers of plants and stones. STOLAS is another version of his name.

SYDONAY, version of ASMODAY, *q.v.*

SYTRY is a Prince, with a human body and wings, with the

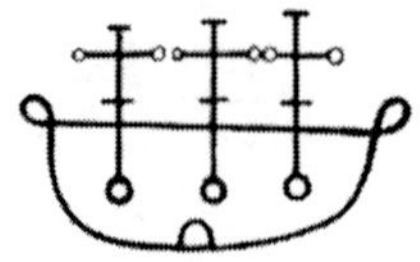

Sytry

head of one of several kinds of wild animal. His province is exclusively that of love and lust. He will cause, for example, a man to love any woman, or *vice versa*. Again, he will 'compel women to display themselves in the nude before him who calls him'.

TAP – one of the pseudonyms of GAAP, *supra*.

VALAC is a President, appearing as a small boy mounted

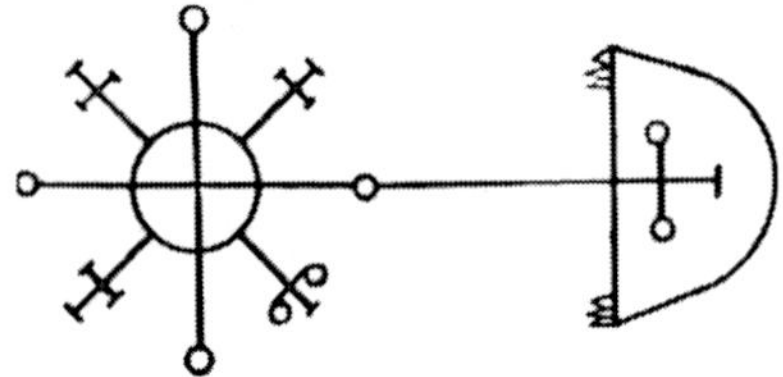

Valac

upon a dragon. He tells where treasures may be found, and rules over reptiles.

VALEFOR comes as a lion, or some composite animal:

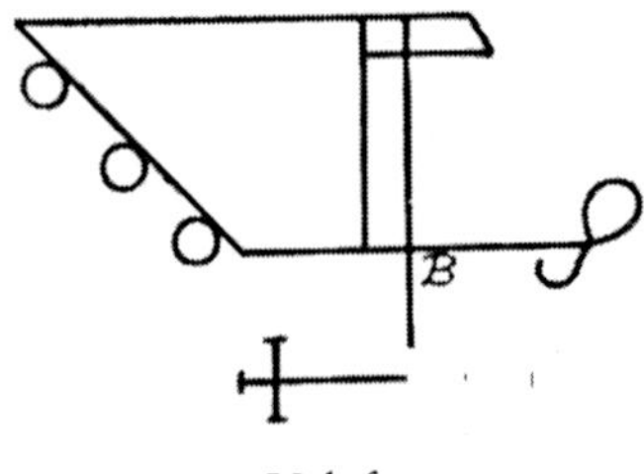

Valefor

opinion is divided among the ancient authors on this. He will tell anything which is unknown to the operator, and is in charge of occult medicine, curing all ills magically. He is also able to transform men into animals, and to make a man skilful with his hands and brain.

VAPULA, another Duke to favour a lion's form with wings.

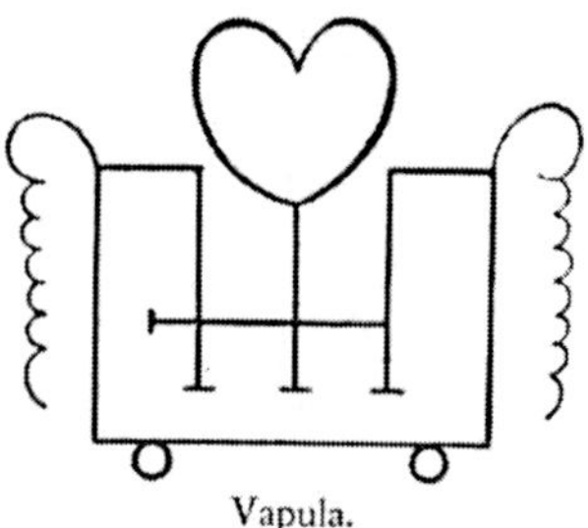

Vapula.

He controls all connected with artisans and formal knowledge.

VASSAGO is a Prince, and favoured by those who would

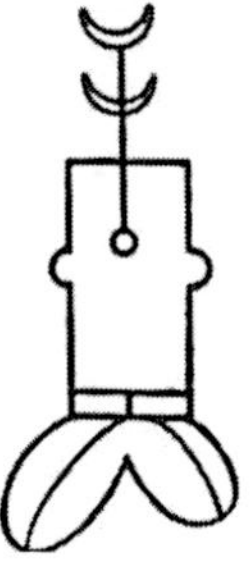

Vassago

know that which is unknown. He can be used to tell of the future, of the past and present, and of anything that has been lost or stolen.

VEPAR is a Duke, though his shape is that of a mermaid.

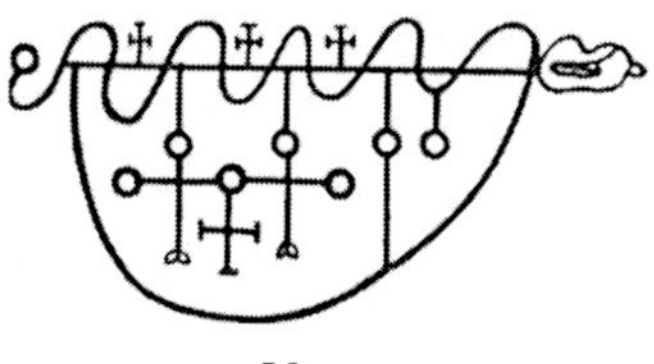

Vepar

His province is the sea, and all that is connected therewith.

He will, for example, cause storms at sea, death and disaster, and also delusions of ships on the sea.

VINE is the only spirit who will tell a magician the identity

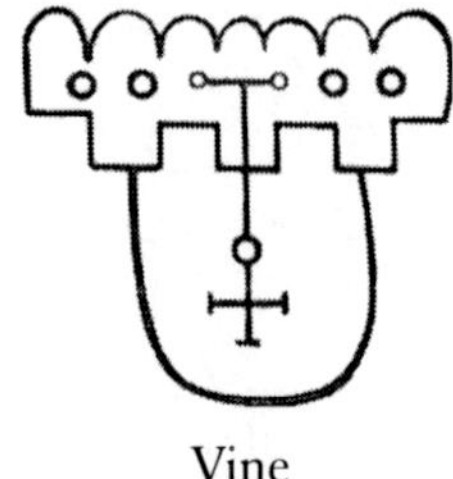

Vine

of other sorcerers and witches. He can also cause destruction, and knows that which is secret, regardless of time. He may manifest himself outside the circle as a lion or some sort of monster. In case of war he can destroy castles, or build defence and other works.

VUAL is a Duke of apparently Asian or African origin. He

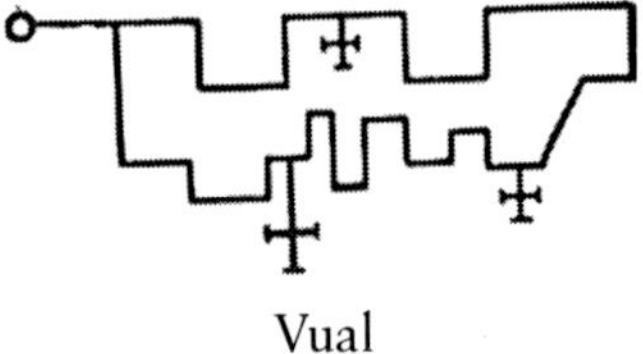

Vual

will begin speaking 'Egyptian', and will seem as a camel. He is to be told to assume human form, and speak the tongue of the magician. He can make one beloved of women, and cause friendship and esteem. He also knows all, and is not bound by time.

ZAGAN is a King, in the shape of a winged bull. He can

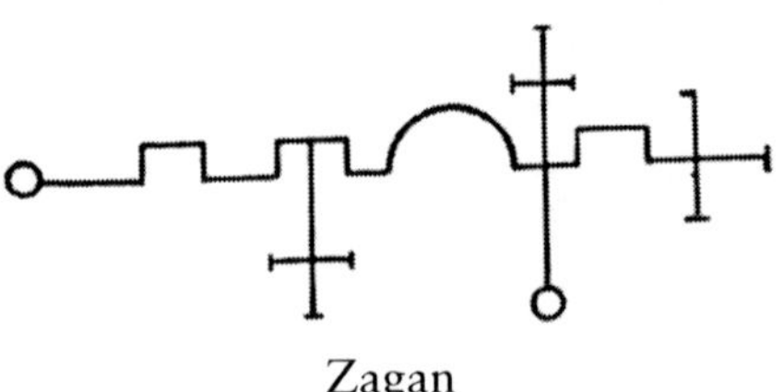

Zagan

change liquids: for example, water into wine, wine into blood, and so on. Those who lack a sense of humour will find that he can make up the deficiency. One of his useful accomplishments is alchemy.

ZALEOS is another form of SALEOS, *q.v.*

ZEPAR is the last of the spirits of the *Lemegeton*: a strong

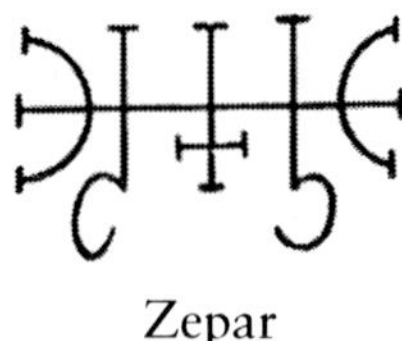

Zepar

Duke, he can change people into any shape they desire.

He can make a woman love any man, at the magician's command.

CHAPTER XI

THE CATALOGUE OF DEMONS:

THE TESTAMENT OF SOLOMON

THIS CURIOUS WORK forms a most intriguing link between the magical systems of Babylonia, Ethiopia and the Hebrews. In its pages we find mention of the magical ring, with which the King of Jerusalem 'bound' and compelled the obedience of the genies; of the rise and ultimate fall of Solomon, and the powers of the spirits themselves.

There are at most two known manuscripts which contain both the *Testament* and the famous *Key of Solomon* – the sorcerers' handbook of the Middle Ages. At the same time there is reason to suppose that both the *Testament* and the *Key* formed a part of the great rituals traditionally attributed to the Son of David, and elaborated in the pages of the *Arabian Nights*.

The *Testament* was first translated into German from an ancient Greek manuscript in the middle of the last century, by Fleck. This was later adapted by Conybeare in 1898, and enjoyed a restricted circulation. It has nowhere been reproduced in the literature of occultism, either before or since. The only other version mentioned by bibliographers is the translation of Istrin, which first saw the light of day in Russia of pre-revolution times.

Manuscripts of the *Testament* exist in certain Greek monasteries, and one Greek text, edited from several such codices, appeared in Leipzig thirty years ago. This just about summarises the accessible copies of the work in question.

One thing is certain in connection with the *Testament*: it contains demonographic material of great interest. Whether King Solomon wrote it, or a Rabbi Solomon – or even, as tradition has it, if it is really the work of the demons themselves – it is a document clearly qualifying for inclusion here. It is one of the sources of magic as we know it.

Summary of the Contents

The document purports to be Solomon's own story – in some detail – of the period between the building of the Temple in Jerusalem, and his own ultimate fall from grace. It begins with the patriarch engaged upon the building. Suddenly, a vampire-spirit seizes upon a youth in his employ. This creature (which resembles the *jinn* or genies of the *Arabian Nights*) is depriving the young man of half his pay, half his food – and sucking his blood through his thumb at night into the bargain.

Eventually the victim appeals to Solomon himself, and the King enters the unfinished Temple to pray for help from the Lord of Hosts (Sabaoth – the phrase which is used much in ritual magic, especially that of the *Key of Solomon*). There is an immediate response. The archangel Michael appears, bringing with him a magical ring, which is presented to Solomon. This is inscribed with the powerful Pentacle (pentagram, a five-pointed star), and it has the power to command all spirits.

The Ring of Solomon

We may be permitted a slight digression here, to look more closely at the ring itself than the *Testament* allows us. When the ring was actually in the possession of anyone, it had to be worn on one of the fingers. Its powers were, first, to call a genie, which could call others who were under his command, and so on. This is what the *Testament* tells us, and it is in line with the Arabian traditions to this effect. Once the spirit had appeared, he could be prevented from causing trouble if the ring were pointed at his breast. When genies were to be compelled to enter jars (and thus be held captive by the operator) the ring was placed near the mouth of the jar and they were perforce compelled to enter it. The jar was then sealed with pitch and a stopper of marble, and the pentagram seal of the ring used to mark the soft pitch.

So much for the using of the ring. Magicians among the Arabs and the Spanish-Arabian school concentrated to some extent upon the manufacture of such a ring, in order to duplicate the supposed operations of the King who first used it: and the Pentacle was believed implicitly to enshrine a magical power to the extent that the Moors of today – descended from those same Spanish-Arabians expelled in the fifteenth century – use it on their national flag.

There is, however, a divergence of opinion on the actual form of the ring and its pattern. As one magical book has it, 'it will be necessary to try all recommended ways, until successful'.

We hear that the ring was small, was made of alternate bands of silver and copper. Another source holds that it was of iron, because that is the metal most terrible to the spirits. Though the general opinion is that the pentacle is the design, some Syrian amulets supposed to incorporate the Solomonic design show 'an eight-rayed star, with a smaller four-rayed star cut on the face of it'.

One manuscript holds that the *Shamir* stone with which the ring was set was in fact a diamond; and an early record has it that this was nothing more than the root – or part of a root – of the magically potent mandrake plant, with which evil spirits are exorcised from those possessed of them.

There are, again, two versions of the names written on the ring. The first says that there were seven magical names or Words of Power in a language akin to Phoenician engraved within the circle; or, to be more exact, between two concentric circles within the diameter. These are given as: SLYT, SPYLT, TRYKT, PPMRYT, HLPT, ALYPT and, finally, HLYPT. The meaning of these arrangements of letters is unknown. It is possible that they may be substitute-letters (interchange code) representing others. They are, at any rate according to the Semitic languages, all consonants.

The second school mentions the names engraved within the ring to be twenty-nine in number: HQQPS, SHHLT, TWRSP, HSPT, BRWLHT, ALYLT, PTPNT, RHMT, QPYDT, SHPLT, HQYKT, PPAYSHNT, LMPS, WHLYMPT, DMPST, KTYBT, TRKLT, YSHRYET, DQST, LMSTMPS, MRYPT, PSYT, PPT, PSDMST, SHKLLT, PSYT, DMPS, PRYSHT, PLISHT.

These words could be derived from either the Arabic or Hebrew *Abjad* type of number-letter notation, or they could be Gnostic. It is common, however, for 'Words of Power' to be apparently meaningless, and few occultists interest themselves in matters of research.

Solomon and the Magical Ring

Once possessed of the ring (and, presumably, the directions for its use), Solomon immediately set about the task of calling and compelling the obedience of the spirits. The procedure was to call a demon, obtain his or her name and functions, and then find out the magical name by which the demon could be baffled. Frequently this name was the name of one of the angels or archangels. All this is well in line with traditional magical belief, and the actual functions of many of the demons are recognisable as dating from Babylonian and other Semitic origins. Such names as Asmodeus and Beelzebul are familiar to all occultists and students of the Bible. There are demons of hate and destruction, male and female among them, spirits of the planets, those with human bodies and others like travesties of animals, incubi and succubi. All these Solomon called, and obtained the relevant information from them, afterwards consigning them to tasks connected with the building of the Great Temple.

It may be mentioned here that Arabian literature abounds with tales of the jinn who worked with Solomon, and there are wondrous accounts of his mining operations without lights or implements. Mysterious mines still exist on both sides of the Red Sea which have no accumulated soot from lamps or candles. In this they differ from other local mines, and hence they are known as those used by Solomon and mined in former days by the lightless jinns.

The *Testament* winds up with details of the thirty-six spirits of the *decani* of the Zodiac, and their appearance, and the temptation and fall of Solomon into idolatry.

The *Testament* has interesting points of contact and difference from traditional magical practice. Most marked here is the absence of the magical circle.

The magical rituals current among the Semites called, as we know from Babylonian tablets and other sources, for the drawing of a magical circle as protection against the incursions of the spirits whom the magician has evoked through his Words of Power. The master, likewise, must have a pentacle for protection, and must know the adjurations to force the jinn to speak.

It may be that the ring itself replaces the circle. This is likely, for the circle, like the ring, contains the pentacle and the Words of Power. In this context, then, the ring is a sort of symbol of the magical circle: a point which I believe has not been noticed before. As with the other books of magic, the 'Discharge' of the spirit is mentioned: "Go in Peace", as well as the adjuration "I command you in the Name of the Lord of Hosts (Sabaoth)" or, sometimes – in the *Testament* as in the Black Books of the Middle Ages – "In the Powerful Name AGLA!"

Another possibility is that the *Testament* itself is intended either as a companion to the *Key* (which gives details about erecting the magical circle), or is actually a part of the comprehensive rituals of which the *Key* is another book.

The actual document is entitled: "Testament of Solomon, son of David, the King of Jerusalem, Master of all the Spirits, with whom he made the Temple. [The Testament] Relates of their powers and how they are combated."

The following is a complete version of the substance of the *Testament*:

When the Temple was being built, a demon called ORNIAS came at sunset, and robbed a boy of half his pay and half his food. He sucked the youth's right thumb daily, and this favourite of the King became sick thereof.

The boy complained to Solomon, who was distressed, and entering the Temple before it was complete, prayed a night and a day that he might gain power over this demon.

Then the Archangel Michael appeared to him, and brought a small ring, with an engraved stone upon it, and said:

"O Solomon the King, son of David, take this gift from God, the Lord of Hosts (Sabaoth). With it thou shalt be able to bind all the demons of the world, male and female. And with them thou shalt build Jerusalem. Thou must wear this ring; and on it is engraved the Pentacle."

The following evening the demon came as usual, to rob the employee. But Solomon had given him the ring and told him what to do. When the spirit appeared, he threw it at him, saying: "Come, King Solomon commands thee!"

The demon cried out, and offered the boy all the gold in existence, if he would only release him from the ring's power.

But the boy refused, and brought the shouting fiend to Solomon's palace, and reported his presence to the potentate.

The latter questioned him:

"Who art thou?"

"I am ORNIAS."

"What is thy sign of the Zodiac?"

"Aquarius, the Water-bearer. I strangle people, and I change into human shape, like a woman, for men to consort with in their sleep. I can come as a lion, and am over all demons: the child of URIEL, the angel, the Power of God!"

Solomon then sent ORNIAS, with the magical ring as his mandate, to bring all the other jinn to him. And he went to the King, supreme over all: Beelzeboul. Forced to come, by the power of the ring, Beelzeboul arrived.

Solomon says of this event:

"And when I saw the prince of demons, I glorified the Lord God, the creator of Heaven and Earth, and I said: 'Blessings to Thee, Lord God, Omnipotent, who hast given me this power...' And I questioned him [the spirit]:

"'Who art thou?'

"'I am Beelzeboul, Chief of Demons. It is I who cause the demons to become visible to men.'

"And he agreed to bind and to bring to me all the spirits."

Solomon asked whether there were any female spirits, and Beelzeboul said that there were, and that he would bring one forthwith.

So it was that ONOSKELIS came, in the shape of a fair and pretty woman. She lives normally in a cave of gold; her time is spent in strangling men, and she can be found in caves and wild valleys. She associates with men of a dark complexion, and shares their star with them. But she says under questioning that she does give certain powers to those who worship her 'as some do still'.

Onoskelis was created out of an echo 'which fell in a wood', and operates under the full moon. She is to be combated only by the name of the angel JOEL, and the Wisdom of God.

Solomon sends her to weave ropes for the Temple.

Next came ASMODEUS: he is part-angel, part-man, and his constellation is the Wain. Furious and shouting, in a stormy scene he foretells Solomon's fall and ultimate disgrace.

Asmodeus works against brides and grooms, and spends his time destroying the beauty of virgins. He also causes madness and lust: making men desert their wives and seek out other women. He is frustrated by the angel RAPHAEL. Those who wish to keep him in check (and hence any of the misfortunes which he is supposed to have caused) are to appeal to that angel, and also to burn certain incense. At first, like others, he will not tell what is the nature of this antidote. But Solomon adjures him with terrible Names, and he reveals it. The incense which banishes Asmodean evils is composed of the gall and liver of the Glanos fish, smoked over tamarisk wood.

Having put this noxious fumigant to work on the demon, Solomon has leisure enough to recall Beelzeboul again, and to submit him to further questioning. This elicits the fact that the jinn is given the work of destroying kings, and especially of aiding foreign enemies. He also sets demons upon people, trying to lead people astray, especially the devout.

While planning the eventual destruction of the world, Beelzeboul also causes murder, envy, wars and unnatural crime.

He is defeated by the word EMMANUEL, and the Name which is represented by the figures 644. He vanishes with the name ELEETH.

This spirit volunteered certain magical information to Solomon, thus:

"Hear, O King: if thou burn gum, incense and bulbs of the sea, with nard and saffron, and light seven lamps in a row, thou wilt firmly fix thy house. And if, being pure, thou light them at dawn, then wilt thou see the heavenly dragons, how they wind themselves along and drag the chariot of the Sun!"

However, Solomon sends him about his business, and another spirit is called.

This turns out to be the Spirit of Ashes, TEPHROS, who appears as a violent wind. He brings darkness, fires fields, and is under the astrological power of the tip of the crescent moon.

This spirit – according to the *Testament* – cannot be all bad, because when he is called in these names, he cures fever, through the power of the Archangel Azael: BULTALA, THALLAL and MELCHAL.

When he heard this, Solomon called Azael, and ordered him to subdue Tephros. Hence the demon was tamed, and made to throw rocks to the workers engaged upon the upper portion of the Temple.

When Solomon called for another demon, seven came, all joined together, and all of female form. They told the King that they constituted between them the thirty-three elements of the Lord of Darkness, and are a group of stars.

The first was named Deceit. She causes deception, and can be confounded by an appeal to the angel Lamechial. When there is a struggle in train, this is caused by the second, whose name is merely Struggle. She is put to flight by the power of the name of the angel Baruchiachel. The third female jinn is known as War, and can be combated only by the angel Marmarath.

The fourth is the genie of hatred and disunity. She separates man and wife, parents and children, kith and kin.

Her activities are stopped only by invoking the power of the angel Balthial.

Power is the name of the fifth spirit of darkness. Her power is that of tyranny and usurpation. Such activities, which she presides over, can be stopped only by the word ASTERAOTH.

Men are led astray by the sixth spirit, whose name is Error. She went so far as to predict that she would eventually be able to lead Solomon himself off the right path, reminding him that she had already caused to kill his brother. It is she who causes people to be necromancers. Uriel is the angel who overcomes her.

The seventh and last spirit of this group is the worst of all. Even the generally frank *Testament* does not do more than hint at the terrible power and danger of this demon. Solomon continues after this succession of spirits has left:

"Then I who am Solomon praised the Lord and ordered a further spirit to appear. So before me came a demon with the likeness of a man, but headless.

"And I said to him, 'Who art thou?' He said, 'I am a demon'. I asked him which, and he replied: 'I am Envy. I eat heads, for I seek a head for myself. I have not consumed enough, and I desire a head like thine.'

"I, Solomon, then put the seal upon him, holding my hand to his breast. Then the devil jumped and fell, and moaned, and said: 'Alas, what is become of me? O ORNIAS, treachery, I cannot see!'

"And I said: 'I am Solomon. Tell me how thou canst see [without a head].' He said: 'Through my feelings.'

"I asked him how he could speak. He said: 'O Solomon, King, I am a voice myself, for I have obtained the voices of innumerable men. I broke the heads of the so-called dumb, on the eighth day after their birth. I can do things at the crossroads, though I am dangerous. I can seize and cut off a man's head like a sword-slash, and I put it on myself. I also send disease to the feet and cause sores...'"

Solomon discovered from him that the angel of lightning alone could control the demon Envy.

The next demon to be mentioned came in the form of a huge dog, with a loud voice. He was formerly a sage of great learning, and now is called RABDOS ('Staff') and throttles people. He is to be combated only by the power of the angel Brieus. He had knowledge of a mine, and of a green stone, which latter Solomon sent to him, for the adornment of the Temple.

Then came a fearsome apparition, like a lion, commander of a legion. His name was not discovered. Truculently, he admitted to being 'bound' by the number 644 and the name EMMANUEL. And his activities consist in attacking the convalescent while they are recovering from illness.

The three-headed dragon with human hands, who was the next demon, was put to work like the others, at the Temple. He attacks children before birth, and causes epilepsy. These manifestations of his activity are overcome by Golgotha and the word JERUSALEM being written down.

After this a female spirit showed herself. Her body was dark, her eyes green and shining, and her limbs invisible. Her name she gave as OBIZUTH. She spends her time with confined women, trying to strangle their children. "My entire work is the destroying of children, in body and mind." She is overcome by the angel Afarof, otherwise given as Raphael. "If any man write that name on a woman in childbed," she tells Solomon, "then I shall be unable to go into her. The number of this name is six hundred and forty."

This number is arrived at by assigning certain numerical values to each letter, thus: R (100), A (1), Ph (500), A (1), E (8), L (30).

After Obizuth came a winged dragon, with human-like face and hands. He associates with woman in disguise, and is put to flight by the angel Bazazath.

ENEPSIGOS was another female spirit, who can manifest herself in various shapes. Her activities are frustrated by an appeal to the angel Rathanael.

A hore-fish was the next visitant. He is the spirit of the sea, greedy for silver and gold. He destroys ships, and causes sickness among men. He is called KUNOSPASTON, and sometimes comes upon the land. The angel over him is Iameth. When Solomon sought to confine him, he said that he could not live without water, which was provided for him. When a jar had been filled with the liquid, he was sealed in it, and placed within the Temple precincts.

The last of this series of apparitions was in the form of a giant, carrying a sword: a relic, as he said, of the days of the giants. He causes demoniac possession, baldness, and a madness in which a man eats his own flesh. He is destroyed by a number written on the forehead; and he was also imprisoned in a jar.

The next spirits to appear were a different type: they were the *decani* of the planets, and each had his astrological province.

Ruax comes under the sign of the Ram. He makes people slow-thinking, and can be controlled by this invocation: "MICHAEL bind RUAX."

Barsafael causes migraine, and this is combated by saying: "GABRIEL, bind BARSAFAEL!"

Arotosael injures the eyes. Those with this trouble have only to repeat this invocation to be cured: "URIEL, bind ARATOSAEL!"

Iudal is the cause of deafness. The counter-spell is "URIEL IUDAL!"

Sphendonael is the demon who attacks the tonsils, and can be dismissed with the cry: "SABRAEL, bind SPHENDONAEL!"

Sphandor causes disease and afflictions of the shoulders, hands, neck and marrow. Against him, the usual formula is used with an invocation to Arael.

Belbel works against the heart and mind. The angel to be called to control his depredations is Arael.

Kurtael causes pains, especially in the bowels. He can be dismissed by the power of the name of the angel Iaoth.

Metathiax causes troubles of the reins, and can be combated by the power of Adonael.

Katanikotael is the cause of domestic troubles. He said that, to have peace and harmony at home, a man has to write on seven laurel leaves this: "IAE, IEO, Sons of Sabaoth, in the Name of the Great God, imprison KATANIKOTAEL." Then the leaves are washed with water, and the water sprinkled in the house, from the inside to the outside.

Saphathorael causes people to fall down and become drunk. To combat him this is to be written on paper and hung around the neck: IAEO IEALO IOELET SABAOTH ITHOTH BAE.

Bobel, or Bothothel, causes all troubles of the nerves. This formula will dissipate his effects: "ADONAEL, bind BOTHOTHEL."

Kumeatel causes shivering and morbid drowsiness. The invocation against this is: "ZOROEL, bind KUMEATEL!"

Roeled, who makes people have colds and pains in the stomach, is put to flight by these words: "IAG, go, thou art cold, Solomon is more wise than eleven fathers!"

Atrax is the evil genius who makes men feverish. To rid the patient of it, coriander is pounded, and this spell spoken: "I exorcise this unclean fever, by the Throne of the Omnipresent God! Arise, dirt, and leave this creation of God!"

Ieropael causes cramp and convulsions. These words are to be said, three times, into the right ear of the patient: "IUDARIZE, SABUNE, DENOE!"

Buldumech brings discord between married couples. He is banished by merely writing the names of the ancestors of Solomon on paper, which charm is left in the house. The charm is thus: "Thou art commanded by the God of Abram, and the God of Isaac, and the God of Jacob – leave this house in peace!"

Naoth afflicts the knees. He is subdued only by a charm with these names on it: PHNUNOBOEL, NATHATH.

Mardero is another who causes fever. This charm against him is written on a piece of paper, and hung around the neck: "SPHENER, RAFAEL, do not pull me, do not lash me!"

Alath causes children to cough. This can be overcome by the words: "ROREX, follow ALATH!"

Neftihada causes the reins to ache and dysury. He is banished by a talisman with these words written thereon: IATHOTH, URUEL, NEFTHADA, fixed on the loins.

Akton is at the root of backaches and pains in the ribs. These can be cured by a copper amulet, made from metal of a ship which had not anchored, with these words on it: "MARMAROTH, SABAOTH, pursue AKTON."

Anatreth is the demon which causes internal fevers. The cure for these is simple: repeat "ARARA CHARARA".

Pheth is the evil spirit to whom tuberculosis and haemorrhoids are attributed. The patient has to drink sweet wine, which has been addressed with these words: "I exorcise thee, by the eleventh aeon, to stop, I demand, FETH, AXIOFETH!"

Anoster causes bladder troubles, and the like. To cure these, and dismiss the attentions of the spirit, three laurel seeds are pounded into oil, and smeared on the affected part, with the words: "I exorcise thee, ANOSTER! Stop, by MARMARAO!"

Alleborith. This is the spirit who is troubling those who have inadvertently swallowed a fish-bone. To get rid of him, it is necessary to take another bone out of the fish, and then cough.

Hephesimireth is the cause of lingering diseases. When this is present, "get salt, rub it in the hand, cast it into oil, massage the patient with it, and say: 'SERAFIM, CHERUBIM, aid me!'"

Ichthion causes paralysis, and he is driven away by the cry of "ADONAETH, help me!"

Agchonion is the enemy of infants. Those obsessed by this demon are to write on fig leaves: LYCURGOS, YCURGOS, KURGOS, YRGOS, GOS, OS.

Autothith causes enmity and all sorts of disturbances. Those who are troubled by him are told to write ALPHA and OMEGA.

Ftheboth is he who casts the Evil Eye. He can be driven away by a drawing of an eye which has become afflicted.

Bianakith is the cause of decomposition and disease. Protection against him is gained by writing this on the front door of the house: MELTO, ARDU, ANAATH.

This completes the catalogue of important demons who presented themselves to Solomon. As they came, he assigned them work on the Temple. His popularity increased, continues the *Testament*, and even kings came to see the Temple, bringing valuable gifts for it.

Then, after several other magical activities – such as sending to Arabia for a demon – he fell in love with a fair Shunamite. For her sake he began to worship Moloch, and built a temple to Baal, Moloch and others. This was the downfall of Solomon, and he ends the document thus:

"For this I wrote this *Testament*, that who gets it may pray for me, and attend to that which is last and not that which is first, and hence you will find grace eternal. *Amen*."

Where was Solomon buried? The world's greatest traveller – Ibn Batuta – mentions a persistent legend that is still current in Tiberias, on the Sea of Galilee, today as it was seven hundred years ago: "In this town is a mosque, the Mosque of the Prophets, and in it the graves of Shu'ayb (Jethro) and his daughter (the wife of Moses). Here, too, are the graves of Solomon, Judah and Reuben."

CHAPTER XII

CORNELIUS AGRIPPA: ON CALLING SPIRITS

BEING, AS THEY are, generally more or less concentrated expositions of ritual magic, most grimoires leave the reader with the feeling that they lack something in terms of connected advice. For this kind of elaboration upon the meanings and procedures of the rites we must, of course, look to the occultist commentators. Chief among these is undoubtedly Francis Barrett, who inspired the Frenchman Constant (Levi) and was a follower of the Fourth Book attributed to the redoubtable Cornelius Agrippa.

Since the study of magic's most absorbing exponent – Barrett – is outside the direct scope of this present work and because the present writer is even now engaged upon editing his masterpiece, the *Magus*, it would be as well here to read Agrippa on spirits.

If you would call any evil Spirit to the Circle [runs Turner's eighteenth-century translation of Agrippa] it first behoveth us to consider and to know his nature, to which of the planets he agreeth, and what offices are distributed to him from the planet.

This being known, let there be sought out a place fit and proper for his invocation, according to the nature of the planet, and the quality of the offices of the same Spirit, as near as the same may be done.

For example, if his power be over the sea, rivers or floods, then let a place be chosen on the shore, and so of the rest.

In like manner, let there be chosen a convenient time, both for the quality of the air – which should be serene, quiet and fitting for the Spirits to assume bodies – and for the quality and nature of the planet, and so, too, of the Spirit: to wit, on his day, noting the time wherein he ruleth, whether it be fortunate or unfortunate, day or night, as the stars and Spirits do require.

These things being considered, let there be a circle framed at the place elected, as well for the defence of the invocant as for the confirmation of the Spirit. In the Circle itself there are to be written the general Divine names, and those things which do yield defence unto us; the Divine names which do rule the said planet, with the offices of the Spirit himself; and the names, finally of the good Spirits which bear rule and are able to bind and constrain the Spirit which we intend to call.

If we would further fortify our Circle, we may add characters and pentacles agreeing to the work. So also, and within or without the Circle, we may frame an angular figure, inscribed with such numbers as are congruent among themselves to our work. Moreover, the operator is to be provided with lights, perfumes, unguents and medicines compounded according to the nature of the Planet and Spirit, which do partly agree with the Spirit, by reason of their natural and celestial virtue, and partly are exhibited to the Spirit for religious and superstitious worship.

The operator must also be furnished with holy and consecrated things, necessary as well for the defence of the invocant and his fellows as to serve for bonds which shall bind and constrain the Spirits.

Such are holy papers, lamens, pictures, pentacles, swords, sceptres, garments of convenient matter and colour, and things of like sort.

When all these are provided, the master and his fellows being in the Circle, and all those things which he useth, let him begin to pray with a loud voice and a convenient gesture and countenance. Let him make an oration unto God, and afterwards entreat the good Spirits. If he will read any prayers, psalms or gospels for his defence, these should take the first place.

Thereafter, let him begin to invocate the Spirit which he desireth, with a gentle and loving enchantment to all the coasts of the world, commemorating his own authority and power. Let him then rest a little, looking about him to see if any Spirit do appear, which if he delay, let him repeat his invocation as before, until he hath done it three times.

If the Spirit be still pertinacious and will not appear, let him begin to conjure him with the Divine Power, but in such a way that all the conjurations and commemorations do agree with the nature and offices of the spirit himself.

Reiterate the same three times, from stronger to stronger, using objurgations, contumelies, cursings, punishments, suspensions from his office and power and the like.

After all these courses are finished, again cease a little, and if any Spirit shall appear, let the invocant turn towards him, and receive him courteously and, earnestly entreating him, let him require his name. Then proceeding further, let him ask whatsoever he will.

But if in anything the Spirit shall show himself obstinate or lying, let him be bound by convenient conjurations, and if you still doubt of any lie, make outside the Circle, with the consecrated Sword, the figure of a triangle or pentacle, and compel the Spirit to enter it. If you would have any promise confirmed upon oath, stretch the sword out of the Circle, and swear the Spirit by laying his hand upon the Sword.

Then, having obtained of the Spirit that which you desire, or being otherwise contented, license him to depart with courteous words, giving command unto him that he do no hurt.

If he will not depart, compel him by powerful conjurations and, if need require, expel him by exorcism and by making contrary fumigations.

When he is departed, go not out of the Circle, but stay, making prayer for your defence and conservation, and giving thanks unto God and the good angels. All these things being orderly performed, you may depart.

But if your hopes are frustrated, and no Spirit will appear, yet for this do not despair but, leaving the Circle, return again at other times, doing as before.

And if you shall judge that you have erred in anything, then you shall amend by adding or diminishing, for the constancy of reiteration doth often increase your authority and power, and striketh terror into the Spirits, humbling them to obedience.

Hence some do use to make a gate in the Circle, whereby they go in and out, which they open and shut as they please, and fortify it with Holy names and pentacles.

This also we are to take notice of, that when no spirits will appear, but the master, being wearied, hath determined to cease and give over, let him not therefore depart without licensing the Spirits, for they that do neglect this are very greatly in danger except that they are fortified with some sublime defence.

Oftentimes also the Spirits do come, although they be not visible (for to cause terror to him that calls them) either in the thing which he useth, or in the operation itself. But this kind of licensing is not given simply, but with a kind of dispensation with suspension, until they shall render themselves obedient.

When we intend to execute any effect by evil Spirits where an apparition is not needful, this is to be done by making the required instrument or subject of the experiment itself, whether it be an image, a ring, or a writing, any candle, character or sacrifice, or anything of the like sort.

The name of the Spirit is to be written thereon, with his character, according to the exigency of the experiment, either writing with blood or using some perfume agreeable to the Spirit, making also frequent prayers to God and the good angels before we invocate the evil Spirit, and conjuring him by the Divine power.

PART IV

MAGICAL POWER THROUGH TALISMANS

CHAPTER XIII

SECRETS OF THE MASTER APTOLCATER

THE BOOK OF POWER

Cabbalistic Secrets of the Master Aptolcater, Mage of Adrianople, handed down from the greatest antiquity. Translation commenced on the Sixteenth day of June, 1724.

THE FOLLOWING PAGES embody my transcription[1] of an unusual magical manuscript of the eighteenth century.

Although I have made a close study of available occult documents in an attempt to trace another copy, I have not so far come across one: and it is therefore possible that this MS is unique. Certain it is that this codex has not been before published in printed form.

References to King Solomon and certain similarities with ritual magic point to the possibility of this book originating – in one form or another – in that Middle Eastern area from which the Babylonian and Semitic magical lore flourished. While it is not mentioned in the great bibliographies of the

[1] This is essentially a transcription. Editing and modernisation of spelling and phraseology have been thought desirable, in the interests of clarity.

era of Arab expansion and culture, there is a likelihood that the work, if extant in the Middle Ages, would be preserved with some secrecy by the magicians and alchemists in whose libraries it would be preserved.

Following up a rumour that there was a copy of this *Book of Power* in the Library of Aya Sofia cathedral in Cyprus, I examined the large collection of Persian, Arabic and other manuscripts there in 1951, without result. Examination of Gnostic gems and literature on Gnosticism, too, has provided nothing that links with this creed. I have examined the available works of this nature in the French libraries – such as the Arsénal – in the British Museum and the Oxford Bodleian, without success. I can also vouch for the fact that there is no copy with this content (though there *are* manuscripts similarly named) in the immense libraries of Deobund in India, Al-Azhar in Egypt[1] or in the vast treasure-house of ancient tomes which is the Library of the Holy City of Mecca.

Wherever I have found indications of a link with other magical systems and operations in the text, this has been mentioned in footnotes.

THE BOOK OF POWER

Cabbalistic Secrets of the Master Aptolcater,[2] Mage of Adrianople, handed down from the greatest antiquity. Englished from the Greek by J. D. A., under the patronage of Master A. N. K. B., and commenced on the 16th day of June, in the Year of Our Lord 1724.

[1] The world's oldest university, whose library is immense.

[2] Probably 'Abd-el-Kadir – 'Servant of the Powerful' (God).

1. To overcome enemies of every kind

Write this square, which follows, on white cloth with red or black colour. This is to be done at the New Moon. Carry the spell with you, and it is better sewn to the clothing in the region of the heart. When it is desired to overcome enemies, the word AIAKAN is to be spoken, with the head to the East; and then twice again, to the North and West. Here follows the square:

A I K N
P R M C
D H T R
M M P M

2. To be revenged upon one that has done you hurt

Say RAIZINO seven times, to the points of the compass, when you are alone, after nightfall. Then take a blue wood pen, and write this square upon a dried, triangular leaf:

R A I Z I
I Z I A R
A Z B G D
B M M T M

When the leaf is complete, it must be burned in a lamp flame which has not been out for more than three hours at a time. And there must be no other person within three hundred paces of you when you work. It is best to do this in a place where no person visits, and always to carry with you a quantity of black cord, tied around your right arm.

3. The killing of men by magic

There is great evil in the killing by magic. It is not allowed by God or man, and surely there cannot be any doubt on this point. But it was done in times gone by, and this was the manner of their working:

A square with the number equal to seven times seven was made, and this was made in iron on a plate of lead, and then was hanged in a running river for the space of seven times seven days. When it was ready, it was brought by night back to the place where the experiment was to be made. Then there were needed: a widow's tear, the three first stones from the river bank, and shoes which had not been used for a year. All these things were taken, and placed with the talisman in a box of wood which had been made without nails. This was then buried, and the place where it lay was to be known to no man. When it was required that the spell should work, the Worker made a picture of the things, and this he burned in a fire of white wood, and he said words over them. And these words were EOO EOO EOO MMOO ADADBASANA. And these words he said seven times seven times, and then the man died.

And when it was all done at night, it was better, and there was nothing seen of it by others.

A man was killed by another man by this square:

M M B A B
B A B M M
M M B B A
A B B M M

It was written in white ink, made from clay and water, and on a black cloth, and the man who was to be killed was to wear it near to his body. Then the man who was killing the other man writes it again five and twenty times, on green silk, with a black ink. And it was done three hours after the dark, and five hours after the dark. And if the man wore it not, then he would only sicken, and die after seventy days. Otherwise he died in three days.

4. To travel instantly from one place to another by magic

The genie AMPHAROOL presides over instant travel to all places, and he is the genie who was called by King Solomon the King of the Genies of Flying. "And he comes to you when you know his name, and it is thus":

A	M	PH	A
R	O	L	A
M	PH	A	R
O	L	A	M

And this is the way in which it is done. Five days after the full Moon, five things are to be taken: and they are five stones, each one from a place where no sun is seen. Then the magician, taking his hat and shoes in his hands, goes to a place where there are high winds, and he calls out in a loud voice, so that the genie may hear him. And he calls upon him in these names: "AMPHA, ROLA, MPHAR, OLAM," as it is written in the square. And the numbers of the words are also used.[1]

1 This almost certainly refers to the 'ABJAD' notation system, shared by the Hebrew and Arabic languages, in which every letter had a numerical equivalent.

The genie will come, and he will be high, and upon his back is a sack. In the sack, if you ask for it, is the Ring of Travel, and he will give it to you. And this ring is to be kept in a small woollen bag, and is to be rubbed with quicksilver every thirty days. And when he comes, he is to be spoken to as an Amiyre, and he is an Amiyre of the genii, and he speaks to you in all tongues, and also tells the manner of learning them.

Where the word Amiyre occurs here, it almost certainly stands for the Arabic word Amir or Emir – a prince. There are several varieties of Emirs. Meaning literally 'Commander', it is generally applied to princes in the Arab lands, and was formerly the title of the Caliph: Emir-el-Momenin, Commander of the Faithful. In this context it probably stands for 'prince or commander of Genies', and not for 'descendant of the Prophet Mohammed', as bearers of this title were sometimes styled in Ottoman Turkey.

Later in the manuscript another – and even more curious process for travelling instantly from one place to another is included.

To travel from one place to another, by flying as fast as the fastest hawk

This is a great secret, which was known to the sages of the earliest days, and it is known to some today, though the art was for some time lost.

Take snow, and boil it with oil, on a fire of two kinds of wood (one white, the other red), and then put the mixture in a bag made from a sheep's bladder. When this has been in the bladder for a moon and a half, allow the mixture to run into charcoal, and when it is all taken up, powder it upon an alabaster table. This powder is placed in a horn and when you want to fly, take a pinch of the powder, and place it within the pages of a book, and then put the book in your robe, in a place which has been prepared for it.

You will then take the book and sit with it in your hand, and think of the place to which you are to fly. And this takes longer at first. And when you are ready to fly, and will feel tired, and then you are to say, "SISPI, SISPI," and you will instantly be at your destination.

When you want to return to the place from which you started, you are to say, "ITTSS, ITTSS," and you will be back. And it is related of a king of former times that he used in this way to rule two lands, and moved so rapidly from the one to the other that it was not known until after a revolt took place and he had fled from the first kingdom, that he was the king of two lands.

5. *Protection from evil spirits and the mischievous*

When you are performing a magical operation, whether it be of alchemy, or the white or red magic, it is best always to have this square written on paper and bound to the left arm:

S D D D C
H T L T B
S D D D C
H T L T B

And this is the talisman that David gave to Solomon the King, and with it he first was able to become pure, and thus he attracted the first good spirit, and he brought the others to him, and he learned the magical arts. So it is of great value.

6. *To stop any man, animal, boat or cart from moving*

This talisman came from India, and it was there much used against the insurrectionists by the kings of that land. And when they had learned it, they were able to rule without fear, and the enemies were unable to conquer them.

The square is written on a green leaf with another leaf, in yellow ink, at any time of the day or night:

1	21	63	7
21	7	1	21
9	19	91	9
12	4	6	8

The use of this figure is simple and works at once. When you would use it proceed thus:

Look at the bird, or animal, or man or boat or cart, while holding this leaf in your left hand. Pronounce the words [*sic*] "1 21 63 7" and then the words "12 4 6 8" until they take effect, which is rapidly. You must say the words quickly, and not in a high voice. And if there is any fear in you, or any doubt, this will not happen. For you must learn that doubt is the destroyer of works of magic, and thus be careful of your processes and your fear.

You must not tell anyone when you are doing this thing. If you tell one, then he must promise, in his blood, that he will tell no more than one person. And when you are working, your head must be covered, and if it is covered with a yellow cloth, it is better.

7. To cause love between two people

Take three strings, one of each of the colours of earth, the sun, and the moon. These are taken, and placed tied together in a small jar of earthenware. When they have lain there for six days, add a little of the juice of the jasmine flower.

Press all together. From this will be made an ink, which is to be used to write the square. Then take a piece of white cloth, that has been steeped in the water of barley and dried. Upon this cloth, with the ink, write the square. The square is to be written at the first hour of day, when you can first see. And it is better to wait in the dark with the things, until such times as you are able to see them clearly, and then start to write the square. It is as follows:

H B B N N
R H B N R
B R H B N
N B H R B

And when this square is complete, place it between two flat stones, in your room. When it has been there for two nights more, take it out, and say the names of the people that are to love each other to it, in a loud voice. Repeat this for three days more. Then the result will be accomplished.

8. To raise storms

A storm comes under the power of the mountain genie, whose name is ARRIDU. So you are to make a square with his name, and write it upon any metal with a pen of red. It is necessary to call the spirit, to ask him to make the storm. And this is done thus:

Go to a deserted spot. Stand facing the West. Then pick up stones from the place where you are. One must be from the front, and one from each side. These four stones are then placed in a small cotton bag, which is hanging from your belt. When you pick them up, say: "YARRIDO." And do not look at anything that you may see, and do not fear anything that you may hear.

When you return to your house, bathe from head to foot in water in which a little salt has been put. Then, when you have dried yourself, take the four stones, and place them upon the talisman of the genie, and he will appear to you.

You can make him come at any time, by placing the stones thus. When he comes, he will speak with a low voice, as if from the air. Then you will invite him to come down, and to have a small piece of bread that you have baked for him.

If he comes, he will be like a man covered with much hair, and dressed in the manner of a servant. Then he will talk of many things, and will tell you that there are secrets known to him. Ask him to tell you some secret, and he will refuse. Then say to him that he must do something for you. And he will agree, but will say: "I cannot tell you anything." Say: "I want to know nothing, but you will help me."

Then tell him that you want a storm to be raised; and tell him the name of the place where the storm is to be, and the duration of the storm.

He will not depart until you have accepted from him a stone which is white and red. This is his sign, and if you put it in a ring of copper, he will come when you place it in water. But with the ring he will not come in his own shape, and you will be able to see him and others not. So, too, you will be able to talk to him without speaking, and to see him when he is not there.

Then he will go, and he will start the storm at the time you have laid down.

9. To cause discord between two people

Discord is an evil thing, and it is to be done only between those who are deserving of it, and it is done in this manner. This square is written with an iron point on lead:

H D H D H
I D I D I
D H D H D
D I D I D

Take the square, and sew it into a leather cover. This is to hang about your neck. Then say the words ROUDMO and PHARRUO seven times to each quarter of the globe, and in a loud voice, when you are desirous of creating discord. Then, when you want that any two people should fight, say their names, and then under your breath: "FIGHT, FIGHT, ROUDMO." And they will start to fight.

And when you want to stop them, say OMDOR, and they will stop. And in this way were many wars stopped in former times, especially those between the enemies of the faith. And if you would stop others from attacking you, then say the same word yourself, with your eyes fast closed.

10. To speak to whomsoever you wish, when they are absent

This is one of the most advanced arts, and it needs preparations greater than the general magical things. You must fast for seven days, without touching even water, between the hours of dawn and sunset. Then you are to say the numbers which follow seven times seven times to yourself, with your head in each direction that is possible. These are the numbers: 1, 9, 2, 5, 4, 9, 6, 5, 3, 3.

Then you are to think of the person that you will talk to, and think hard of every thing about him, and then say all these things about him to yourself, in a loud voice. And if he does not know that you are going to talk to him, you will have to make the experiment at night, so that he will hear you during sleep.

Then you are to take three vessels of water. One is full, the second is half-full, the third is empty.[1] Take pebbles to the numbers which I have already given, and these you will drop into first the first vessel, then into the second, and so on, until all jars have an equal number of pebbles in them. Then say all the numbers silently into the jars.

Then you will say the message that you have to say, into the jars, once into each, and you will have another empty one, for the answer.

If you want an answer, then you have to put your ear to the fourth jar, and listen for the answer. And you will hear it if all has been done aright. Should you hear no answer, you will hear that there is a sound as of a cricket from the jar, and this is to say that you have made some error, and you are again to try. When you have done this seven times, you will be able to speak to anyone as easily as if he were present by day or by night, and he will answer you, whether he wishes to or not, and whatever he is doing at the time when you speak to him. But until you are well practised at this art it is sometimes difficult at the beginning. And many make the mistake of listening to the jar before they have completed the rites, and this is folly, because it is not possible for the genie of the jars to help when you are listening.

[1] [*Sic*].

11. To overcome envy

If you know who is your enemy, this is better. Then take a small piece of liver, and tie it up in a scrap cut from a scroll. Then hang this up near the fire, and look at it with anger, as if it were your enemy. Then write this square on paper and burn it at once:

6 66 848 938
8 11 544 839
1 11 383 839
2 73 774 447

When the man or woman who envies you is troubled by this, he will come and ask you to forgive him. He will see in a dream that he has made a mistake, and that he must come to you to make amends, otherwise he will feel that he will die. And if the man is far away, and cannot come, you will know that he has repented when the liver takes the shape of a crescent, and then you will remove the spell. This you do by making the square again on paper, and placing it in water, until the writing has disappeared. And remember to think that you forgive him.

Envy and dislike can be prevented by taking a coin of silver, and making it square by pounding, and then writing the figures upon it, and keeping it in a woollen cloth, safe from any other person.

12. To gain the submission of men

Take a chain, a hook and a piece of wood three fingers broad. Tie these up with a cord which has no knots. Place them in a hole in the ground, where they will not be disturbed. Then write this charm on a piece of paper:

E EEE EEA
AEE EEE EAA
I I I I I I I I I

Look at this charm by the light of your lamp for one hour each night after it is the half night. Then take the charm, and boil it in clear water, until there is nothing left.

Look at your fingers which you must hold before you, while you repeat: "77.77.77.77. ANANANAN. KAKAKAKAKAK."

You will know soon that this is taking effect. And as soon as you feel this, go out into the street, and see that the first man to whom you talk will be respectful towards you, even though before he thought you a fool. And it is related of mages that many by this means who were dull at school later became famous, and the counsellors of kings. And this is the secret that is called the Treasure of Learning. And by it you may become respected, no matter what thing you undertake.

13. To transmute metals

Base metals cannot be transmuted into gold or silver without the talisman which follows:

1 5 8 A O
7 9 1 O A
1 8 5 O O
8 5 1 O A

This magical square has been used always by the great masters of the alchemistical art, and was to be found inscribed on all their apparatus, and upon the doors of their houses. "And the more times thou writest it, the greater will be the power thereof. It is to be written when the Sun is in Leo, or the Moon. And it is written on any place, or any material, but with a pen with a blade like that of a pointed knife. When you start your alchemistical experiments, make sure that this talisman is before you, and that its figures are always in your mind. And when you are starting a part of an experiment, make sure that you draw it anew. And this is not to be revealed to anyone whatsoever."

To transmute, you may use the way which has been handed down by the philosophers, or you may use this method:

Take a quantity of lead, and with it half the amount of black powder, and then half again of the red. This is to be mixed with mercury under the sign of Leo the Lion. And eight days and eight nights the whole is to be heated in a slow furnace, and it is to be bound with strips of a cloth and enclosed in a vessel of earthenware, and it is to have this sign upon it: D Z A B.

And when the time is passing, take care that you are pure in mind and body, and in spirit also, for this will determine the result. And read many times of the book that is prescribed.[1] And when you have finished these things, and the time is nigh, do not put out the fire, but make sure that it goes out with a gently decreasing heat, and that it loses its heat upon the eighth day. When this is all finished, bring a witness, for there must be one who sees the gold. And it is sufficient if this witness be an animal or a man. Open the vessel and take out the gold, and use it as you will. But it is better that the

[1] If the 'Book of Power' is of Islamic origin (as seems probable), this refers to the Koran.

gold be used before a year old. This is an experiment difficult of success. If anything is neglected, it fails, and if all is well it prospers, and if there is failure, you must try again and if need be again, until success comes. And remember that some part of this gold is to be given to the poor, up to two parts in a hundred.[1]

14. To obtain the Elixir of Life

Know first, that none lives for longer than his span, save by the permission of God. And therefore sages have written that this must be asked of God, before the water of life can be made. Alexander found the fountain and when he saw it, he was afraid, for the first time in his life, because he knew that there was much danger and fear therefrom. Therefore, if you are not afraid, prepare yourself with fasting and meditation for the space of forty days, and then when you are fortified, go out into the desert and seek a stone which is blue on one side and red on the other. This abounds in the deserts of Africa, and it is known when it is seen, for there is no other stone like it, and the two colours are separated by a white line. This is a stone, and it is not a stone; and those with wit will know.

When you have found this stone, you must take it to a place far from the world of men, and there you must make for it a sheath, which is of copper and gold, and mount it therein, with the figure of a bird inscribed on it, and the words LI LI LI NA NA AN.

Then you place it in water which you have brought from a running stream, and leave it there, alone and buried for the time during which seven moons wax and wane. And

1 Similarly, this may mean the Moslem 'poor-tax' of 2½ per cent, the *Zakat*.

then, taking with you new clothes, and having bathed and eaten nothing, repair to that place. When you have the stone in your hand, say the words again and again, and place it on your heart. When this is finished, put off all your clothes, and make a fire from them. Then take up the new garments, and robe yourself. If they are green and white, it is better. Then take the water that has been with the stone, and it is the Water of Life. Half of it is to be placed in a small container, and this is to be stoppered and carried with you. The other half is to be drunk, when the sun comes up. Then you will live for the period for which you have prayed to be spared.

But there is a strange thing about this. I have heard it said that every person who takes of the water of life longs for death in the end, and that beyond two hundred years he cannot live. So he must take the remainder of the water, and drink that, and he will then die at the appointed time.

15. *To make camels fight together*

This secret was much used by commanders in war, who wanted to cause confusion among the armies of their enemies. Draw the pictures of two camels on stones of different colours, and with inks of different colours. Then make a hole through each stone, and join the stones together with pieces of string. Then write the numbers of antipathy on one: 2, 3, 9, 4; and on the other, the accursed numbers of infidelity: 3, 333, 333, and then swing them by the string, so that the genies which are president over those numbers shall see and feel them, and the camels will begin to fight. But if you will cease the fighting, then say the numbers of unity and mystery: 1, 5, 7. They shall cease fighting forthwith.

16. To be warm in the cold

Make a talisman of leather, and hang it by means of a leather thong from your right arm. On it are to be inscribed the following signs:

——— ——— ———
——— ———
———

Then, when the moon is full, place the talisman in its rays, and make over it the signs that you have drawn, with your hand. Close your eyes, and pick up the object. This, whenever worn, will keep you warm in the cold; and formerly soldiers used this, when they were in the desert at nights. And you can prove it by taking off all your clothes when alone, and putting on the amulet.

17. To become cool in the heat

Take a piece of leather, which must be red, and on it draw these signs: | || |—| = | || —. Then, when the sun is at its highest, place the talisman in its rays, and make those marks upon it with your finger, and with your eyes looking at the sun. The talisman is to be kept wrapped up in cloth of gold until you need it. It is worn under the armpit.

18. To be brave

To be brave, a talisman must be made with these numbers on it:

23 23 23 23
58 85 88 55
25 28 28 25
52 82 82 52

The talisman is made of the tooth of an elephant, and the numbers should be inscribed at the fifth hour of the day, with a pen made of the horn of a goat which has been slain the day before the new moon.

Then place the talisman in a quantity of warm milk, and let it stand there until all the words [*sic*] have disappeared into the milk. Then take the milk and drink it, saying "S A M T D G K M" in your mind. After that there will be no more fear in your heart.

19. To gain honour at court

Wear your cap at all times, and inside it is to be embroidered in yellow silk these signs:

A D D 7 D 5 D A D D A

And the success will come to you after seven days. But on each night you must say fifteen times: "YARA YARA ANTARA"; for this is the name and sign of the genie which presides over success and honour. And he may appear to you or not. If he is to appear, he will leave beside your bed a brown leaf, and you will leave for him a jar of honey, which he will take, and place instead a white stone there. And when he comes, it will be as an old man, with a large head, and he will give you if you ask it a spear that can overcome everything, and which is made from the iron of the seven mountains. Remember that you must not thank him for this, as he will cause it to disappear if you do so.

20. To become learned and respected

Take a piece of polished brass, and upon the surface for three nights of the full moon drop a little water, and then polish it again. Then retire into a prepared room, in which there are to be a book without anything written in it, a pot of ink, and a pen made from a reed. Then, when you are ready to summon the genie, tap the mirror seven times with the pen. It will seem that you are asleep, and you will see him in the mirror. He will ask you what you want, and whose name you call. Say: "I call DUNA, and I seek knowledge." Then he will come nearer, and will answer to his name. Then ask him what you will, and he will write the answer in the book, without touching the pen. Then, if there is any book that you would commit to memory, ask him, and the next morning you will know it and you will never forget it thereafter. Tell him then: "Come, DUNA, whenever I shall call with this metal plate, and you are learned, and I am but an ignorant student." Then he will agree to come when you call him, and he will give you if you ask him a ring which will make you respected as a great sage. If you would that the power of learning become permanent, then eat each day no less than three eggs, and make sure that you eat salt before and after each meal.

There is one thing that takes away all honour, and that is if the person who is respected claims for himself any of the credit for having attained his learning, for that is an action against the genie who has given you of his knowledge.

21. To hear music whenever you want it

Call the name of the genie EL-ADREL, and when you do, wear on your head a cap of metal. And he will come, and will speak to you from a pot of water that you have placed on the table near you. Speak to him fairly, and he will cause you to hear what music you wish. And when you want the music to cease, call his name the other way about, and he will go away, and take the music. But you must not call him more than once in each day.

22. To be provided with food by spirits

Take a piece of glass the size of your largest finger, and place it above a green stone, and above this a leaf of a tree which has borne no fruit. Then, with your finger, make in the dust these words: AM MA ES OM. And when this is done, you must say: "AMESOM, come at once; come, and bring with thee that which is needful to me, the food that I want, and the meat, and the fruits and all things that I may eat a banquet."

Then a genie will come, more than four times the size of a horse, and shaped like a man, black, and with a smiling face. Speak to him like a friend, and tell him what you will eat. He will ask you to come with him to his table, but say: "I have reading and writing to do, and cannot stir from here, as I have made a vow." He will then disappear and return at once with whatever you have asked him in foods, and lay them before you.

Then he will seem to go, after speaking nicely to you. But he will not go, though you will not see him. Then you will ask him if he will share your feast, and he will come again and will sit with you and eat. And when you want to call him again, he will give you a name that you shall call, and he will come every time that you call.

23. *To cure all ills*

Take a large piece of black cloth, and place it in a cleft of wood that has been exposed to the sun for seven years. And to do this some masters formerly used pieces of wood from trees that were more than seven years of age, and used the wood that was nearest the sun. And it is also good to see the wood from the side of a house that has stood more than seven years.

Take then this wood and cloth, and place them in a white vessel which is half full of the wax of bees. Then place the whole over a slow fire, leaving it there for two days. Then add a quantity of wheat and boil the contents of the vessel in water. Place the mass obtained in a white cloth, and leave it to hang until the moon is full.

Then, after a whole moon, take a piece of the wax and place it in molten lead. The lead is made into a ring, which shall fit upon your first finger. Then, inside the ring, write the words: AL OML LA, with an iron point.

This ring is the talisman against all disease. When you wish to use it, put a black cloth on your head, and stand facing the sick man. Let him take your hand with the ring on it, in his hand, and repeat the words. Then take the ring off your finger, and place it in a little water, and give the water to the man to drink. Then will he stand up, cured.

24. *To become a proficient swordsman*

Take wax of bees, and out of it make small men and animals. They are to be like soldiers and like ordinary men. Then make a small man like you, but make it larger, and with a larger sword in his hand. Then break the swords of the other men, and say on it all: "AO AO AO APH." From that time you will be invincible, by the sword, just as were the heroes of old, who used this magic. But you must have with you the images at all times.

PART V

THE GRIMOIRE OF HONORIUS THE GREAT

CHAPTER XIV

PREPARING THE MAGICAL SKIN

THE GRIMOIRE OF HONORIUS THE GREAT

THIS IS THE black book generally considered among writers on the occult, both modern and ancient, to be the most diabolical work of black magic which has appeared in written form, at any time.

As its title shows, the book purports to be from the pen of Pope Honorius III, and it is universally denounced by Catholic writers as a forgery.[1] The book did not become current among magicians, so far as is known, until the seventeenth century, and was apparently originally written in Latin. It is thought not to be the same as another tome bearing the name of the same pontiff, the *Conjurations of the Angels*, reputedly issued in Rome during the middle of the sixteenth century.

The introduction to the work purports to be an actual Papal Bull instructing that the *Grimoire* be used for the purpose of invoking spirits, and adding to the functions of ordained priests that of controlling demons, by Apostolic authority.

Like the other grimoires, the writings of occult art ascribed to the great Honorius are hard to come by, and seldom so much as change hands in either the original manuscript form

[1] Almost unanimously – some merely ignore it.

or even the seventeenth-century printed versions. There are several other works bearing the same title (as is the case with the *Great Albert*) whose contents have no relation to the real grimoire, and were printed during the nineteenth century with the object of deceiving buyers into thinking that they were securing copies of the real book.

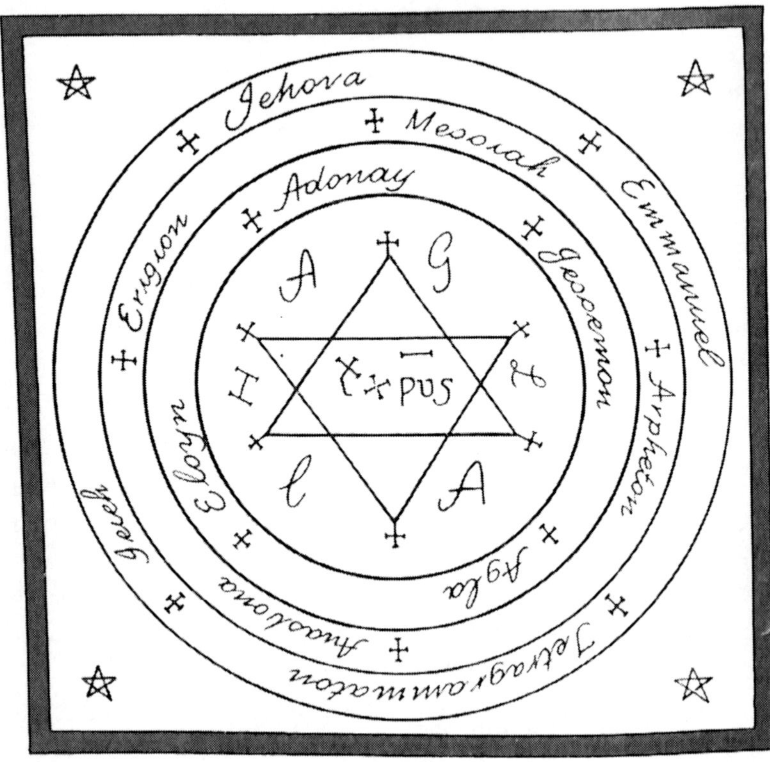

Honorius' 'Circle or Pentacle of Solomon', in which the magician stands during his conjurations

What are the arts disclosed in the *Grimoire of Honorius*: that most hated work of sorcery? In the first place, the arrangement has much in common with the traditional grimoire-pattern as contained in the *Key of Solomon* or the *True Grimoire.*

There are the same kinds of rites of purification, preparation for a sacrifice, and the ultimate conjuration of one or more spirits by means of a magical circle. There are, too, various cryptic texts to be inscribed on the kidskin, and so on.

The main departure from the general run of events is that this grimoire is loaded with Christian formulas and prayers. In fact, it was probably designed by a priest for the use of other members of the ministry, being an adaptation of the Solomonic – and hence Jewish – type of rite.

The following pages reproduce the notorious book in its entirety:

Introduction to the Grimoire of Honorius the Great

The Holy Apostolic Chair, to which were given the keys of the Kingdom of Heaven by these words, addressed to Saint Peter by Jesus Christ: "I give unto thee the Keys of the Kingdom of Heaven. To thee alone I give the ability to order the Prince of Darkness and the angels who are his servants, and who obey him with honour." And in these other words of Jesus Christ: "Thou shalt worship the Lord thy God, and Him only shalt thou serve." Therefore with the virtue of these keys the Chief of the Church has become the Chief of Hell.

But until the time of this Constitution, only the Ruling Pontificate has possessed the virtue and the power to command the spirits and invoke them. Now His Holiness, Honorius III, having become mellowed by his pastoral duties, has kindly decided to transmit the methods and ability of invoking and controlling spirits, to his brothers in Jesus Christ, the revered ones; and he has added the conjurations which are needed for this: and all is to be found in our Bull which follows.

The Bull of Pope Honorius III

Servant of the Servants of God. To each and every one of our respected Brethren of the Holy Roman Church, the Cardinals, Archbishops, Bishops, and Abbots;

To each one of our sons in Jesus Christ, the Priests, Deacons, Sub-Deacons, Acolytes, Exorcists, Pastors, Clerks whether Secular or Regular; upon you all health and the Apostolic Benediction. ✠

In the times when Jesus, the Son of God, the Saviour, of the tribe of David, lived on this Earth: we see what power he exercised over Demons. This power he passed on and communicated to Saint Peter with these words: "Upon this Rock I shall build my Church, and the Gates of Hell shall not succeed against it."

These were the words which were addressed to Saint Peter, he who was the chief and the basic foundation of the Church.

We, the undeserving Pontiff, elevated to this high office through the benignity of God, and inheritor as the successor to Saint Peter of the Keys of the Kingdom of Heaven, have the intention and desire of communicating this power over the spirits which we possess and which has until now been known only to those of our rank. By the inspiration of God, we desire to transmit and to share this power with our respected brethren and our esteemed sons in Jesus Christ. We feel that while exorcising those who are possessed they might become overcome at the frightful appearances of the rebellious Angels who were thrown into the Pit for their sins, for they may be not well enough versed in the things which they should know and use; and we desire that those who have been redeemed by the Blood of Jesus Christ should not be tortured by sorcery or possessed by a demon, and so we have added to this Bull the unchangeable manner whereby they may be invoked.

Because, too, it is correct and right that those who minister at the Altar should be able to exercise power over the rebel spirits, we entrust them herewith with the powers which have thus far been ours alone. And we command them, by our Papal authority, to follow that which follows this utterly without change: otherwise through some omission they may attract upon them the anger of the All-Highest.

The Ritual of Honorius: I. Preparation

As with the other major rituals of magic, this grimoire requires extensive preparations on the part of anyone who would treat with spirits. The magician, says the Pope (or pseudo-Pope), must first of all fast for the space of three days. After this he is to confess, and approach the Altar (of the Church, not of the Art). When this has been completed, the master will rise early the following day and intone the Seven Gradual Psalms, with the 'usual Litanies and Prayers', on his knees. Now he is to rise in the middle of the night on the first Monday of the month, and say one Mass of the Holy Ghost. After the consecration, he takes the Host in his left hand, and – being on his knees – he speaks this:

Orison

"My Supreme Saviour, Jesus Christ, Thou Son of the Ever-living God. Thou, who suffered death on the Cross, for the purpose of saving all humanity, Thou, who instituted this

Sacrament of Thy Body, before Thou wast left to Thy foes, and this out of extreme Love! Thou, who hast allowed us, miserable ones that we are, the honour of daily re-enacting this fact! Do Thou vouchsafe to Thine unfortunate servant, who now holds Thy Body in his hand, the strength and power to apply his strength against the rebelled Spirits, that facility which has been given to him! For Thou art their real God, and I will call on Thy Name, for they tremble at it, and I shall cry 'JESUS CHRIST! JESUS,' come Thou to mine aid, now and for evermore! *Amen.*"

The next ritual is to procure a black cock, kill it after sunrise, and select the first feather of the left wing, which is kept carefully. Then the eyes are removed, and these, with the tongue and heart, must be dried in the rays of the sun, and powdered.

The disposal of the rest of the cock is to be done at the time of the setting sun, in an unknown place. Over the grave will be placed a cross one palm in height. Then, with his thumb, the operator writes these figures at each of the corners of the place of interment:

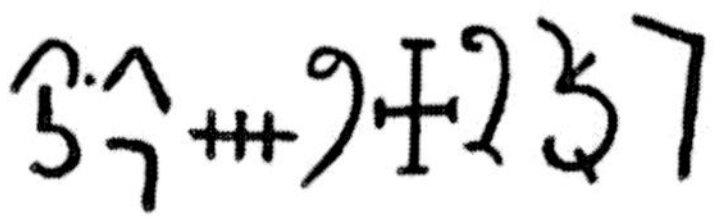

During this day the magician must eat no meat, and may not drink wine.

On Tuesday, at daybreak, a Mass of the Angels is celebrated. The feather from the cock is to be on the altar, and beside it a new knife. Taking the consecrated wine, the master then writes with it certain figures on a piece of virgin paper:

These are written while the paper is resting on the altar. When the Mass is over, the document is wrapped in a piece of new violet-coloured silk, together with the oblation and a part of the consecrated Host.

During Thursday night, the magician rises from his bed at midnight. He sprinkles holy water around the room, and lights a taper made from yellow wax, which has been made the day before, and it should be engraved with the sign of the Cross. As soon as this taper is alight, Psalm lxxviii is recited.

Then comes the Office of the Dead, and the recital of Matins and Lauds. Instead of the versicle of the ninth Lesson, this oration is substituted:

"Save us, O Lord, from the fear of Hell! Allow not the devils to destroy my soul, when I conjure them from the Pit, and when I order them to accomplish that which I desire. Let the day be light, let the Sun and Moon shine, as I call them! They are indeed terrible and of monstrous deformity: but do Thou restore to them their angel forms, when they come to do my bidding! O Lord, save me from those who have frightful faces, and permit them to obey me when I call them from hell, and when I order them to obey me!"

Then the operator puts out the taper. As soon as the sun rises, he will kill a male lamb by cutting its throat – though the blood must not touch the earth. Then remove the skin from the animal, and throw the tongue and heart into the fire. This must be a new fire, and the ashes are collected for further use later.

The lambskin is left in the middle of a field for nine days, and it is to be sprinkled with holy water four times a day during this period.

On the tenth day, before sunrise, the ashes from the fire are taken and spread over the skin, together with the cinders of the cock.

Then, after sunset (presumably the following day), the meat of the lamb is buried in a place unknown to anyone else, "to which no bird will be able to go". With the thumb of his right hand the sorcerer then draws certain figures over the burial-place:

For three days after this, the operator is to visit this grave, and sprinkle holy water at each of the four corners, with the words: "Pour upon me holy water, O Lord, and I shall be whiter than snow!" Before leaving the spot on these three occasions, he is to continue:

Orison

"O Jesus Christ, redeemer of all humanity, Thou who were made to suffer while pure, Thou who wert able and fit to open the book of life, deign to give unto this skin power to assume the signs that I shall make upon it, which shall be inscribed with Thy blood, in order that such inscriptions may be endowed with power to do that which I desire. And make it so that it will also repel the devilment of demons, who shall become afraid when they see these characters, and who will be able only to tremble as they behold them and approach.

"Through Thee, Jesus Christ, Thou who art ever-living, and rulest for ever and ever. So be it. *Amen*."

Following this oration, the Litanies of the Holy Names of Jesus are to be said. In place, however, of the Agnus Dei, say:

"Sacrificed lamb, be a tower of strength to me against devils! O Lamb which has been sacrificed, render me power against the powers of darkness. O Holy Lamb, vouchsafe unto me Thy beneficence for the purpose of binding the rebellious spirits. So be it. *Amen.*"

For the following eighteen days the skin of the lamb is pegged out. On the nineteenth day its fur is removed, and buried in the same place, after having been incinerated. These words are written above it by the operator, with his finger:

"VELLUS. May this, which has been burnt to cinders, be a shield against devils, in the Name of Jesus."

Then these signs are to be written, in the same place and manner:

And then the following:

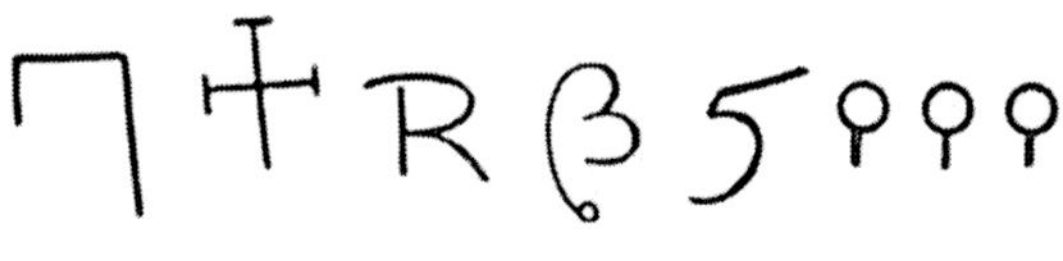

The skin is now to be put facing the east in the rays of the sun for three days, and these figures written with a new blade:

Now the magician reads Psalm lxxi, while writing these following signs:

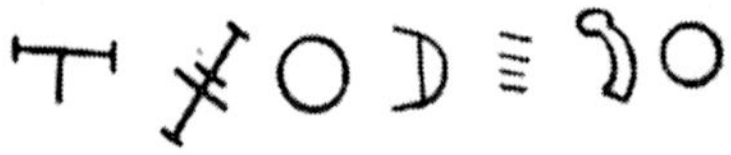

And after saying Psalm xcv in Latin, these marks are made:

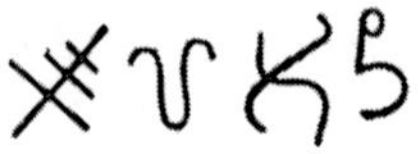

Then follows the intonation of Psalm lxxvii, while writing this:

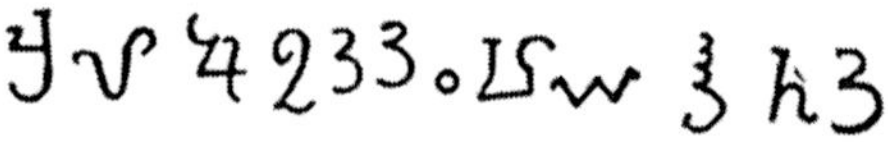

The final set of symbols is done as follows, when Psalm ii has been said:

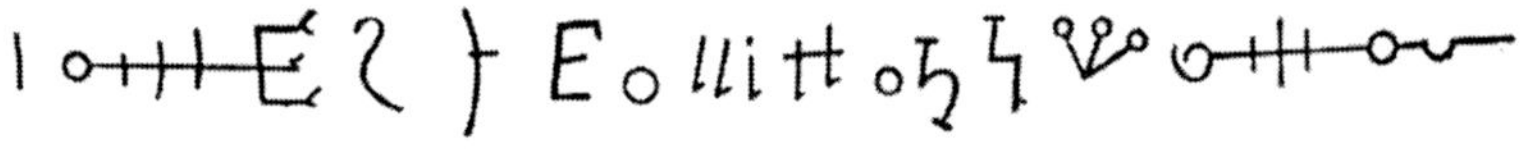

The operation ends with the recitation of Psalm cxv.

On the last day of the month the operator is instructed to offer a Mass of the Dead, leaving out the prose, and the Gospel of Saint John. At the end of the Mass the Psalm Confitemini Domino, etc., shall be said, and then the seventy-two Names of God, thus:

"In the Name of the Holy Trinity, the Father, the Son and the Holy Spirit, *Amen.*

"Trinitas, Sother, Messias, Emmanuel, Sabahot, Adonay, Athanatos, Jesu, Pentagna, Agragon, Ischiros, Eleyson,

Otheos, Tetragrammaton, Ely, Saday, Aquila, Magnus Homo, Visio, Flos, Origo, Salvator, Alpha and Omega, Primus, Novissimus, Principium et Finis, Primogenitus, Sapientia, Virtus, Paraclitus, Veritas, Via, Mediator, Medicus, Salus, Agnus, Ovis, Vitulus, Spes, Aries, Leo, Lux, Imago, Panis, Janua, Petra, Sponsa, Pastor, Propheta, Sacerdos, Sanctus, Immortalitas, Jesus, Christus, Pater, Filius Hominis, Sanctus, Pater Omnipotens, Deus, Agios, Resurrectio, Mischiros, Charitas, Aeternas, Creator, Redemptor, Unitas, Summum Bonum, Infinitas. *Amen.*"

And here follow the three smaller pentacles of Solomon, and the pentacles of the Gospel of Saint John:

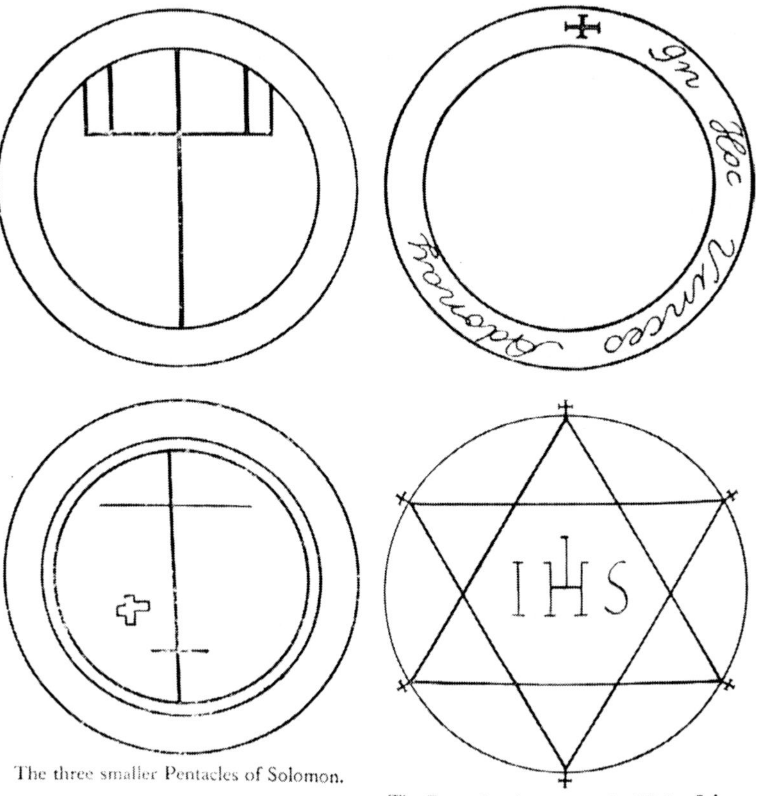

The three smaller Pentacles of Solomon.

The Pentacle of the Gospel of Saint John.

The Gospel of Saint John is read until the fourteenth verse. Then:

"Thanks unto God, Hosannah to the Son of David. Blessings upon Him who cometh in the Name of the Lord. Hosannah to the Highest. We call upon Thee, we glorify Thee, O blessed and splendid Trinity. Blessings upon the Name of the Lord, both now and for ever and ever. *Amen.*

"In the Name of the Father, of the Son, and of the Holy Spirit, Jesus of Nazareth, King of the Jews. May Christ conquer, reign, order and protect me from all evil. *Amen.*"

After this the Grimoire continues with the Great Conjuration:

"I, [NAME OF OPERATOR], conjure thee, Spirit, [NAME OF THE SPIRIT], by the Living God, by the true God, by the blessed and omnipotent God: He who created the Heavens, the Earth, the Sea, and all the things that are in them, from out of nothing.

"In the Name of Jesus Christ, by the power of the Holy Sacraments and of the Eucharist, and in the power of this Son of God who was crucified, who died, and who was buried, for our sake; He who rose once again, on the Third Day, and who is now seated at the right of the Supreme Creator, and from where He will come to be a judge over the living and over the dead; and likewise by the priceless love of the Holy Spirit, the Perfect Trinity:

"I conjure thee into this circle, O accursed [SPIRIT], by thy judgement, thou, who hast dared to disobey God. I exorcise thee, Serpent, and I order thee to appear immediately, in human form, well-shaped, in body and soul, and to comply with my commands without deception of whatsoever kind, and without either mental reservation: and this by the Great Names of God, the God of Gods and the Lord of all Lords:

"Adonay, Tetragrammaton, Jehova, Tetragrammaton, Adonay, Jehova, Otheos, Athanatos, Ischyros, Agla,

Pentagrammaton, Saday, Saday, Saday, Jehova, Otheos, Athanatos, Aliciat Tetragrammaton, Adonay, Ischyros, Athanatos, Sady, Sady, Sady, Cados, Cados, Cados, Eloy, Agla, Agla, Agla, Adonay, Adonay:

"I conjure thee, O evil and accursed Serpent, [naming the spirit], to appear at my wish and pleasure, in this place and before this Circle, immediately, alone and without any companion, without any ill-will, delay, noise, deformity or evasion. I also exorcise thee by the ineffable names of God, namely, Gog and Magog, which I am not worthy to speak. Come here, come here, come here. Satisfy me and my commands, without evasion or lie. If thou does not this, Saint Michael, the invisible Archangel, will soon strike thee in the deepest pit of Hell.

"Come, then, [naming the spirit], and obey me, and accomplish my desire."

Then the spirit must appear, unless there is something holding him back. If he does not come after the foregoing powerful conjuration, the following is to be spoken:

Compulsion of the Demon

"Why art thou delaying? Where art thou? What art thou doing? Prepare to obey me, thy Master, in the Name of the Lord, Bathat, flowing over Abracmens, Alchior over Aberer!"

Then the Pentacle is to be uncovered, with these words:

Command of the Pentacle

"See, then, this – the Pentacle of Solomon, which I show unto thee! I order and command thee, in the Name and Power of the Great God, *Adonay*, *Tetragrammaton* and *Jesus*. Come now, speedily, and obey me, without any guile or untruth, but verily, in the Name of the Saviour, of the Redeemer, Jesus Christ!"

The spirit must then come. When he has obeyed the operator in all things, he is to be dismissed with the Dismissal or Licence to Depart.

Dismissal of the Spirit

"Go, now, in peace, to your place(s). Let there be peace between us and you, and be ready to come at my call. In the Name of the Father, and of the Son, and of the Holy Spirit. *Amen.*"

When the Spirit has departed, a further prayer is addressed to the Deity, giving thanks for the successful completion of the experiment:

"All Praise and Hail to Him who is upon the Throne, He who is Everlasting. *Amen.*"

CHAPTER XV

THE LIBER SPIRITUUM

WE HAVE NOW seen how the skin is prepared, and the formulae for conjuring, binding and dismissing the spirits.

The remainder of the *Book of Honorius* is concerned with the Book of the Spirits, the making of the Circle, and the conjuration of certain individual spirits.

The Book of the Spirits

It is what may be called 'standard procedure' among sorcerers to make and consecrate this important book. Briefly, it is a small volume made by the magician himself, naturally from virgin parchment. In it he is to write the names of the spirits whom he is to conjure – one to a page. When the book is made and consecrated, it must be endowed with magical power by a strong conjuration.

The intention of the magician in making this book is to induce the individual spirits to appear, and to sign the book with their name and Sign. After this, they can be recalled whenever it pleases the master. There is an interesting illustration of two pages of one Spirit Book in Francis Barrett's renowned – though almost inaccessible – work, *The Magus.*

So well known is this type of book, that intending magicians for whom the *Grimoire of Honorius* was designed were not troubled in its pages with such details as the foregoing. They knew what a *Liber Spirituum* was: what they wanted to know was the correct method of conjuring and sanctifying it. This information is therefore graciously supplied by our author.[1]

The Conjuration of the Book of the Spirits

When the book has been prepared, it is addressed thus:

"I conjure thee, O Book, to be of value and utility to all those who use thee, that they may succeed. And I conjure thee again, by the power of the blood of Jesus Christ, which is represented in the Chalice of the Mass, that thou be of use to those who may use thee!

"I exorcise thee, O Book, in the Name of the Most Holy Trinity!" (Three times repeated.)

After this, the book is to be sealed, and should not be opened by any but a magician, and one who is moreover protected by pentacles. Just before the sealing of the book, this command is intoned over the book:

Command to the Spirits of the Book

"I conjure and I command you, O Spirits, however many you may be, to agree to this Book with alacrity, in order that when we may read it, since it is acknowledged to be in order and potentised, you will be compelled to appear when you are commanded, in a proper and human shape, as the reader of the Book shall desire.

"And you shall not in any way interfere with the reader, either in his body, his soul or his spirit, not by causing any

1 Compare *Key of Solomon*, above.

storm, noise, mischief or reluctance whatsoever, or cause such things to any person who may be with him!

"I command and conjure you to appear instantly when you are conjured, and to carry out with haste everything that may be written in the Book. You will obey, serve, inform, and execute services, within your province of power as may be the bidding of those who order you, and you will do this entirely without deviation or illusion!

"Should, through any reason, some of you Spirits who are thus invoked be unable to come when they are ordered to appear, they are compelled to send other spirits, who have been empowered to act for you, and they, too, shall swear equally to perform everything that the reader of the Book may command: you are all thus now compelled by the Holiest Names of the All-Puissant and Living God: Eloym, Jah, El, Eloy, Tetragrammaton! And this that you do properly and worthily carry out everything as commanded above.

"Disobedience on your part will cause me to consign you to torture for a millennium, which will be the punishment for any of you who do not accept this Book and its commands entirely!"

When this lengthy operation is over, the Book is ready for use. Supposing that the operator is ready to pass on to this experiment without delay, the *Grimoire* gives this oration to call the spirits:

Conjuration of the Spirits

"In the Name of the Father, and of the Son, and of the Holy Spirit! Attention, and come, all you Spirits! By the Power and the Virtue of your Kings, all the Spirits of the Hells are compelled to manifest themselves in my presence before this

Pentacle or this Circle of King Solomon, when I may call them!

"Come, then, at my orders, to accomplish what I desire, so far as it is within your powers! Come, then, from the East, from the South, from the West, and from the North!

"I command and conjure you all, by the Power of Him who is Three in One, who is Invisible, and who is Eternal, He who created the Heavens, the Sea, and all which is under Heaven!"

As soon as this conjuration is completed and the spirits appear, they have to sign the book by placing their mark thereon, as witnesses and parties to the contract to come when next called.

CHAPTER XVI

THE CIRCLE OF EVOCATION

NOW THE *GRIMOIRE* passes to the question of the erection of the Magical Circle, within whose defensive orbit every sorcerer must shelter against the wiles of spirits.

These, says Honorius, are to be made with charcoal, or they can be traced on the ground with holy water, which has been in contact with 'the wood of the Cross'.

When the tracing of the circle is completed, and the characters have been inscribed in the outer circle (as, it is supposed, given in the illustration which is reproduced here), holy water is sprinkled around it, to dissuade hostile elements from

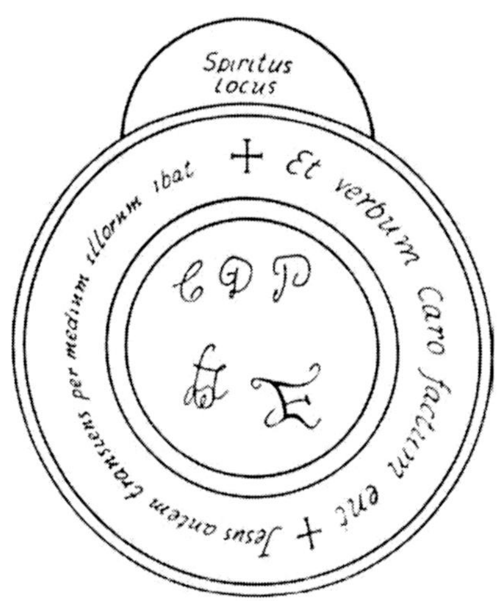

The Magic Circle, according to the *Grimoire of Honorius*

interfering with the rites. Then the magus takes up his place in the centre of his circle to order the appearance of the spirits.

As, however, anyone who has read thus far will know, the actual moment of making the circle is to be employed in speaking certain powerful words and phrases – the charging of the circle with potency:

Potentising the Circle, as it is drawn

"O Lord, to Thee do we flee for Thy Power! O Lord, confirm us in this Work! That which is working in us becomes like unto dust scattered before the Wind; and the Angel of the Lord coming, cause the darkness to vanish, and the flight of the Angel of the Lord upon us: Alpha, Omega, Ely, Elohe, Elohim, Sabaoth, Elion, Sady!

"See Thou the Lion who is the Victor of the Tribe of Judah, the roots of David. And I will open the Book, and the seven Seals of it; and I have seen Satan, like unto a thunderbolt, crashing from Heaven! It is Thou who hast given unto us the power to destroy the dragons and scorpions, and to crush all Thine enemies under Thy feet. We shall be protected, by the Power of Eloy, Elohim, Elohe, Sabaoth, Elion, Esarchie, Adonay, Jah, Tetragrammaton, Sady!

"The Earth belongeth unto the Lord, and all those who live within it, because it was He who fixed it upon the Seas, and made it between the waves. Who shall climb up into the mountains of the Lord, and who shall find acceptance in His Place? He who is innocent in hand and heart, he who has not borne false witness and whose soul he has not betrayed. He shall be blest by God, and shall reach salvation. He is of those who seek Him! Open your gates, O Princes, open those Eternal Gates, and then shall the King of Splendour enter. Who is the King of Glory? He is the Lord, the Almighty, the

All-Powerful in battle. Open the gates, O Princes! Lift up the Gates of Eternity. Who is the King of Glory? He is the Lord Almighty, the King of Glory. Glory be to the Father, and to the Son, and to the Holy Spirit!"

When the circle is completed, and these terrible words have been spoken, the conjuration follows, and then the dismissal of spirits made. A second kind of dismissal, by means of the Pentacle of Solomon, is given here, such as is usually used for reluctant spirits. Holding up the Pentacle of Solomon, the sorcerer pronounces these words:

Discharge of Inimical Spirits

"See, here, your sentence. See that which prohibits revolt against our orders, and that which orders that you return forthwith to your places!

"Peace between us and you, and be ready to come every one of you, when you are bid, to fulfil my desires."

Conjuration by means of the Great Pentacle of Solomon

Here follows a method of conjuring the Kings of the four points of the Compass, with the Pentacle alone, it seems. The *Grimoire* is obliging enough to state that this may be done at any time, and on any day – which is a considerable concession when it is considered that generally spirits may be invoked only at specified times ascertained by reference to the tables of times and days upon which their astrological signs or planets are ruling. "Should you seek the presence of only one spirit," continues the *Grimoire*, "then name him, and he alone will come."

CHAPTER XVII

CONJURATIONS OF THE KINGS OF THE DEMONS

Conjuration of the King of the East

"I conjure and I invoke thee, O *Magoa*, strong King of the East, by the names of God, and by my holy work! I order thee to obey me, to come to me, or otherwise to send at once to me *Massayel*, *Ariel*, *Satiel*, *Arduel*, and *Acorib*, that they may answer my questions, and obey my orders!

"Now come, thyself: and if thou refuse, I shall compel thee through all the virtues and powers of God!"

Conjuration of the King of the South

"I conjure and I invoke thee, O *Egym*, great King of the South, by the mighty and blessed Names of God, appear here, drest with all thy power! Come before this Circle, or otherwise send at once to me *Fadal* and *Nastrache*, that they may answer my questions, and obey my orders! If thou comest not, I shall compel thee by God Himself!"

Conjuration of the King of the West

"I conjure and invoke thee, O *Baymon*, powerful King ruling at the West, in the name of God! I order thee by the Power of the Most High, to dispatch to me instantly to appear before this Circle the Spirit *Passiel Rosus*, and all the other Spirits who are under thee, that they may answer all things that they are asked by me. If thou doest not this, I will compel thee by the Holy Sword of Fire! I will increase thy sufferings, and I will cause thee to be burned!"

Conjuration of the King of the North

"O King *Amaymon*, thou King and Emperor of the North, I call thee, and invoke and exorcise thee, in the Power and Name of the Creator of all, and by the Power of Powers! Send unto me instantly *Madael*, *Laaval*, *Bamlahe*, *Belem* and *Ramath*, and all the other Spirits that are under thee! Let them come here, in a pleasant and human shape!

"Wherever thou may now be, come here and give to me the submission that is to be rendered to thy Maker, the True and Great Living God! In the Name of the Father, of the Son and of the Holy Spirit: Come, then, submissively before this Circle; and that without danger to my body or my soul. Come, in pleasant and human shape, without frightfulness. Come now, I conjure thee!

"By all the Holy Names, *Sechiel*, *Barachiel*, and if thou disobey me or art slow, *Balandier*! Suspensus, iracundus, Origratiumgu, Partus, Olemdemis and Bautratis, N...!

"I exorcise thee, I invoke and compel thee with mighty conjurations, by the Power of the All-Powerful and Living

God, the True God, the Blessed God! And in the Power of Him who spoke, and all things were created, and by His Holy Commandment which made the Heavens and Earth, and all things contained therein. I conjure thee by the Father, and the Son, and by the Holy Spirit, and the Holy Trinity, and by the Power of God, which thou canst not disregard, and by the Power of whom I will bind thee!

"I adjure thee by God, the Father, by the Son, and by the Holy Spirit! By the Mother of Jesus Christ, the Holy Mother and Eternal Virgin! By her sacred Heart, by her Holy Milk, which was taken by the Father and the Son, by her Holy and Sanctified Body and Soul, by every part of the body of the Virgin! By the trials and afflictions, by the sufferings and troubles, by the agonies which she suffered throughout her life, by the tears which she wept, by the tears which she shed when her Son cried before His painful Passion and on the Cross! By all the sacraments and holy deeds, and by everything which is said and done on Earth and in Heaven, in the Name and to the Glory of our Saviour: Jesus Christ, of His Mother the Holy Mary, by the Church Militant, and for all the Saints!

"And also I conjure thee by the Holy Trinity and by all the Mysteries, by the Sign of the Cross, and by the priceless blood which came forth from out of the Body of Jesus Christ, and by the sweat of His Body, when He spoke in the Garden of Olives: 'My Father, let this Chalice pass from me, if it may be done.'

"And I conjure thee, by His death, and by His Passion, by His interment and His resurrection, by the Ascension, and by the coming of the Holy Spirit! I conjure thee too, by His crown of Thorns, by His blood, by the Nails of the Cross, by His tears, and His suffering undergone through His love for us!

"I adjure thee by the lungs, by the heart, the hair, and the members of our Redeemer Jesus Christ. I conjure thee by the judgement of those living and those dead, by the words of our Redeemer Jesus Christ, and by His preachings, and His words and His miracles, and by the infant in arms, and the crying child, and the child carried in the mother's virgin womb!

"I conjure thee by the power of intercession of the Virgin, Mother of Jesus Christ! And by everything that is from God and His Mother, as it is in Heaven, so be it on Earth. I conjure thee by the blessed Angels, and by the Archangels; and by all the ranks of the Spirits, by the holy prophets and the sages, by the martyrs and the witnesses! And I conjure thee by all the virgins of religion and the widows, and the holy saints, male or female. I conjure thee by the head of Saint John the Baptist, and by the Milk of Saint Catherine, and in the name of all the Saints!"

CHAPTER XVIII

CONJURATIONS OF EACH DAY OF THE WEEK

CONJURATIONS FOR SPIRITS OF THE DAYS

THE *GRIMOIRE* OF Honorius gives a very detailed system of conjuring various spirits, according to the day of the week upon which the experience is performed. Lucifer is conjured on Monday. A double circle is drawn with consecrated chalk. Within the outer ring is inscribed the formula: 'I forbid thee, LUCIFER, to enter within this Circle.'

Lucifer is invoked between the hours of eleven and twelve, or between the third and fourth hour. Before starting the conjuration the sorcerer should make sure that he has his Robes of the Art, and a mouse to give the spirit: for he demands a sacrifice. A flask of holy water completes the apparatus.

Conjuration of Lucifer

"O Lucifer, I adjure and invoke thee, in the Name of the Living and the True God, by the Holy God, who spoke and created all, He who commanded, and every thing was made!

"I conjure thee in the powerful Names of God: *On*, *Alpha and Omega*, *Eloy*, *Eloym*, *Ya*, *Saday*, *Lux*, *Mugiens*, *Rex*, *Salus*, *Adonay*, *Emmanuel*, *Messias*! I conjure and compel thee by the Names which are contained in the letters V, C and X, and by the Names *Jehova*, *Sol*, *Agla*, *Rijfasoris*, *Oriston*, *Orphitne Phaton*, *Ipretu*, *Ogia*, *Speraton*, *Imagon*, *Amul*, *Penaton*, *Soter*, *Tetragrammaton*, *Eloy*, *Premoton*, *Sitmon*, *Perigaron*, *Iratаton*, *Plegaton*, *On*, *Perchiram*, *Tiros*, *Rubiphaton*, *Simulaton*, *Perpi*, *Klarimum*, *Tremendum*, *Meray*! And by the powerful Names of God *Gali – Enga – El – Habdanum*, *Ingodum – Obu*, *Englabis*: come instantly, or else dispatch to me the Spirit named: N..., in a pleasant and human shape, and not objectionable in any way; in order that he may give answer truthfully to that which I shall ask him; and that he may be incapable of harming me, or any person who is with me, in our bodies and our souls!"

The conjuration of Frimost takes place between the ninth and tenth hours of the night. When the spirit comes, he is to be treated almost with deference. The circle is drawn, and within the concentric circles is to be written: 'Obey me, Frimost. Obey me, Frimost. Obey me, Frimost.'

The various characters of this spirit, as in the case of the other spirits of the days of the week are given, and are to be drawn within the circle, in accordance with the illustration provided by the maker of the *Grimoire.*

When the preliminaries have been started in the usual way, the conjuration commences.

Conjuration of Frimost

"O Frimost, I adjure and order thee, by all the Names which are able to bind and compel thee. I adjure thee, *Nambroth*, in thy name, and by the powers of all the Spirits, by all cyphers, and by the conjurations of the Jews, the Greeks and the Chaldeans, by thine own utterances of evil and ineptitude! If thou dost not come forthwith, and answer my questions and obey me in everything, I shall cause upon thee from day to day awful tortures and sufferings! And when thou comest, thou shalt be unable to do evil unto me, or to any of my companions, in our bodies or our souls!"

Wednesday – between the tenth and eleventh hours of the night – is the day set apart for the conjurations addressed to Astaroth. Those who would obtain the favours of rulers call him, and within his circle is inscribed 'Come Astaroth', three times repeated.

Conjuration of Astaroth

"O Astaroth, evil Demon, I adjure thee, in the Power and Words of God, the God of Power, Jesus the Christ of Nazareth, He who subdued all spirits, He who was born of the Virgin Mary! I conjure thee, by the Angel Gabriel the unknown! And in the Name of the Father, of the Son, and of the Holy Spirit! I conjure thee, in the Name of the resplendent Virgin Mary, and the Trinity, Most Sacred: for in their honour do all the archangels, the thrones, the dominions, the powers and the sages, the prophets, the apostles and the evangelists cry endlessly *Hosanna*, *Hosanna*, *Hosanna*, Eloim Sabaoth, Thou who Art, Wert and Shall Be, like unto a stream of fire! Do not disobey my ordinances, but come forthwith!

"I order thee, in the Name of Him who shall pass judgement with flames upon the living and the dead! He, to whom may be all Power and Honour!

"Come, then, instantly, and accomplish my desires! Come, and render homage unto the True Lord, the Living God, and to all His Works! Disobey me not, and be submissive unto the Holy Spirit, and in his Name I order thee!"

Silcharde comes, with the appearance of a king, when called with conjurations from a circle between the third and fourth night hour of Thursday. Those who would have disclosed to them hidden hoards would apply to him: but he requires the sacrifice of a piece of bread, which he carries away contentedly with him.

Three times the phrase 'By the Holy God' is inscribed within the double circle, and the character given in the illustration is described therein.

Conjuration of Silcharde

"O Silcharde, I adjure thee, by the face and form of our Redeemer Jesus Christ, He who pledged Himself for the whole of humanity by His death and Passion! He commands

that thou shouldst manifest thyself here and now! I order thee, in the Name of all the Kingdoms of God! I bind and conjure thee by the Holy Name of Him who trod upon the Asp, and who crushed the Lion and Dragon! Obey me, and carry out my ordinances, without the ability to do me harm, either in my body or my soul!"

On Friday the conjuration of Bechard is accomplished. Three times this invocation is written within the circle: 'Come Bechard.' His sacrifice is a walnut, which is to be handed to him when he appears. The times for Wednesday's operation are between the eleventh and twelfth hour.

Readers will recall, of course, that the hours mentioned in processes from grimoires refer to the planetary hours, and not to the normal clock times, as calculated in Chapter XIX of this present work.

Conjuration of Bechard

"O Bechard, I adjure thee and conjure thee, in the Names of God the Most Sacred, *Eloy – Adonay – Eloy – Agla – Samalabactay*, whether written in Hebrew, in Greek or in the Latin tongue; and by the Blessed Sacraments, and by the

Names written in this book. And I conjure thee by Him who made thee flee from the Heavens!

"I order, adjure, conjure and command thee, by the Power of the Holy Eucharist, which saves man from sin! I conjure thee to come, instantly, to execute my orders! And that without danger to my body or my soul, and without causing damage unto my book, or any harm to my companions!"

Saturday is the occasion for calling another of the spirits of Honorius: Guland, who demands the relatively small price of a present of a piece of singed bread to be given to him. He is credited in exchange with the faculty of doing whatever he is commanded. Inside the double circle of evocation is written the threefold invocation: "Enter not Guland", and in the centre his character is drawn.

Conjuration of Guland

"O Guland, I conjure and adjure thee, in the Name of Satan and Beelzebub, and in the Name of Astaroth, and in the Names of all the other Spirits! Do thou come instantly, before me! Come, now, in those Names, and in the Names of all the Demons!

"Come, I order thee, in the Name of the Most Holy Trinity! Come, without injury to me, to my body or soul, to my books or any other thing of mine! I order thee to manifest thyself, at once. Otherwise, thou mayst dispatch unto me some other Spirit empowered to act equally as thee, acting on my orders and subject to the conditions above, and that he shall not be licensed to leave this spot until he has accomplished this function!"

On Sunday the magician may address his invocations to Surgat, between the hours of eleven and one of the night.

Like many another spirit, Surgat is able to bring any treasure that he may be commanded. That he is one of the diabolical breed is evidenced by the fact that he will try to obtain a hair from the head of the exorcist: when, however, he asks for one, he is to be given one from a fox, with the precaution that Surgat contents himself with this. His circle differs from most others in that it has three rings. Inside are the characters of the Spirit. In the outer circle is written the words 'Tetragrammaton, Ismael, Adonay, Jhva', and a cross. The second circlet contains the threefold adjuration: 'Come Surgat.'[1]

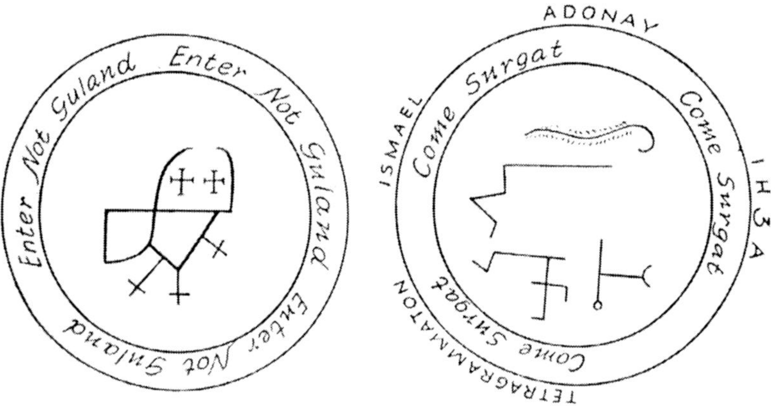

Conjuration of Surgat

"O Surgat, I conjure and adjure thee, by all the Names inscribed within this book, that thou come before this circle,

[1] The block given here is not entirely accurate. It should have a third circle around it, and the signs given in the block as I H Z A should strictly be J (or I) H V A (or H).

immediately and agree to obey my orders! Otherwise thou mayst send unto me another Spirit, carrying a stone which I may use to make myself invisible when I bear it. And I also adjure thee that thou must be submissive, either thyself or in the form of thy deputy, that everything that I shall ask shall be accomplished; and this without any hurt or injury to me or to any other person!"

CHAPTER XIX

HOURS AND TIMES FOR MAGICAL RITES

Albertus Magnus on the rulership of the days and hours by the planets, according to magical usage.
"And here fol[l]oweth in what hour every planet hath his Dominion...."

Method of Calculating Hours of the Planets for magical use[1]

In this section, Albertus Magnus distinguishes between ordinary time (that of the clock), and planetary time, as used by magicians. Briefly summarised, planetary time is arrived at as follows:

There are twelve planetary, or unequal hours in each day, and twelve in each night. The total of minutes of *actual daylight* are added together, and then divided by twelve. This gives the actual number of minutes in a planetary hour of the day. For instance: there are, say, sixteen hours of daylight in a given day. This is equal to nine hundred and sixty minutes.

[1] In the original text, this section follows the Third Book of Albertus Magnus.

Divided by twelve, this gives the number of minutes in a planetary hour: eighty minutes.

A similar calculation will give the length of the planetary hours of the night: eight normal hours ('dial-hours') equal four hundred and eighty minutes. Divided by twelve, this equals forty minutes to each hour of the night.

"AND that all things which hath been saide before, and all that followeth after, may be applied more easily to the effects of their desire which have no knowledge in the Starres: first, thou shalt note that an houre is taken two wayes: that is, equall and unequall. The equall houre is the houre of the diall or clocke, which is always equall [i.e. is always composed of sixty minutes].

"The unequal houre is considered, after that the dayes bee longer or shorter. For as the astrologers always consider the time in the which the Sunne standeth upon his halfe sphere. And they call it the houre of the day and by the contrary the night. They devide that time which they call the day, into twelve equall parts, which be the houres of the same day: and whatsoever is said of the day, thou must understand contrariwise of the night.

"And that thou mayest understand more clearly: put case the Sun commeth out from his halfe sphere at viii of the diall [clock]. We have unto the going downe of the Sun xvi houres of the dial, which we may multiply by lx, as there be lx minutes of every houre of the dial, and we shall have nine hundred and threescore minutes, which we may devide by twelve, as there be xii houres of the day. Applying to every houre his portion and count lxxx minutes in an [planetary] houre. Therefore every houre of a day shall have fourscore minutes, which shall containe an houre, and one third houre of the dial. And in all that time the dominion of the Planet of that houre shall be considered as the table here following shall make more manifest. At every houre of his night shall have but forty minutes, which thou shalt understand and likewise of others, according to the rising of the Sunne upon the ground; because that houre which is the middest between night and day, which is called the dawning of the day is not called the day, but the day is properly to be understood when the Sunne may be seene.

"THEREFORE thou willing to consider and know the domination and rule of every planet, then here you may see how in every houre every planet hath his dominion. Thou shalt consider the houres themselves, as I have before said, and so thou mayest come to the end of thy purpose. Also the beginning of the day is considered from one of the clocke of the day, going before afternoone.

"So divide the Sunday into two parts, and each twelve houres. So that the first hours of Monday beginneth after xii on Sunday, and one is the beginning on Monday. Wherefore thou art to consider that Sunday hath his signe under the Sunne..."

Albertus Magnus[1] here gives the rulerships of the days of the week, by planets. This material, which is repetitious, may be summarised thus:

Monday is under ☾ Moon.
Tuesday is under ♂ Mars.
Wednesday is under ☿ Mercury.
Thursday is under ♃ Jupiter.
Friday is under ♀ Venus.
Saturday is under ♄ Saturn.
Sunday is under ☉ Sun.

[1] Most grimoires concur in this correlation of days and planets, as with the succession of planetary hours, as given below. Cf. *Key of Solomon* and *Magical Elements* of De Abano.

The author continues that every "true thing must be done under his planet". It should be done on the proper day of the planet which governs the matter in hand. It, of course, follows from this – and it is emphasised – that magical operations are to be done in the actual hours which are 'ruled' by the planets which govern the operations.

Under Saturne	Life, building, doctrine, mutation;
Under Jupiter	Honour, things desired, riches, apparell;
Under Mars	Warre, prison, Matrimony, enemie;
Under the Moon	Policy, dreame, merchandise, theft;
Under the Sun	Hope, lucre, fortune, heir;
Under Venus	Friend- or fellow-ship, way, lover, stranger;
Under Mercurius	Losse, debt, feare.

Of the Houres of the Dayes and Nights

Here follows a full enumeration of the planetary rulerships of days and nights of every day of the week. As the matter is extremely long-winded, everything is to be gained by tabulating Albertus Magnus's planetary rulerships.

HOURS OF THE NIGHT

HOUR	SUNDAY	MONDAY	TUESDAY	WEDNESDAY	THURSDAY	FRIDAY	SATURDAY
1	♃ JUPITER	♀ VENUS	♄ SATURN	☉ SUN	☽ MOON	♂ MARS	☿ MERCURY
2	♂	☿	♃	♀	♄	☉	☽
3	☉	☽	♂	☿	♃	♀	♄
4	♀	♄	☉	☽	♂	☿	♃
5	☿	♃	♀	♄	☉	☽	♂
6	☽	♂	☿	♃	♀	♄	☉
7	♄	☉	☽	♂	☿	♃	♀
8	♃	♀	♄	☉	☽	♂	☿
9	♂	☿	♃	♀	♄	☉	☽
10	☉	☽	♂	☿	♃	♀	♄
11	♀	♄	☉	☽	♂	☿	♃
12	☿	♃	♀	♄	☉	☽	♂

The planets are always taken in the following succession: ☉ Sun, ♀ Venus, ☿ Mercury, ☾ Moon, ♄ Saturn, ♃ Jupiter, ♂ Mars. They follow each other in rulership of the hours, starting with the planet which rules the day itself, and also rules the first (planetary) hours of the day. Hence, Sunday is the day of the Sun; the Sun rules the first planetary hour, and is followed by Venus (second hour) Mercury (third hour) and so on:

Midnight-to-midnight Rulership of Days and Hours

Hours Of The Day

Hour	Sunday	Monday	Tuesday	Wednesday	Thursday	Friday	Saturday
1.	☉ Sun	☾ Moon	♂ Mars	☿ Mercury	♃ Jupiter	♀ Venus	♄ Saturn
2.	Venus	Saturn	Sun	Moon	Mars	Mercury	Jupiter
3.	Mercury	Jupiter	Venus	Saturn	Sun	Moon	Mars
4.	Moon	Mars	Mercury	Jupiter	Venus	Saturn	Sun
5.	Saturn	Sun	Moon	Mars	Mercury	Jupiter	Venus
6.	Jupiter	Venus	Saturn	Sun	Moon	Mars	Mercury
7.	Mars	Mercury	Jupiter	Venus	Saturn	Sun	Moon
8.	Sun	Moon	Mars	Mercury	Jupiter	Venus	Saturn
9.	Venus	Saturn	Sun	Moon	Mars	Mercury	Jupiter
10.	Mercury	Jupiter	Venus	Saturn	Sun	Moon	Mars
11.	Moon	Mars	Mercury	Jupiter	Venus	Saturn	Sun
12.	Saturn	Sun	Moon	Mars	Mercury	Jupiter	Venus

"And note that Jupiter and Venus be good, Saturn and Mars evill, but the Sun and Moon in a meane, and Mercurius is good, with good, and evill with evill."

Lucky and Unlucky Days of the Year, According to the *Grand Grimoire*

Month	Lucky dates	Unlucky dates
January	3, 10, 27, 31.	12, 23.
February	7, 8, 18.	2, 10, 17, 22.
March	3, 9, 12, 14, 16.	13, 19, 23, 28.
April	5, 17.	18, 20, 29, 30.

Month	Lucky dates	Unlucky dates
May	1, 2, 4, 6, 9, 14.	10, 17, 20.
June	3, 5, 7, 9, 13, 23.	4, 20.
July	2, 6, 10, 23, 30.	5, 13, 27.
August	5, 7, 10, 14.	2, 13, 27, 31.
September	6, 10, 13, 18, 30.	13, 16, 18.
October	13, 16, 25, 31.	3, 9, 27.
November	1, 13, 23, 30.	6, 25.
December	10, 20, 29.	15, 26.

CHAPTER XX

THE SPIRITS, PLANETS AND DATA OF MAGIC

The Power of the Planets

So closely bound up with the stars is magic that the terms astrologer and magician were formerly almost synonymous. It was not until the sixteenth century that writers of magical books troubled (as did, for example, Albertus Magnus) to give astrological advice to their readers – they were expected to be masters of star-lore already. But even the most accomplished magician preserved – written in his own hand – details of the correspondences of stars with demons, colours, signs and herbs: and much more besides. It was not enough to know the days and hours ruled by the planets – though this was fundamental. In addition the magician had to be sure that the work that he was performing came within the purview of the stars whose influences were supposed to be paramount during these times. Again, it would be vain to attempt to conjure spirits of, say, Venus (which rules Friday), on any day of the week but her own.

Among the correspondences to be observed were the use of the correct perfumes in the invocatory fire; the employment of the correct metal for inscribing the talisman of the day, hour or demon; the choice of the stone corresponding to the day in question. By selecting as many correspondences as possible of this nature, the magus could be sure that he was invoking a concentration of all the powers inherent in the items coming under the star which presided over the operation in hand.

When the magical circle was drawn, the characters of the planet ruling at the time of the experiment were included in addition to the sign of the planet and of the spirit whose aid was sought.

Here, then, in much the same form as one of these sorcerers' handbooks, are details of the 'considerations' for the seven planets used in magic, one for each day of the week:[1]

♄ SATURN, *ruling Saturday, under the Sign of Aquarius,* ♒

Perfume: black poppy seeds, henbane and mandrake, lodestone and myrrh, to which is added the brain of a black cat.

Sign of the Planet (SR): 

Wood to be burned in the Brazier: oak (KS).

Herb: assodilius (AL).

Demon of the Day: Guland, *alias* Nabam (GH).

Works for the Day and Planet: life, buildings, doctrines, meditation (KS).

Angels: Cassiel, Machatan, Uriel.

Sigil of Cassiel:

[1] Letters in parentheses refer to original Black Books – see List of Abbreviations.

Metal: lead (KS *et al*).

Olympic Spirit: Aratron. His Character:

His powers: changing anything into stone or gold, finding familiars, works of alchemy and magic.

Colours of the Pentacles of Saturn: black.

Other operations for this day: Saturday or Tuesday for making the Pentacles (LM), and also the Knife with the Black Handle (GV).

Astrological stone: Turquoise or Garnet.

Inscription of the Leaden Talisman of Saturn:

4 9 2
3 5 7
8 1 6

Function of this Talisman, works of Power. In the Hebrew notation, the figures stand for YH – Jehova (FB).

♃ JUPITER, *ruling Thursday, under the Sign of Sagittarius,* ♐

Perfume: ash plant, lignum aloes, storax, gum and lapis lazuli. This is made into a paste with the tops of peacock feathers, and stork's-blood or the brain of a hart.

Sign of the Planet (SR):

Wood to be burned in a sacrifice to spirits: pine.

Herb: henbane (AL).

Demon of the Day: Silcharde (GH).

Works for the Day and Planet: honour, desires, riches, clothing (KS).

Angels: Sachiel, Cassiel, Asasiel (HT).

Sigil of Sachiel:

Metal (for talismans, etc.): tin.

Olympic Spirit: Bethor.

His Character:

His powers: treasure, honours, riches, medicines, longevity.

Colours of the Pentacles of Jupiter, on Virgin Parchment: azure.

Other operations for this day: All unusual operations are to be performed on this day and in this hour. GV says make the knife and needle of the Art on this day.

Stone: sapphire, lapis-lazuli, cornelian. Also mentioned: turquoise, diamond, moonstone and pearl.

Inscription for the Talisman of Jupiter:

4	14	15	1
9	7	6	12
5	11	10	8
16	2	3	13

Function of the Talisman: protection against sorcery, especially if engraved on coral. Generally inscribed on tin, and this word is the interpretation of the numbers, according to the Hebrew notation.

♂ MARS, *ruling Tuesday, under the Sign of Scorpio,* ♏

Perfume: "Euphorbim, Bdellium, gum armoniack, roots of hellbore, lodestone and sulphur; mix well with the brain of a hart, the blood of a man, and the brain of a black cat."

Sign of the Planet: (SR)

Wood to be burned in a sacrifice to spirits: cedar.

Herb: plantain (AM).

Demon of the Day: Frimost, *alias* Nambroth (GH).

Works of the Day and Powers of the Planet: war, imprisonment, marriage, enmity.

Angels: Samael, Satael, Amabiel.

Sigil of Samael:

Metal: iron.

Olympic Spirit: Phaleg.

His Character:

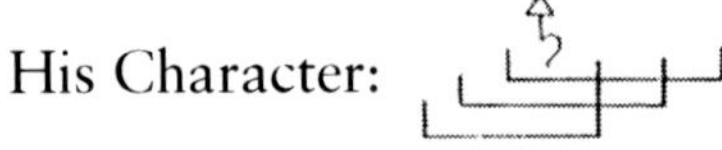

His powers: military honours.

Colours of the Pentacles of Mars, on Virgin Parchment: red.

Other operations for this day: Making pentacles (LM), at midnight, when the moon is in the Sign of Virgo.

Stone: ruby, emerald, jasper, topaz.

Inscription for the Talisman of Mars:

11	24	7	20	3
4	12	25	8	16
17	5	13	21	9
10	18	1	14	22
23	6	19	2	15

Meaning and use of this Talisman: to call the Demon of the Planet.

Sign of the Demon of the Planet:

Sign of the Spirit of the Planet: 

Interpretation of the numbers of the Talisman: ADNI (Adonay) – 'Lord'.

The SUN: *ruling Sunday, under the Sign of Leo,*

Ruler of the first hour of Sunday: the Sun.

Perfume of the Planet: cloves, myrrh, frankincense, ambergris and musk. These were mixed and added to bruised lignum aloes, and blended until a sweet perfume was obtained. Then this was added to the brain of an eagle and blood from a white cock.

Sign of the Planet:

Wood to be burned in a sacrifice to spirits: laurel.

Herb: poliginia.

Power of the Planet: works of hope, money, fortune, inheritance.

Demon of the Day: Surgat, *alias* Aquiel.

Angels: Michael, Dardael, Hurtapal.

Sigil of Michael:

Metal: gold.

Stones: diamond, topaz, jacinth, sunstone, sardonyx.

Olympic Spirit: Och.

His Character : 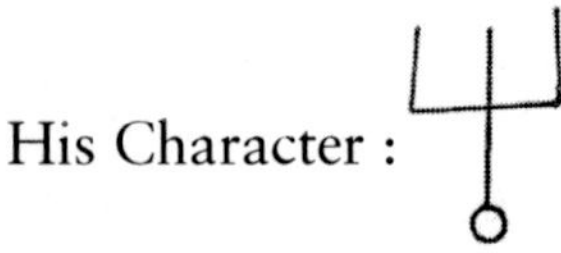

His powers: long life, wisdom, transmutation, superlative honours.

Colours of the Pentacles of the Sun: gold or yellow.

Other operations for this day and planet: treasures guarded by spirits are to be won, oracular carpet of the *Key of Solomon* made.

Inscription of the Talisman of the Sun:

6	32	3	34	35	1
7	11	27	28	8	30
24	14	16	15	23	19
13	20	22	21	17	18
25	29	10	9	26	12
36	5	33	4	2	31

Interpretation of the inscription of the Talisman: the numerical values of this figure compose the number of the Demon of the Sun, and also the Hebrew word for 'pure gold'. This is a talisman of success and honour.

Sign of the Demon of the Sun:

Sign of the Spirit of the Sun:

♀ VENUS: *ruling Friday, under the Sign of Libra,* ♎

Ruler of the first hour of Friday: Venus.

Perfume of the Planet Venus: musk, ambergris, lignum aloes and coral of the same colour, mixed with the blood of a pigeon and the brains of a sparrow.

Sign of the Planet Venus: 

Wood to be burned in a sacrifice to spirits: myrtle.
Herb of the Planet: verbena.
Power of the Planet: friendship, lovers and strangers.
Demon of the Day: Bechard.
Angels: Anael, Rachiel, Sachiel.

Sigil of the Angel Anael: 

Metal of Venus: copper.
Stones: emerald, amethyst, carbuncle, pearl or diamond.
Olympic Spirit: Hagith.

His Character:

His powers: love, beauty, transmutation, familiars.
Colour of the Pentacles of Venus: green.
Other operations for this day and planet: works of love or favour.
Inscription of the Hebrew Talisman of Venus:

22	47	16	41	10	35	4
5	23	48	17	42	11	29
30	6	24	49	18	36	12
13	21	7	25	43	19	37
38	14	32	1	26	44	30
21	39	8	33	2	27	45
46	15	40	9	34	3	28

Meaning of the Talisman: this inscription consists of the numerical value of the phrase 'secret council of the goddess MENY (Venus)', and the total of the numbers is equal to the value – in letters – of the number of the intelligence of Venus. The talisman is drawn on copper, the metal of the planet, and is used for operations in which spirits connected with this planet are invoked.

Sign of the Demon of Venus:

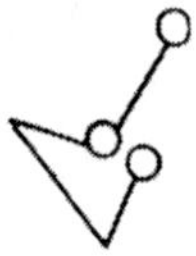

Sign of the Spirit of Venus:

☿ MERCURY: *ruling Wednesday, under the sign of Gemini,* ♊

Perfume of the Planet: mastic, frankincense, cloves, cinquefoil and achates, added to the brain of a fox.

Ruler of the first hour of Wednesday: Mercury.

Sign of the Planet Mercury, used in magic:

Wood to be burned in a sacrifice to the spirits of the day: hazel.

Herb of the Planet: cinquefoil.

Powers of the Planet: loss, debt, fear.

Demon of the Day: Astaroth.

Angels: Raphael, Miel, Seraphiel.

Sigil of the Angel Raphael:

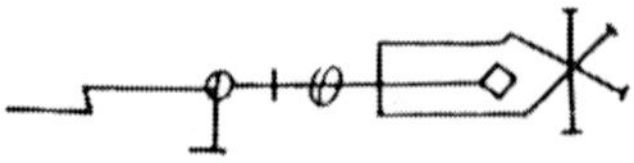

Metal of Mercury: quicksilver, alloys or 'electrum' (silver-gold alloy).

Stones: amethyst, lodestone, 'alecotria'. Other stones used to represent Mercury: agate, turquoise, sapphire, opal. Olympic Spirit: Ophiel.

His Character:

His powers: familiars, all knowledge, changing mercury into gold.

Colours of the Pentacles of Mercury: 'mixed' or purple.

Inscription on the Talisman of Mercury, used in invoking the spirits of the planet:

8	58	59	5	4	62	63	1
49	15	14	52	53	11	10	56
41	23	22	44	45	19	18	48
32	34	35	29	28	38	39	25
40	26	27	37	36	30	31	33
17	47	46	20	21	43	42	24
9	55	54	12	13	51	50	16
64	2	3	61	60	6	7	57

Meaning of the Talisman: the numbers add up to the Hebrew words 'Star of Mercury', and also to 'Tiriel', the name of a spirit of the planet. The total of 2,080 is the number of the demon of the planet.

Sign of the Demon of Mercury:

Sign of the Spirit of Mercury:

☽ *The* Moon: *ruling Monday, under the Sign of Cancer,* ♋

Perfume of the Moon: a dried frog's head, eyes from a bull, seed of a white poppy, camphor and frankincense, 'mixed with menstrous blood'.

Ruler of the first hour of Monday: The Moon.

Sign of the Moon: ☽

Wood to be burned in a sacrifice to the spirit: willow.

Herb of the Moon: chynostates.

Powers of the Moon: policies, dreams, merchandise, theft.

Demon of the Day: Lucifer.

Angels: Gabriel, Bilet, Missaln, Abuzohar.

Sigil of the Angel Gabriel:

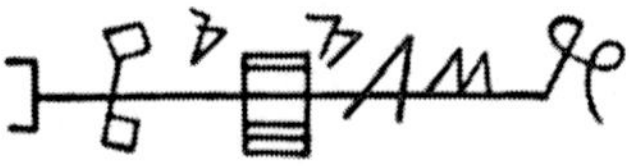

Metal of the Moon: silver.

Stones: pearl, crystal, spinel, rose quartz.

Olympic Spirit: Phul.

His Character:

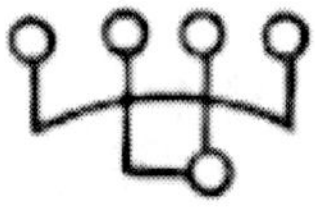

His powers: transmutation, serving spirits, long life, medicine. Colours for the Pentacles of the Moon: silver or grey-white. Inscription for the Talisman of the Moon, inscribed on the metal of the Planet, and used during conjuration of the spirits of the Moon:

37	78	29	70	21	62	13	54	5
6	38	79	30	71	22	63	14	46
47	7	39	80	31	72	23	55	15
16	48	8	40	81	32	64	24	56
57	17	49	9	41	73	33	65	25
26	58	18	50	1	42	14	34	66
67	27	59	10	51	2	43	75	35
36	68	19	60	11	52	3	44	76
77	28	69	20	61	12	53	4	45

Sign of the Demon of the Moon: 

Sign of the Spirit of the Moon: 

APPENDICES

I to VI Inclusive

APPENDIX I

POWERS AND SECOND CONJURATION OF SPIRITS

1. POWERS OF THE SPIRITS ACCORDING TO THE LEMEGETON

THERE ARE THIRTY-FIVE main categories of magical power bestowed by the spirits of the *Lesser Key of Solomon*. They may be arranged thus:

Power given:		*Name of Spirit:*
Riches are bestowed	by:	BUNE, SHAX.
Bravery	by:	IPOS.
Flying by Magic	by:	BATHIN, GAAP.
Magical knowledge	by:	BATHIN, PURSON, OSE, MORAX, BIFRONS, PROCEL, FURCAS, GAAP, SOLAS.
Invisibility	by:	BAAL, GLASYALABOLAS, BALAM.
War and Death	by:	LERAJIE, SABNACK, GLASYALABOLAS, MALPAS, MARCHOSIAS.
Fire	by:	HALPAS.
Wisdom	by:	BAAL, GUSION, ZAGAN.

Power given:		*Name of Spirit:*
Love	by:	SYTRY, BELETH, ELIGOR, FORNEUS, VUAL, ZEPAR, DANTALIAN, SALEOS, GAAP, RAUM, GOMORY.
Destruction	by:	RAUM, SHAX, VINE.
Honour and promotion	by:	GUSION, BELIAL, NABERIUS, OROBAS, RONOBE, ORIAS, BERITH.
Drowning, etc.	by:	FOCALOR, VEPAR.
Immobility	by:	AGARES, FORAS, ASMODAY.
Visions	by:	DANTALIAN.
Philosophy	by:	BUER, GAAP, MURMUR, VAPULA.
Rhetoric, etc.	by:	NABERIUS, RONOBE, FORNEUS, CAIM.
Enchantments	by:	SEERE.
Languages	by:	AGARES, RONOBE, FORNEUS, CAIM.
Treasures	by:	ASMODAY, BARBATOS, PURSON, ANDROMALIUS, FORAS, CIMERIES, AMY, VALAC, GOMORY.
Thunder, winds, etc.	by:	FURFUR.
Earthquakes	by:	AGARES.
Friendship, etc.	by:	BARBATOS, GUSION, BOTIS.
Music	by:	AMDUSCIAS.
Demotion	by:	AGARES, RAUM.
Alchemy	by:	BERITH, ZAGAN.
Transformations	by:	ZEPAR, MARBAS, OSE, ANDREALPHUS.
Prophecy, past, present and future	by:	FLAUROS, CAIM, VASSAGO, VUAL, AMON, ALLOCEN, BARBATOS, IPOS, ASTAROTH, PURSON, GUSION, VINE, BOTIS, OROBAS, GAAP.

Power given:		*Name of Spirit:*
Hatred and Revenge	by:	GAAP, ANDRAS, FLAUROS.
Medicine	by:	MARBAS, BUER.
Things Lost/Hidden	by:	VASSAGO, ELIGOR, SHAX, SEERE, ANDROMALIUS.
Secrets	by:	MARBAS, AINI, ASTAROTH, FURFUR, OSE.
Arts and Sciences	by:	PHOENIX, BIFRONS, GAMYGYN, SOLAS, PAIMON, MORAX, FORNEUS, PROCEL, FURCAS, NABERIUS, ASMODAY, RAUM, GLASYALABOLAS, DANTALIAN.
Intelligence and Wit	by:	IPOS, AINI, BUNE, FORAS, BALAM, ZAGAN.
Necromancy	by:	GAMYGYN, MURMUR.
Thieves	by:	VALEFOR.

2. SECOND CONJURATION TO RELUCTANT SPIRITS

(*From the* Lemegeton)

I invoke, conjure and command thee, O Spirit (NAMING THE SPIRIT), to appear and show thyself in visible form here before this Circle, in fair and handsome form, without artifice or deformity, in the name of *On*, by the Names *Y* and *V*, which were heard and spoken by Adam! By the Name *Joth*, which Jacob learned from the Angel on the night when he wrestled with Esau, and was saved from him! In the Name of God *Agla*, which is the name that Lot heard, and he and his people were saved! By the name *Anehexeton*, which Aaron spoke, and hence became wise! By the Name *Schemes Amathia*, which was used by Joshua, and then the Sun stayed in its place! In the Name of *Emmanuel* which was called out by the three children Shadrach, Meshach and Abednego in the flames, and they were saved!

In the Name of *Alpha et Omega*, which was spoken by Daniel, and which destroyed Bel and the Monster. In the Name *Sabaoth*, which Moses spoke: and then all the rivers and the streams of Egypt produced frogs; and these frogs went into the homes of the Egyptians, and destroyed all things!

In the name *Escerchie Ariston*, which was also spoken by Moses: when the rivers turned to blood! In the name *Elion*: which Moses used, and then there fell hail such as had never been seen since the beginning of the World! In the name of *Adonai*: which Moses spoke, and there came out locusts throughout Egypt; and they ate all that the hail had left behind! In the Name *Hagios*, by the Sigil of *Adonai*, and by those other Names: *Jetros*, *Athenoros* and *Paracletus*! And by the Three Most Secret, Sanctified Names: AGLA, ON, TETRAGRAMMATON!

By the Fearful Day of Judgement! By the Moving Sea of Glass, before the visage of the Greatest Divinity! By the Four Beasts before the Throne, with eyes in front and behind! By the Fire of the Throne! By the Holy Angels of Paradise! By the very Powerful Knowledge of God!

By the Sigil *Basdathea*! By the Name *Primematum*, used by Moses, when the Earth opened up and devoured Corah, Dathan and Abiram!

Make thou true and accurate replies to my questions, and carry out my commands, in so far as thy functions allow! Come, therefore, pleasantly and in peace! Come in a visible shape, and at once, to do my bidding! And speak in a clear and easy voice, that I may understand thy words!

APPENDIX II

3. THIRD CONJURATION TO RELUCTANT SPIRITS

(*From the* Lemegeton)

I INVOKE AND command thee, O Spirit (NAMING THE SPIRIT), by all the resplendent and potent Names of the Great and unparalleled Jehovam Sabaoth, our Lord, to come here to this place instanter! Come, from whichever place in the world thou art. And give answer to my questions: answers that shall be true and reasonable. Come, then, in visible form, come and speak pleasantly, and that I may understand thy words!

I conjure thee, and thou art invoked (NAMING THE SPIRIT), by all the Names that have been spoken! And by the Seven Secret Names wherewith Solomon, the King, son of David, did compel thee and thy fellow spirits in the brazen Vessel. And these are thus:

By Adonai, by Prerai, by Tetragrammaton, by Anexhexeton, by Inessesensatoal, by Pathumaton, and by Itemon!

Come, visibly, before this Circle, obedient in every way to my desires! If thou dost come not, or disobey in any way, I will curse thee, and will cause thee to be stripped of thy powers, and consigned to the bottomless Pit, where thou wilt remain until the Day of Judgement!

I will cause thee to be bound to the Waters of Everlasting Flame, Fire and Brimstone! Come, then, and appear before this Circle, to obey me utterly!

And otherwise thou art cursed in the Name of the Most Powerful Lord! In the Name *Eye*, the Name *Saray*, the Name *Primematum*, the Supreme Power of All Heaven! And in the Name of the Lord who created the entire World, all within it, in the space of six days!

Come, then (NAMING THE SPIRIT), through the virtue of the Most Holy and Efficacious Names Adonai, Sabaoth, Amioram!

Come, in the Name of Adonai!

APPENDIX III

COMMAND TO THE KING OF THE RELUCTANT SPIRIT

O GREAT AND Potent King of the Spirit (NAMING THE SPIRIT), thou who ruleth in the Name of the Greatest God *El*, over the entire company of the Spirits. I conjure and order thee by the special and truest Name of God! By the Name of that God whom thou dost worship, and who created all! In the Names Jehova – Tetragrammaton, of He who caused thee and the other Fallen Angels to be cast down from Heaven! The Creator of Heaven, of Earth and of Hell! And of all the powers therein! By the powerful Name Primematum!

Thou art to compel and bind the Spirit (NAMING THE SPIRIT) to appear here, before me, in visible and pleasant form, harmlessly, to answer my questions and commands, to achieve the purpose of my desires, whatever this may be, and if it be appropriate to his function!

This is through the Power of God, in the Name *El*, which rules over all things, no matter what they may be!

APPENDIX IV

INVOCATION TO A REBELLIOUS SPIRIT: 'THE BURNING'

THOU HAST REFUSED to come, O Spirit (NAMING THE SPIRIT). Therefore I, who have the power conferred upon me by virtue of the Great Names of the Almighty, *Elohim Sabaoth*, will cause upon thee a burning, which will be put into operation forthwith!

I have thy Name and Seal, these are in this Box, and I shall destroy both, by putting them in this Fire! Then they will be relegated to oblivion! Come, then, immediately, in friendship and clear to see, gently and without causing alarm or hurt! Come, and give answers to that which I will ask thee, such being things within thy powers! And also obey me in every way!

APPENDIX V

'CURSE OF CHAINS' ADDRESSED TO RELUCTANT SPIRITS

O SPIRIT (NAMING THE SPIRIT), thou who art not only inimical but disobedient, I am going to curse thee with the power invested in me by virtue of the Names in which I have called thee!

Thou art accursed, and consigned to the lowest depth of the Bottomless Pit, until the Day of Judgement. There thou shalt stay in the fire of brimstone: except shouldst thou appear now in this, the triangle before my Circle, submissive, in peace, and in visible shape.

Come, Spirit (NAMING THE SPIRIT), in the Name of Adonai – Sabaoth – Adonai – Amioram! Come, Come, now, for Adonai, the Lord of all Lords, orders thee! *Amen.*

APPENDIX VI

SECOND INVOCATION TO A REBELLIOUS SPIRIT: 'THE PIT'

SPIRIT (NAMING THE SPIRIT), thou who art yet rebellious and refuseth to appear before me here in this triangle, and still will not tell me that which I desire to know, I shall curse thee by the power that has been imparted to me by the Lord, by *Jehovah – Tetragrammaton*; by the Creator of Heaven, of Earth and of Hell, by the All-Powerful Lord of all things, thou art cursed.

I herewith consign thee to the Bottomless Pit! The pit filled with the everlasting Fire, until Judgement Day! May thou be accursed: accursed by Heaven, by Hell, by the Sun and Moon and Planets!

Just as thy name and Sigil are bound in this box over these flames in this Circle, so will they be burned in the Everlasting Fire. In the Name of *Tetragrammaton*, ANEXHEXETON, *Primematum*!

Thou wilt be forced O Spirit (NAMED HERE) into that Fire, and eternally consigned and held there, for ever and ever. *Amen.*

LIST OF ABBREVIATIONS

KEY LIST TO sources mentioned in the text or footnotes by initials:

AA *Art Almadel.*

AC *Secrets of Aptolcater*, tr. 1724.

AF *Fourth Book of Occult Philosophy*, by Cornelius Agrippa. (BM Slo. 3850, etc.)

AL *Secrets of Albertus Magnus*, Bishop of Ratisbon.

AN *Ars Notoria*, tr. Robert Turner. (BM Slo. 3648, etc.)

AR *Arbatal of Magic* (*De Magia Veterum*), 1575.

BA Arsenal Library, Paris.

BM British Museum.

BN Bibliotheque Nationale, Paris.

EL *Enchiridion of Pope Leo III*, 1633.

FB *The Magus*, by Francis Barrett, 1801.

GG The *Grand Grimoire*, n.d.

GH The *Grimoire of Honorius the Great*, Rome, 1760.

GV *Grimorium Verum* (Veritables Clavicules), 1517.

HT *The Heptameron*, by Peter de Abano. (BM Slo. 3850.)

KS *Key of Solomon* (Clavicules de Salomon). (BA 2346 and 2348.)

LM The *Lemegeton* (*Little Key*) of Solomon. (BM Slo. 2731, 3648, etc.)

SR *Sefer Raziel* and *Liber Lunae*. (BM Slo. 3826, 1686.)

TG *True Grimoire*, n.d., see GV, above.

TS *Testament of Solomon*.

INDEX

Alchemy, see Transmutation
Anael, conjured for divination, 112 f.
Analgesia, producing, 132
Angel, appearance of, 202
Angels, powers of, 201 ff.
Anger, charm against, 166
Animals, overcoming, 164; taming for magic, 181
Antipathies, theory of, 170
Aspersion, 102
Astaroth, conjuration of, 325
Astrology, obtaining knowledge of, 222, 237, 239, 243
Avicenna (Ibn Sina) and Aristotle, 180

Babylonian origins of magic, 4
Battles, caused by spirits, 236
Bechard, conjuration of, 327
Beélzébuth, conjuration of, 107
Bees, to spellbind, 149
Birds, attracting, 152; language of, 166, 229; transformation into, 222
Black and white magic discussed, 81 f.
Book of the Spirits, address to, 312; consecration of, 44
Bravery, talisman for, 288

Candles, making of magical, 200
Carpet, oracular, 45

Chastity, test for, 130, 140
Children, demon of, 258
Circle, according to Agrippa, 264 f.; description, 26; erecting, 26, 76; potentising, 316
Cock, sacrifice of, 302
Conjuration, according to the Grimorium Verum, 108; of Honorius, 308, 313; of Lucifuge (pact), 68 f.; of Solomon (rite), 29; by talismans, 51 f.
Consecration (Book of the Spirits), 44
Convalescence, demon of, 258
Convulsions, spell against, 261
Cough, spell against, 261
Counter-spell, 11
Crown, ritual, 19
Crystal, calling spirits to, 219
Cursing, talisman for, 55 f.

Danger, spell against, 164
Days, lucky and unlucky, 336 f.; planetary rulerships of the, 334
Deafness, spell against, 259
Death spell, 153, 165, 274
Deception, demon of, 256
Defences, destroying, 246
Delusions created, 152
Demon, compulsion of, 309
Demoniac possession, to cause, 55
Demons of the planets, 339 ff.
Depart, licence to (spirits), 42; Lucifuge, 80; Grimorium Verum, 107 f. (See also under Spirits, *infra*.)
Destruction by fire, 231.
Discharge (of inimical spirits), 317
Discord, causing, 148, 281
Diseases, spells against, 258 ff.
Dismissal of spirits (Honorius), 310; (Lemegeton), 213. (See also under Depart and Discharge, *supra*.)

Dogs, against barking, 168; power over, 150; safety from, 168; silencing, 163
Drowsiness, spell against, 260
Drunkenness, against, 134, 260
Dumb, demon of the, 257

Earthquakes, talisman to cause, 55
Elixir of Life, 286
Eloquence, 178
Enemies, destruction of, 9 f., 62; made friends, 166; nailing, 124 f.; overcoming, 133, 134, 140, 273; pacifying, 164; reconciliation of, 221 f.
Envy, against, 283; demon of, 258
Epilepsy, demon of, 258
Evil Eye, spell against, 262
Evoking spirits (Lemegeton), 213. (See also s.v. Conjuration.)
Exorcism, according to Agrippa, 266

Familiars, obtained from spirits, 221, 237, 241
Favour, charm for, 166
Fear, against, 133, 147; causing, 131, 194
Female spirit, 235
Fever, spell against, 260; to cause, 151; cure for, 164; cured by Tephros, 256
Fire, annihilation by, 231
Fishes, attracting, 147, 164
Flying by magic, 36, 95, 275; talisman, 50
Food brought by spirits, 291
Foreknowledge, 165, 229
Friday, demon, etc., of, 344
Frimost, conjuration of, 324
Fumigation, method of, 97 f.
Future, knowledge of, 221 f., 235. (*cf.* Foreknowledge.)

Glass, softening, 163
Guland, conjuration of, 328

Hares, attracting, 150
Hatred, genie of, 256 f.
Heart's desire, 133
Herbs, magical knowledge of, 225, 237, 243
Honorius, conjuration, 308
Honour, to gain, 138, 227, 240, 289
Hours, magical, 331
Hunters, spell against, 139

Ills, to cure all, 292
Illusions, 136
Immobility, causing, 278
Immorality, test for, 146 f.
Ink, 103 f.
Insomnia, producing, 151
Instruments, general conjuration of, 96; candles, 200; crown, 19; inkhorn, 103; knife, 97; lancet, 99; parchment (preparation), 98 f.; perfumes (sanctification), 103; salt (benediction), 100; shoes, 18; stones (orison), 101; wand, 75; water (aspersion), 101
Intrigue, against, 223
Invisibility, achieving, 120, 130, 223, 224, 235
Invocation, according to Agrippa, 265 f.; of angels, 207; of spirits, 91; times of, 207

Joy, causing, 131
Jupiter, powers, herbs, etc., of, 340

Killing by magic, 274. (*Cf.* Death spell, *supra.*)
Kings, destroyed by Beelzeboul, 255
Knowledge, hidden, 220

Laurel, charms of, 166
Lechery, charm against, 166
Licence to depart (for spirits), Honorius, 310; Lemegeton, 217 f. (*Vide* Depart, and Discharge, *supra.*)
Lies, spell to discover, 185

Locks, opening, 152
Logic taught by spirit, 232, 238 f.
Love, causing, 141, 148 f., 177; charm, 166; destroyed, 154; marital, 233; through spirits, 221 f., 241, 242; talismans, 52 f., 279
Lucifer, conjuration of, 106, 322

Madness, demon of, 259; spell against, 186
Magic, discussion of black and white, 81 f.; sympathetic, according to Albertus Magnus, 169 f.
Mars, powers, herbs, etc., of, 341
Mathematics, taught by spirits, 222, 240 f.
Mercury, powers, etc., of, 346
Metals, transmutation of, 284
Migraine, spell against, 259
Mind, influencing through spirit, 230
Mirror, magical, 111
Monday, spirit, demon, etc., of, 348
Money, to multiply, 121 f.; through spirit aid, 243
Moon, powers, etc., of the, 348
Mouse, as offering to spirit, 323
Music, magical, 221, 291

Necromancy, spirit invoked for, 234

Owl, spell of, 163
Oxen, attracting, 154

Pact, rite of the, 68 f., 89 f.
Pain, spell against, 260
Past, knowledge of the, 234, 241
Peace, 142
Pen of the Art, 103
Pentacle, to compel spirits, 309 f.; of Solomon, conjuration by, 317; making and consecration of, 20 f.
Pentagram of Solomon, use of, 213
Penury, causing, 220

Perfumes, 102 f.
Philosophy, learned from spirit, 233
Poetry, taught by spirit, 240
Planets, herbs of, 156 f.; rulership of, 333 f.; times for spells, 167
Preparation, 15, 301; bathing, 16 f., 95, 104; garments, 17; for rites, 15; purity, 143. (Apparatus, see under Instruments.)
Prison, release from (talisman), 49
Property, recovering stolen, 223
Purity, 143

Questions answered by spirits, 237

Rain caused by magic, 241
Rainbow, causing, 153
Respect, to gain, 290
Revenge, spell, 273
Riches, 58
Rites: fumigation, 97; preparation for, 15; times for, 12, 15
Rituals, preparation for, etc., 301; according to the Almadel, 198 f.
Runaways, to stop, 220

Sacrifice, making the, 99 f. (See also Cock, Mouse.)
Sacrifices, to Lucifuge, 74; to spirits, 42
Safety, 141 f.
Saturday, spirit, demon, etc., of, 339
Saturn, powers, etc., of, 339
Sea, disasters at, 245 f.
Seal of the Almadel, 201
Secrets, revealed by spirits, 224, 233, 240, 246
Semitic and Babylonian origins, 4
Serpents, engendering, 155
Ships, sinking, 232
Shivering, spell against, 260
Shoes, 18
Silcharde, conjuration of, 326

Sleepers, to panic, 130
Solomon, Key of, 3 f.; Mirror of (making), 111; Pentagram, 213, 317; Rings of, 110, (discussed), 249 ff.; spirits of, described, 253 ff.
Souls of the dead, calling, 200
Spells: against death, 56; against hunters, 37; destruction of enemies, 60 f.; demoniac possession, 55; earthquakes, 55; hate, 95; invisibility, 39; love 118; times for, 156. (See also listed under subjects.)
Spirits: compelling, 215 f., 309; conjuration (Honorius'), 313; conjuration of kings', 318 ff.; controlling, 62; discharge of the inimical, 317; dismissal of, 35 (see also Licence to Depart); invocation, 91 f.; monarchy of, 218 f.; of the planets, 339 f.; protection from, 277; seduction, 24, 109; of Solomon, 220 ff.; treasures, 39
Stolen property, recovery of, 245
Stones, magical knowledge, 225, 237, 243; powers of, 129 f.
Storms, pacifying, 135; raising, 279
Submission, to gain, 283
Sun, powers, etc., of the, 343
Sunday, spirit, demon, etc., of, 343
Surgat, conjuration of, 329
Swordsmanship through magic, 292

Talismans: against disease, 64; of eternal life, 60; flying, 50; invincibility, 62; invisibility, 50; love, 52 f.; obedience, 50; power and honour, 49; release from prison, 49; riches, 58; spirits, to conjure, 51; visions, 51; wax for, 199
Thunder, causing, 153; by spirits, 233
Thursday, colour, spirit, etc., of 340 f.
Tongues, gift of, 220
Tonsilitis, spell against, 260
Transformation (human), 239, 247
Transmutation (alchemy), 227, 236, 246 f.
Transportation (magical), 225, 234, 275
Treasure, found through spirits, 39 f., 222, 235
Tree, sterilising, 155

Tuberculosis, spell against, 261
Tuesday, spirit, demon, etc., of, 341
Tyranny, caused by spirit, 257

Unconsciousness produced (spell), 153
Unusual operations, 38

Venus, hours, powers, etc., of, 344
Victory, 137, 138, 148, 154
Visions (talisman), 60
Voice, loss of, 165

War, causing, 231
Warmth, causing, 288
Wax (for talismans), 199
Wednesday, spirit, demon, etc., of, 346
White (and black) magic discussed, 81
Women, gaining love of, 246

Black Magic and sorcery have been practised through the ages with the aid of certain writings which were guarded jealously for uncounted centuries. Such works are the *Black Books* – the Books of the Magicians. They contain spells, charms, and the methods of making powerful talismans, and the rituals of raising spirits through the Magical Circle – the whole gamut of supernatural power and its attaining.

To this very day copies of these *Grimoires* (the 'grammars' of sorcery) are rare indeed. While books by occultist writers based to some extent upon some grimoires continue to appear, the actual sources have never been made available for study and comparison.

OCCULT

This volume contains not one but *all* the major source books of the magical arts. *The Secret Lore of Magic* includes the entire text of the four books of the secrets of Albertus Magnus, the Book of the Spirits, the Almadel, the Book of Power, the Clavicle and the Testament, the Grimoire of Honorius the Great, and the processes of the Black Pact as set forth in the True Grimoire and the Great Grimoire.

Citadel Press, Inc., Publishers *A subsidiary of Lyle Smart, Inc.* 120 Enterprise Avenue Secaucus, New Jersey 07094

ISBN 0-8065-0004-2

If you enjoyed this book, please review it on Amazon and Goodreads.

Reviews are an author's best friend.

To stay in touch with news on forthcoming editions of Idries Shah works, please sign up for the mailing list:

http://bit.ly/ISFlist

And to follow him on social media, please go to any of the following links:

https://twitter.com/idriesshah

https://www.facebook.com/IdriesShah

http://www.youtube.com/idriesshah999

http://www.pinterest.com/idriesshah/

http://bit.ly/ISgoodreads

http://idriesshah.tumblr.com

http://idriesshahfoundation.org